ARCHITECTURE AND POLITICS
IN AFRICA

MAKING AND REMAKING THE AFRICAN CITY: STUDIES IN URBAN AFRICA

Series Editors

Taibat Lawanson, Marie Huchzermeyer, Ola Uduku

Series description

This series is open to submissions that examine urban growth, its delivery and impact on existing and new populations in relation to the key issues of the moment, such as climate control, sustainability and migration. Showcasing cutting-edge research into how the African city and urban environments are being made and remade across the continent, the books in this series will open up debate on Urban Studies as a dynamic social interaction and urban encounter, and bring a fresh perspective to its exploration. Broad-ranging and multidisciplinary, the series will be mainly monographs, but we also welcome edited volumes that enable a continental, multidisciplinary approach. Innovative, and challenging current perspectives, the series will provide an indispensable resource on this key area of African Studies for academics, students, international policy-makers and development practitioners.

Please contact the Series Editors with an outline or download the proposal form at www.jamescurrey.com

Professor Taibat Lawanson, Professor of Management and Governance, University of Lagos: tlawanson@unilag.edu.ng

Professor Marie Huchzermeyer, School of Architecture and Planning, University of Witwatersrand: Marie.Huchzermeyer@wits.ac.za

Professor Ola Uduku, Head of School, Liverpool School of Architecture: O.Uduku@liverpool.ac.uk

ARCHITECTURE AND POLITICS IN AFRICA

MAKING, LIVING AND IMAGINING
IDENTITIES THROUGH BUILDINGS

Edited by
Joanne Tomkinson, Daniel Mulugeta
and Julia Gallagher

JC JAMES CURREY

First published 2022
James Currey

ISBN 978 1 84701 332 3

James Currey is an imprint of Boydell & Brewer Ltd
PO Box 9, Woodbridge, Suffolk IP12 3DF, UK
and of Boydell & Brewer Inc.
668 Mt Hope Avenue, Rochester, NY 14620–2731, USA
website: www.boydellandbrewer.com

This title is available under the Creative Commons license CC-BY-NC-ND.
It is based on research that received funding from the European Research
Council (ERC) under the European Union's Horizon 2020 research and
innovation programme (grant agreement No 772070)

A CIP catalogue record for this book is available
from the British Library

CONTENTS

ILLUSTRATIONS

MAP

FIGURES

NOTES ON CONTRIBUTORS

Irene Appeaning Addo is a Senior Research Fellow at the Institute of African Studies at the University of Ghana and a practising architect in Ghana. She holds a PhD from the University of Ghana. She has a postgraduate degree in Architecture from Kwame Nkrumah University of Science and Technology, Ghana, and a Master's degree in Housing and Inner City Revitalisation from the Institute of Housing and Urban Development Studies (IHS), Rotterdam. Her research focuses on African architecture and urban housing in West Africa.

Innocent Batsani-Ncube is a Post-Doctoral Researcher in the Politics Department at SOAS, University of London, where he completed his PhD on Chinese Government-funded parliament buildings in Lesotho, Malawi and Zimbabwe in 2022. His research explores the interaction between African states and state and non-state actors from China, India and Brazil. He is interested in understanding whether Africa's relationships with these actors from the Global South are potentially transformative, or again playing out in dependent form.

Daniel Mulugeta is a Lecturer in International Politics of Africa and UK Research and Innovation Future Leaders Fellow at SOAS, University of London. His interdisciplinary research focuses on the ethnography of the state in Africa, materiality and regional politics, cutting across the fields of politics, anthropology and sociology. His Future Leaders research focuses on understanding the gap between pan-Africanism as an ideal and pan-Africanism as a policy tool, in the contexts of security and development in Africa and Black identities in the diaspora.

Dawit Yekoyesew is a Lecturer and social researcher in the Department of Sociology at Addis Ababa University, Ethiopia. His main research interests are social development and the interface between social sciences and health. He has engaged in evaluating development projects in Ethiopia.

Julia Gallagher is a Professor of African Politics at SOAS, University of London. Her research builds on a long-standing interest and engagement in statehood and international politics in and about Africa. She has published *Zimbabwe's International Relations, Images of Africa* and *Britain and Africa under Blair*. She currently leads a five-year research project on architecture and politics in Africa.

Marie Gibert is an independent scholar and secondary school teacher of history and geography, based in Lille, France. She lived and drove through Nairobi's legendary traffic jams from 2016 to 2021. Her PhD, from SOAS, and post-doctoral research focused on Africa's international relations.

Tonderai Koschke is a visiting student at Harvard Graduate School of Arts and Sciences and is completing a Master's degree in architecture from the Technical University of Munich. She has practised at Boltshauser Architekten in Zürich as well as worked in project management at Architangle publishers in Berlin. Her research interest within these fields is in post-colonial identities.

Kuukuwa Manful is a trained architect and PhD candidate in the Politics Department at SOAS, University of London. Her British Library-funded project has digitised endangered architectural documents produced in Accra from 1904 to 1947. She has Master's degrees in Architecture from the Kwame Nkrumah University of Science and Technology, Ghana, and African Studies from the University of Oxford, UK. Her current research examines nation-building, social class, and modernity through a study of the architecture of schools in Ghana.

Yah Ariane Bernadette N'djoré is a PhD candidate in Communication Science at Université Félix Houphouët-Boigny of Cocody in Abidjan (Côte d'Ivoire). Her research interest is in the Science of Education and she explores on various themes around violence in education, inclusive education, higher education and Islamic schools. Her collaboration with Julia Gallagher has led her to study the politics of public buildings in Western Africa, especially in Côte d'Ivoire.

Emmanuel K. Ofori-Sarpong is an architect and Lecturer at the School of Architecture and Design (SADe) in Central University, Ghana. He has a Master's in Architecture from Kwame Nkrumah University of Science and Technology. His current research explores how various ideologies and historical events give shape to large-scale urban developments, civic spaces, cultural buildings and housing.

Yusuf Patel is a South African architect, who practises in Johannesburg, South Africa. He has two Master's degrees from the Graduate School of Architecture at the University of Johannesburg (Master's in Architecture and MA in Design and Theory). He takes up a PhD project in 2022 at Newcastle University (UK) to further his interest in prison architecture.

Laura Routley is Senior Lecturer in Politics at Newcastle University, UK. She is the Principal Investigator on the Leverhulme Trust funded project *Afterlives of Colonial Incarceration: African Prisons, architecture and politics* which explores the memory politics of former sites of colonial imprisonment in Ghana, Kenya, Nigeria, and South Africa. The project engages with questions about how the architecture of colonialism continues to mark African cities. These interests emerged out of her research on prisons in West Africa. She has also previously worked on NGOs and corruption.

Joanne Tomkinson is a post-doctoral researcher in the Department of Politics at SOAS, University of London. Her PhD thesis in Development Studies from SOAS was a comparative political economy examination of the challenge of late development in the age of neoliberalism in Ethiopia and Vietnam. Her current research explores the role of airport buildings and infrastructure in national development strategies, focusing on Ethiopia and Ghana.

Tony Yeboah is a PhD candidate in History at Yale University. His dissertation examines the entangled themes of colonial power, the built environment, and community making in one of the greatest West African capitals, Kumase. Tony is a contributor for the OER (Open Educational Resources), project and his works have appeared in *History in Africa*, the *Journal of West African History*, the *Conversation* and *Nursing Clio*.

ACKNOWLEDGEMENTS

This book started life in a workshop called 'The Politics of Architecture in Africa' held in Johannesburg and organised by the African State Architecture (ASA) project at SOAS, the Johannesburg Institute of Advanced Studies (JIAS) and the Graduate School of Architecture (GSA) at the University of Johannesburg in December 2019. We would like to thank everyone who helped organising the workshop, particularly Peter Vale, Bongani Ngqulunga and all the team from JIAS, Lesley Lokko and her team at the GSA, and Sunil Pun, Sadeep Rai and Carolyn Charlton at the ASA project.

Most of the papers received a further outing at an online workshop organised between the ASA project and the British International Studies Association in cooperation with their Africa and International Studies Working Group in September 2020. We thank all the people who came along to listen and the many great comments, questions and challenges they put to us.

We are grateful to Jaqueline Mitchell, who has been a keen supporter of this project for several years now. We thank everyone at James Currey, and the anonymous reviewers who shared their comments and ideas with us.

The workshop and research carried out by the ASA team received funding from the European Research Council (ERC) under the European Union's Horizon 2020 research and innovation programme (grant agreement No 772070). The ERC is also supporting the open access costs for this book.

ABBREVIATIONS

AU	African Union
AUC	African Union Commission
CBD	Central Business District
CCAG	Concerned Clergy Association of Ghana
CCG	Christian Council of Ghana
CPC-ID	Communist Party of China's International Department
CPP	Convention People's Party (Ghana)
DPP	Democratic Progressive Party (Malawi)
EAE	Ethiopian Airports Enterprise
EPRDF	Ethiopian People's Revolutionary Democratic Front
FGD	Focus group discussion
GCBC	Ghana Catholic Bishops' Conference
GHC	Ghana Housing Corporation
GNCC	Ghana National Construction Corporation
JPB	Jerusalem Prayer Breakfast
MNA	Consortium of three architectural firms, MD Initiative, Norman & Dawbarn and ABC Design Associates (Malawi)
MRA	Malawi Revenue Authority
MCP	Malawi Congress Party
NGO	Non-governmental organisation
NPP	New Patriotic Party (Ghana)
OAU	Organisation of African Unity
PMFJ	People's Movement for Freedom and Justice (Ghana)
PRAAD	Public Records and Archives Administration Department (Ghana)
PRC	People's Republic of China
PWD	Public Works Department (Ghana)
ZANU-PF	Zimbabwe African National Union (Patriotic Front)

Map 0 Map of Africa highlighting the countries discussed in this book (Sunil Pun, November 2021).

Introduction:
Buildings are the stuff of politics

DANIEL MULUGETA, JOANNE TOMKINSON AND
JULIA GALLAGHER

In 2019, to considerable global fanfare, the new Prime Minister of Ethiopia, Abiy Ahmed, opened the former palace of Emperor Menelik II to the public for the first time. Located in the heart of the capital, Addis Ababa, with sweeping views across the city, the buildings – used by successive Ethiopian regimes since the late nineteenth century – represent some of the most significant centres of political power in recent Ethiopian history. Breaking with centuries' old traditions of secluding state buildings from popular view, the buildings now lie in a vast public complex called Unity Park alongside examples of indigenous architecture from each of Ethiopia's nine ethnic regions. The Park is intended to be a symbolic national site that embodies and condenses Ethiopia's cultural and material diversity. However, from the outset the purpose and official meaning of the Park as a symbol of unity have been contested by alternative narratives, reflecting how architecture and built spaces take on political meanings beyond the expressed intentions of their creators. In particular, the Park is accused of being a foreign-funded political vanity project which represents an oversimplification of the complex history of the country. The site has fuelled wider debates regarding Ethiopian history and politics in relation to where the country has come from, what constitutes its diversity and where it is going.

Such political contestations over the Unity Park underscore how public spaces and buildings function as political texts. The controversy surrounding Unity Park particularly captures how built spaces serve as arenas where national politics and cultural identity are tangibly negotiated across Africa, where buildings are overlaid by complex meanings associated with colonialism, nationalism and globalisation. Maurice Amutabi, for example, describes the powerful political effects of buildings in his account of colonial architecture in Kenya. Enormous buildings erected by the British in Nairobi

were designed to 'civilise' Africans and held many of them 'everlastingly
... spellbound', anxious that they might be 'trespassing', impressed by a
seemingly overwhelming power (Amutabi, 2012: 326).

   Colonial architects often set out to use architecture to entrench dramatically unequal power relations, and to reshape African subjectivities in the
process. Quoting words attributed to Christopher Wren, colonial architect
Herbert Baker, who designed South Africa's Union Buildings, wrote in 1911 to
Prime Minister Jan Smuts: 'Architecture has its political use: public buildings
being the ornament of a country; it establishes a nation, draws people and
commerce, makes the people love their native country, which passion is the
origin of all great actions in a Commonwealth' (Baker, quoted in Metcalf,
1989: 193). The Union Buildings have been the heart of the colonial, apartheid
and post-1994 regimes.

   However, as in Ethiopia, the commissioners and designers of these buildings
did not get to exclusively determine their meanings: public opinion and
patterns of ordinary usage have also defined them and shaped their perpetual
reinvention. The Union Buildings also became the site of popular protest. They
embodied the nation, both as a projection of power and an object of dissent.
Now they house a democratically elected presidency; but also represent the
Women's March against the pass laws in 1958 and Nelson Mandela's 1994
inauguration that overturned its colonial rationale. It is the embodiment of
a different form of nation, still the place to which people take their political
grievances, but also a carrier of a painful history (Gallagher, forthcoming).

   In this way, buildings both describe how political regimes wish to be
perceived by citizens and the international community (see Vale, 1992) and
how they collect and become inscribed with popular descriptions, stories
and myths about political power and social relationships. Public buildings
are the constant referents in everyday urban life and assume significant roles
in the development of national consciousness. Their visibility can provoke
vigorous political controversies and their association with particular identities
can reinforce or challenge insider/outsider status. They host public ceremonies,
political rites and national festivals, serving as the backdrop to the national
drama. Sometimes they embody national aspirations of modernity and techno-
logical advancement; and at other times, ideas of conservation and tradition.
Buildings in Africa, as everywhere else, are thus 'politics with bricks and
mortar' (Beck, 1998: 115). They constitute political space that is normatively
inhabited by politicians and bureaucrats, but also shaped by citizens, who
engage with ideas, policies and practices that shape political imagination such
as the nation, community and society (Milne, 1981).

   The point here is that buildings are the subject of discussions about power,
distribution and identity from the moment they are conceived and for as long

as they are used – and perhaps even longer, if they survive in popular memory. In this sense, architecture is possibly the most political of all the arts, bringing elite and everyday ideas of politics together. As the Ethiopian example shows, this is not just a colonial story – there are powerful examples of the political uses of monumental architecture in pre- or non-colonial Africa (Hughes, 1997; Biruk, 2020). Post-independence elites have similarly used architecture to articulate and exert post-colonial political power (Elleh, 2002). The dynamics of this architecture-as-politics vary enormously – just as architectural styles do – and they can be studied to explain and expose new facets of the nature of political systems and socio-political relationships in different contexts. It is these dynamics then, those created by these most ubiquitous of material representations of political authority, that this book explores.

Stylistically, Africa's rich and varied architectural heritage and building traditions reflect the diversity of material life across the length and breadth of the continent (Adjaye, 2012). Builders across the continent have also adopted and transformed architectural ideas and built forms from other cultures, further adding to diverse local tastes, traditions and building practices (Elleh, 1997). Architecture usually requires large capital investment and tends to be commissioned by political and cultural elites, illustrating and shaping wealth distribution and reflecting the socialised construction of 'taste'. Colonial-era buildings include those in classical European style, such as the Union Buildings, as well as those in the supposedly more locally sensitive tropical modernist style. Post-independence architecture betrays the influences of modernism, as well as pre-colonial architectural aesthetics – all bidding to assert confident new forms of nationhood (Hess, 2006). The continent's recent building boom has seen a plethora of new foreign-financed public buildings that are dramatically reshaping many African capitals once more (Biruk, 2020). These developments have engaged Africa in long-standing debates about the impacts of globalisation, capitalist expansion and cultural homogenisation on architecture (Sklair, 2017). Hybrid physical forms, weaving together local, national and global influences and power relations, thus lie at the heart of architecture in Africa.

Yet, despite the rich and varied politics to which they speak, buildings in Africa receive scant attention in political science literature. This volume sets out to address this lacuna, offering a multifaceted reflection on the dynamic and co-constitutive relationships between architecture and politics and political institutions. The book is distinctive in seeking to understand the materiality, use and meaning of public buildings, and to use them to begin new debates about political life in Africa. The overarching question that frames our analysis is: what can architecture tell us about politics in Africa today? As the contributors to this volume demonstrate, looking at politics through the optics of architecture opens up many new avenues for research, including on popular perceptions of politics in Africa, the legacies of colonial relations, the spatial practices of governance, the gendering of space, in both pre- and colonial contexts, the role of religious architecture in the service of political power, conceptions of modernity and the politics of identity construction.

A significant point of departure for all of the book's contributors is their reading of buildings as part of a repertoire of material culture that structures political imaginaries and social relationships. Yet our conceptualisation of the material is different from the classic formulations used in the African politics literature to date. Here the concept of the material tends to be used in relation to the notion of patronage and distributive politics (Bayart, 2009; Schatzberg, 2001; Chabal and Daloz, 1999). It is in part taken to mean the things that politicians dispense (benefits, salaries, jobs) to their followers in exchange for political support (Bratton and van de Walle, 1997). It is also taken to mean the reverse: the things politicians accept (bribes) in exchange for favours. In its classic sense, the material supposedly demonstrates the distinctively African patron-client model of leadership, that is, the reciprocity of eating and feeding and practices of 'chopping' and looting public resources or 'dividing the national cake' (Isichei, 2004; Schatzberg, 2001). Broadly cast under the catchphrase 'the politics of the belly' (Bayart, 2009), in Africa, the material is usually deployed as a metaphor for practices of corruption and given as a cultural explanation of political behaviour.

In contrast, this book moves the concept of the material in discussions of African politics beyond the confines of the politics of patronage, which although important, offers partial insights into the politics of the continent. By fully engaging with the architectural objects and spaces that help to constitute the political world, we uncover a much broader and more complex set of political stories, encompassing issues of ideology, aesthetics and agency that are channelled through and embodied in public buildings. By taking architecture, not resources, as the material matter of politics, the book provides a richer understanding of the array of relationships, ideas and power that constitute political life in Africa.

The material is viewed broadly, conceptualised both in terms of the assemblage of built forms, physical artistic elements and the political contexts that form the intertwined poetics of socio-political life in Africa. The study of architectural materiality involves looking at building forms, designs and layouts; the political processes of commissioning, financing and producing public buildings; as well as controversies over the selection of sites, stylistic preferences, the choice of architects and material elements (Yaneva, 2016). Hence, the contributors apply the concept of the material to a wide variety of themes in different contexts, taking stock of the physicality and the representational significations of architecture. The authors insist that material and value systems need to be conceptualised as one complex and inter-related phenomenon.

By focusing on the relationships between built and socio-political forms, this book builds on three important existing approaches. The first has been to explore how architecture reflects the societies and cultures that produced it (Lawrence and Low, 1990). Within this tradition, scholars have laid bare the representational mechanics through which buildings can be seen as resonant symbols that evidence broader social, cultural and kinship relations, political contexts and cosmic structures. The built space in this sense is conceived as a purveyor of social and political processes (Bourdieu, 1979; Moore, 1986). Meanings are thought to be inscribed in the built space and the task of the scholar is to decipher and decode their underlying social and cultural messages (see Pierre Bourdieu, 1979; Vale, 1992). A second approach draws on the intellectual tradition deriving from Foucault, wherein architecture is viewed as a medium of social control and power. This approach emphasises the manner in which the hegemonic power structures of what Michel Foucault calls disciplining institutions such as hospitals, schools, the military, factories and prisons, is effected through architectural and spatial practices (see Foucault, 1975; Mitchell, 1988; Barnard, 2005). The third and final influence has been to understand buildings as mediators that can 'transform, translate, distort and modify the meaning or the elements they are supposed to carry' (Latour, 2005: 39). Crucial here is a relational conceptualisation of humans, spaces, objects and events as entangled in constant processes of mutual shaping and reshaping. In so doing, this understanding moves beyond and problematises essential dualisms between agency and structure, human and non-human, knowledge and power, materiality and sociality.

Bringing together these three approaches to the study of architecture illuminates some of the different facets and textured layers of meanings of buildings and how they shape and are shaped by the political system. Buildings as material forms are intertwined with the fabric of social and political life – in Africa as in other contexts – so that their meaning and function are contingent upon their imbrication within the wider relational field in and through which both humans and things are interwoven. Thus, we suggest that balance should be sought between different ways of exploring buildings through their physicality, symbolism and political connotations. This means our approach accounts for symbolic resonances, socio-political practices and material considerations and illustrates the ways in which politics is mediated by concrete, social and sensorial, entanglements (see Ingold, 2013) of different actors and actor-networks (Latour, 2005). We posit that buildings are key symbolic media of social relations and instruments of political power. But they can do more than represent existing social arrangements, cultural and political ideologies, or modes of thought. They can help to create them. Buildings inform thoughts, affect the human, mediating emotions and stimulating imagination and meaning-making. As Martin Heidegger (1971) notes in his seminal study on the relationship between dwelling, living and thinking, buildings are an integral part of human experience and existential meaning-making. We treat buildings as more than an epiphenomenon of social and political processes. Such an approach helps us move away from the patronage literature that compartmentalises socio-political life in Africa into bounded units of material and ideational domains. We suggest that buildings as material allow for a dynamic and multifaceted perspective on political dynamics in Africa.

Constructing the volume: methodological approaches and scope

From inception, this book sought to effect new kinds of dialogue between buildings and the study of politics in Africa. It began life within the interdisciplinary African State Architecture research project based at SOAS University of London, which comprises academics with training in African Studies, politics, architecture, anthropology, sociology and development studies. This has shaped the approach taken to the book which, as it evolved, has been characterised by a keen interest in understanding buildings within the politics which coalesce around, converge within and emanate from their physical forms. In calling for contributions for this volume we were interested in bringing together diverse perspectives on the 'politics' of architecture.

The question of how this was to be done was deliberately left open. It was an intention, in deciding to publish an edited volume, to see what fresh perspectives might emerge from a process of active dialogue between our contributors as the chapter drafts developed. Potential contributors were invited to attend a workshop, entitled The Politics of Architecture in Africa, organised with the University of Johannesburg in December 2019. This proved particularly fruitful for sharing and developing ideas across disciplines and across Africa, many of which have become chapters for the book. Indeed, by bringing together a group of predominantly young, early career scholars, the workshop opened dialogues that were at times challenging and searching. Architects were invited to see the bigger politics that their buildings speak to. Political scientists were encouraged to put more of the building within their work. Political economists were entreated to see beyond the flow of resources and goods and examine the symbolism underlying their buildings of study.

To a large extent, the themes presented at that workshop confirmed our instincts that buildings provide a rich vantage point for the study of elite and everyday politics. They ranged from the quotidian such as gas stations and motels, libraries, shopping malls, houses, airports and prisons to grand institutional headquarters, parliaments, palaces, ministerial buildings and cathedrals, and they took in challenges to 'big-A architecture' made by citizens,[1] and discussed in the ways architecture should be taught, studied and produced. But, in addition, they also unsettled our assumptions and posed distinct challenges. Chief among these was how to ensure the connection between the kinds of politics being found through the study of the building and the debates residing within the literature on African political practices, its international relations and post-colonial state building. The fit between the empirical material and these established intellectual traditions was not always neat, and posed challenges for our contributors in terms of situating their buildings within existing academic conversations. Yet, as well as posing challenges for the authors, looking at African politics from the ground up has also exposed the limits of existing conceptual tools, and we have, as a result, encouraged our authors to tie their studies into such moments of departure.

A second issue was more circumstantial and logistical. With the workshop taking place shortly before the Covid-19 pandemic took root, several contributors had their subsequent research and travel plans disrupted, and have had to adapt and innovate with more collaborative methods of data collection, or by replacing them with virtual interviews. The study of buildings does indeed pose particular kinds of challenges here. Their initial encounters with the structures, followed by subsequent triangulation from more distant sources, have thus provided some insights into how academic work might be rethought going forward.

The methods deployed by authors within the volume are diverse. Many authors begin with the elite agendas driving building conception and construction and use elite interviews, archival, document and media analysis to do so. Several others were more interested in how buildings are understood and perceived by those that use or negotiate them, and so adopted interviews and focus groups with ordinary citizens and users of the buildings, as well as photography, participant observation and techniques from auto-ethnography. Other authors had the challenge of studying buildings that do not yet exist – located in the imaginaries of elites and communities rather than actual bricks and mortar. Yet the politics of these buildings is no less real for that, and their study encompasses much the same methods as their already existing counterparts. This diversity of tools to study the same relationship can provide a guide to others researching Africa, as politics in the continent – as demonstrated

[1] The term 'big-A architecture' denotes prestigious projects designed by named architects. But see Kuukuwa Manful's Afterword, this volume, for an even stronger push back against big-A architecture.

by this book – resides not only in corridors of power and between the flows which pass between elite actors, but in the intersections between place, space, power and perception.

In terms of their original disciplines, many of our participants and ultimate contributors are architects. They brought expertise and precision to the conversations and encouraged new, sharper and more material ways of seeing buildings. Others are historians, political scientists, political economists and anthropologists, and they tended to be looser in their understandings of how politics could be seen through buildings, deploying metaphor where the architects deployed rich description. All contributors' chapters have benefited from the rich and extended exchanges which have occurred as the chapters have evolved.

Even though not all workshop delegates eventually submitted their papers for inclusion in the book, they all contributed to the development of the volume through their ideas, questions and enthusiasm for studying politics through architecture. For this reason we think it important to mention them all here: Irene Appeaning Addo, Awut Atak, Julia Gallagher, Marie Gibert, Tonderai Koschke, Thandi Loewenson, Jabu Absalom Makhubu, Kuukuwa Manful, Daniel Mulugeta, Innocent Batsani-Ncube, Emmanuel Kusi Ofori-Sarpong, Yusuf Patel, Laura Routley, Giulia Scotto, Caio Simoes de Araujo, António Tomás, Joanne Tomkinson and Tony Yeboah. Lesley Lokko from the Graduate School of Architecture at the University of Johannesburg was instrumental in setting up the workshop programme, and read many of the early drafts of papers, even though she was not able to attend.

The mechanics of putting together this volume have also generated some useful lessons. To future research which seeks to centre the study of Africa around the contributions of authors located on and from the continent, and thus to decolonise the sources of knowledge, we would stress the significance of research funding to allow those participants to meet and collaborate together, to build research relationships and networks which transcend country and disciplinary boundaries.

Finally, having sought to define a new way of reading African politics through architecture, we need to point out some limitations of this volume, the main one being the lack of comprehensiveness. We raise many debates, but we cannot pretend to be able to present a complete picture of the architecture, or the politics, or even the politics of architecture in Africa. We explore the politics of buildings in eight countries – in a continent of fifty-four this is necessarily narrow – and there are important gaps, not least in the absence of any Lusophone countries, and limited engagement with Francophone ones (see Map 0, p. xiv). We do not include examples from North Africa in this collection, a departure that would have helped challenge some of the artificial, colonially inspired boundaries erected within the continent. Any collection must choose to make omissions, either in the service of depth, or in the face of practical constraints. Ours were created by a mixture of both, the themes and geographical reach we chose to tackle being those of particular interest to the editors, or those that fell out because of the contributors we were able to assemble.

However, one of the delights of bringing together a variety of scholars working in different contexts has been to trace *both* common themes *and* huge differences that are manifest in African politics. Every story turns up a new variation. We hope that the volume will be read as a provocation to scholars of politics in Africa to understand difference and complexity, rather than through reductive parsimonious theory. More broadly, we do not wish to over-claim on the political stories we can tell through architecture. Our focus on public buildings misses the array of politics that happens beyond them – through commercial exchange, in the media, online, within crowds and open spaces, to give just a few examples. However, although not everything political can be pinned down to a physical form – rhetoric, stories, dreams, financial transactions, secrets, etc. – our point is that buildings can enable us to think about these things in rich, productive ways that help open up the study of African politics.

Contributions in this volume

The book is structured around three themes: making, living and imagining.[2] This framework was designed to help us translate the ways governments and populations have between them shaped their political life through public buildings. 'Making', therefore, highlights the politics embedded in how buildings are produced; the politics that surround their funding, the materials and methods used in their construction, and the ways in which identity is reflected in their aesthetics. The objectives, arguments and outcomes governing these issues tell us about how political elites conceive statehood, how well they can carry their ideas through, the compromises they have to make along the way and the forms of resistance they may encounter. 'Living', in contrast, is about the ways people live in, use and think about buildings, who is allowed in and who isn't, how far their aesthetics are accepted, as well as in what ways they can be resisted and changed. These issues are about how members of society respond to the environment that is shaped around them, and the degree to which they choose, and are able, to reshape it. Finally, 'imagining' is about

---

2   In doing so we are loosely following Heidegger's treatment of architecture as building, dwelling and thinking (1971).

how both elites and citizens think and dream about wider political possibilities, in the ways they imagine what buildings might once have meant, and about what they might mean in the future. In this final theme, we examine the ways people conceive of political possibilities, both as a way to consider existing political realities and to explore how they might be changed. All three themes are explicitly political, involving: the tensions present in power struggles – which ideas are best expressed in the buildings and who gets to choose; the distribution of resources – who pays and who gets to use the buildings; and relationships – how ideas and opinions about the buildings describe the ways in which citizens and users comply and contest elite objectives.

This three-part structure has also allowed us to surface other themes which have added depth to this basic framework. These help to highlight some of the particularities of building and politics-making in sub-Saharan Africa.

'Making', it is clear from the contributions in Part 1, is underpinned by tensions between domestic autonomy and a dependence on foreign actors in the construction process. Debates in these chapters focus on funding, materials and methods, and questions about how to express local identity. The chapters ultimately coalesce around an international/local nexus that sheds light on African agency and struggles for autonomy. Making deals with planning, resourcing and constructing new buildings – the Bole International Airport in Addis Ababa, the planned national cathedral in Ghana, Malawi's new parliament building and the post-war public housing programme in Ghana. All, in different ways explore what dependence on foreign funding does to shape key national building projects, the degree to which local forms are deemed 'good enough' and how modernity is often associated with foreign architecture.

Joanne Tomkinson and Dawit Yekoyesew, in their chapter about Bole Airport, Ethiopia's global gateway and symbol of the country's swift modernisation, explore connections between state-building efforts, national identity formation and international relations on the continent. Bole has been funded by Chinese investment, and has an apparently generic form and aesthetic, raising questions about how far Ethiopian elites have been able to shape it. Tomkinson and Dawit show how assumptions of a zero-sum relationship between the Chinese funders and their 'less powerful' Ethiopian recipients is misplaced – ideas of modernity and internationalism sit (sometimes uneasily) alongside ideas about local aesthetics, revealing the airport to be the site of a deeply embedded and complex domestic state-building project.

While the Ethiopian airport discussion is intensely focused on the country's projection of itself to the outside world, Emmanuel Ofori-Sarpong's chapter on the proposed national cathedral in Accra focuses more on the borrowing of rhetoric and imagery from the outside world to shape and control domestic power struggles. In his examination of the rhetoric and ritual surrounding plans for the new cathedral, Ofori-Sarpong describes how foreign ideas of religious imagery and progress are used to support political power divisions, rather than representing a truly national endeavour. In this account, Ghana's political elites harness the power of foreign ideas for political leverage at home. In particular, the discussion explores how this takes place within the context of a large religious building project, highlighting the important place of religious architecture across much of the continent. Ofori-Sarpong asks what the cost of such activities might be on domestic state-society relations.

If the Ethiopian and Ghanaian elites are able to carve out some space to instrumentalise international relationships, Innocent Batsani-Ncube highlights the limits for Malawian elites in their negotiations with the Chinese Government over their new parliament building. Batsani-Ncube finds the Malawian elites in unempowered relationship with their donor partners and traces the ways in which problems with the building's design highlight the Malawians' relative lack of agency. He further explores how the project has created mistrust of China among the wider population in Lilongwe and uses the parliament building as a template for discussing the tensions, asymmetrical gains and future implications of China-Africa relations.

Finally in this section, Irene Appeaning Addo returns us to Ghana in her exploration of the public housing programmes that shaped the transition to independence in the 1950s. She shows how a series of foreign schemes was brought in to meet high housing demand in expanding urban areas. She highlights the painful tension expressed by a government keen to show its modernising credentials as an independent country but faced with the realities of dependence on ideas and funding from international partners; and she examines the eclectic legacy of a programme that relied on so wide a variety of foreign ideas and capital.

All the chapters in Part 1 demonstrate struggles for independence in one form or another. By focusing on prestigious public architectural projects they show just how high the political stakes can be in creating the material structures of statehood within contexts of unequal international relationships. 'Making' in these African contexts continues to involve managing considerable foreign constraints.

In Part 2, 'Living', we find the idea of inheritance looming large, particularly in popular imagination. The chapters here – about state buildings in Côte d'Ivoire, a shopping centre in Zimbabwe, municipal libraries in Kenya and a police station in South Africa – deal with uncomfortable colonial legacies and the ways in which these can or cannot be domesticated by citizens after independence. None of them reach for easy answers, all detailing the compromises that have been made in accommodating the material reminders of painful histories.

Julia Gallagher and Yah Ariane N'djoré explore citizens' understanding of the state in Côte d'Ivoire by examining popular discourses about the aesthetics of post-colonial state buildings. They show how citizens imagine their state as both beautiful and ugly – at once a source of wonder and fear – and examine the degree to which such an aesthetic reveals a state that appears distant and miraculous, ostensibly local but in many ways alien. Gallagher and N'djoré show how these aesthetic engagements with state buildings enable citizens to measure and manage their relationship with the state.

Tonderai Koschke looks at the Sam Levy shopping centre in Harare, Zimbabwe showing how both the ideas and the physical exclusionary structures of colonialism are reproduced in a commercial space, built after independence but designed to look like a 'little England'. Koschke shows how racial and class exclusivity are embedded in the architecture and spatial design of the centre, discusses how and why colonial tropes persist in Zimbabwe forty years after independence, and explores the continuing damage they do to the social fabric.

Marie Gibert's chapter is about public libraries in Nairobi, Kenya, all built before or immediately after independence, and now being renovated by a local non-governmental organisation (NGO) called Book Bunk. Gibert discusses how colonially gendered spaces and aesthetics erected as a quintessential emblem of European civilisation and embodying its patriarchal structures are being 'decolonised' both in terms of the structures and decoration of the buildings and in the books they stock. Gibert explains the difficult compromises made by Book Bunk, sitting between private and state sectors, and the class dimensions of the effort to create a decolonial library within a politically ambiguous space.

Finally, Yusuf Patel looks at the legacies of a notorious police station, John Vorster Square in Johannesburg, South Africa, used under the apartheid regime as a place to hold political prisoners. Many prisoners died here in unexplained circumstances, and Patel explores the uses of the building itself in forms of torture and murder. His chapter reveals the complicit nature of architecture as an instrument of state violence and addresses the larger challenge facing the South African judicial system of dealing with eye-witness accounts that show agency in memory and architectural contexts.

Together these chapters powerfully communicate the historical constraints of post-coloniality. The buildings they discuss represent these constraints in physical form, but also in the ideas and memories of colonialism. They speak to decolonial debates in painful ways, exploring the enormous difficulties of living with, and seeking to create life beyond, colonial histories.

Part 3 of the book takes on the theme of 'imagining', and the ways in which buildings express ideas of transcendence beyond concrete realities that are often characterised by constraint and contingency. Here, buildings are used to describe an idea or ideal, sometimes by projecting into an idealised past or future, in ways that help highlight critiques of reality and possibilities of change.

Daniel Mulugeta's chapter explores the African Union building in Addis Ababa, Ethiopia, its ability to embody pan-African ideals and its attempts to transcend national difference across the continent. Daniel draws on descriptions of the building from citizens in Addis Ababa and Abuja, Nigeria, to explore the tensions between different strains of pan-African imagination and the ambivalent aspects of people's relationship with the AU. He shows how embedded in the building are both the imagined possibilities of pan-Africanism and the AU's failure to deliver on the ideal.

In contrast, Tony Yeboah looks to the past in his discussions of efforts to rebuild the Asante Kingdom's palace in Kumase, Ghana. Destroyed by the British, the palace has not been rebuilt despite repeated efforts over many years. Yeboah explores the role played by the idea of an imagined ideal past which underpins discussions about rebuilding, and how the failure to give this new palace material form helps to preserve an imagined perfection of the Asante as a political community.

Turning from the past to the future, Laura Routley's chapter examines Freedom Park in Lagos, Nigeria which has been built on the site of a colonial prison. She looks at the ways in which the histories of incarceration are memorialised and imagined in the architecture of the Park and how they are used to produce a hopeful, forward-looking narrative, reinforced by the prosperity and artistic creativity on display. She explores how the Park overwrites Nigeria's colonial history in an act that protects its heritage as well as building beyond it.

Together, the chapters in Part 3 show the ways in which imagination can be used to construct new political ideas, and to escape from political realities. Ultimately, they speak to the role of ideas in political processes and show how these can be explored and extended through physical and aesthetic experimentation.

The book ends with the Afterword by Kuukuwa Manful, in which she challenges the neglect of what is often called 'informal architecture' such as slum dwellings, places of worship, schools and industrial facilities erected without planning permission or the use of an official architect. This architecture makes up the bulk of the built environment in Africa. Manful discusses the political forces that lead to the othering of such 'not-architecture' and argues that its inclusion in a study of architecture and politics will hugely expand our understanding of both.

All the chapters in this book demonstrate the powerful contribution the study of architecture can make to the study of politics, from grand ideas to the mundane processes of making do and making marginally better, to compromises, assertions of strength in the face of greater powers, to tales of countries caught between the drag of history and the unlimited potential of the future. The result is not a neat theorisation of how politics works in Africa, but a complicated, diverse set of conversations, struggles and ideas that are the real stuff of everyday politics. By reinforcing and undermining established conversations about politics on the continent the book provides a fresh agenda for understanding the complexity of contemporary Africa and its place in the world.

PART 1

MAKING

1

Global ambitions and national identity in Ethiopia's airport expansion

JOANNE TOMKINSON AND DAWIT YEKOYESEW

Bole, Ethiopia's chief international airport, bears the marks of the country's recent political history in ways that can help us understand the evolution of the Ethiopian state. The airport was first constructed in the 1960s during a major imperial modernisation drive pioneered by the country's last emperor, Haile Selassie I.[1] It remained in much the same form, although progressively deteriorating, throughout the successor military Derg regime which ruled Ethiopia between 1974 and 1991. Then, in the mid-1990s, not long after Ethiopia emerged from a protracted civil war, the new Ethiopian People's Revolutionary Democratic Front (EPRDF) regime approved its wholesale modernisation and expansion. The expansion of what by then was known as Bole International Airport centred around the construction of a brand-new international terminal building, whose gleaming façade, heavy utilisation of glass, and expansive, high ceilings contrasted sharply with the adjacent modest original 1960s terminal (which was thereafter relegated to largely domestic use). When it was completed in 2003, the apparent incongruity between the country's urgent social and economic needs and the glittering, highly modern new airport prompted criticism that it was a 'white elephant' vanity project, wasted scarce resources, and was premised on an over-optimistic estimate of the airport's growth potential.[2] In a country with a long and rich architectural heritage stretching back to the ancient Axumite Empire, the airport site captures the more contemporary dynamics connecting state building with state buildings, including how architecture is interwoven with state-building and national identity formation in Ethiopia.

---

1   Then known as Haile Selassie I International Airport.
2   See Emmanuel Ofori-Sarpong (Chapter 2 this volume) for a discussion of similar architectural controversies in Ghana.

Figure 1.1 Exterior of Terminal 2 expansion, Bole International Airport (Joanne Tomkinson, November 2019).

The airport also provides an important lens on Ethiopia's international relationships, including its rapidly changing role in the African continent. Since the contested expansion in the early 2000s, Bole International has emerged as a major African aviation hub. As a result, the airport is again expanding, which will give Ethiopia the largest airport on the continent (in passenger numbers), increasing capacity from seven to twenty-two million passengers a year (Embassy of the FDRE, 2019).[3] The second expansion drive has added, at a right angle to the international terminal of the 2000s, a new structure with greater height to the airport site, as well as a new winding road up to the terminal itself, which otherwise blends seamlessly in with the earlier design (see figure 1.1). Internally, the extension gives the new terminal an eerie quiet; a sense of an airport waiting expectantly for the noise and bustle characteristic of airports globally (see figure 1.2). The main driver of the airport's growth is the rise of the country's state-owned flag carrier, Ethiopian Airlines, reflecting

[3]   Passengers at Bole increased from 2.3 million in 2006 to 7.4 million in 2015. Although it is yet to catch up with South Africa's OR Tambo's 19.8 million passengers or Kenya's Jomo Kenyatta's 9.0 million in 2015 (ICAO and UN-Habitat, 2018), its growth trajectory and emergence as an African hub airport puts it squarely among the continent's most significant airports.

Figure 1.2   Interior of Terminal 2 expansion, Bole International Airport (Joanne Tomkinson, November 2019).

long-standing patterns of co-dependency between the airport and airline. For instance, in the 1960s the airport was moved to its present site so the airline could begin using jet aircraft (the first airline on the continent to do so), and now, as the airline's business model has come to depend on vastly expanded continental connections (Ethiopian Airlines, 2019), most passengers transit through Bole en route to somewhere else. With the airport one of the few things passengers ever see of Ethiopia, it is both symbolically and materially a central site through which Ethiopia extends itself outwards into the world and continent.

The airport thus presents a fascinating but understudied vantage point on the international dimensions of state building. Investigations into international relations typically make states their central focus, resulting in a very top-down approach to understanding international politics. This chapter, in contrast, sets out to understand the domestic resonances of the airport and its role in shaping elite and citizens' understandings of Ethiopia's place in the world, and for this, a state-centric focus is only partly useful. As Christopher Clapham (1996) has noted, there is significant value to be gained from adopting a more bottom-up perspective on international relations – in Africa and elsewhere. A more rounded and indeed 'grounded' take on the continent's international relations is therefore provided in the chapter, making use of semi-structured interviews with elites, focus group discussions (FGDs) and archival and document analysis (government plans, funder reports, promotional materials and domestic English-language newspapers). A total of twenty semi-structured elite interviews were carried out between October 2019 and February 2020 with government employees and technical experts such as engineers and architects. These interviews allowed us to capture the elite aspirations and trade-offs driving the expansion. A total of six FGDs were conducted with thirty-six people in Amharic in February 2020. As Julia Gallagher (2017) shows, FGDs can provide a rich and bottom-up vantage point on international relations. Participants were gender balanced, drawn from a cross-section of Ethiopia's ethnic groups, and from across the Ethiopian social spectrum. They included cleaners, construction workers, university students, a local government youth group, as well as government and private sector employees. As participants challenged each other's views during the discussions, we gained an insight into how people understood the nexus between the airport expansion and Ethiopia's international relations. A tour of the airport by Ethiopian Airlines staff also provided the opportunity to observe the site and take photographs within and outside the building.

The central argument of the chapter is that, despite its seemingly globalised appearance, the expanded airport at Bole has deep roots in a complex domestic state-building project. This project has nonetheless been shaped by complex interrelations and interdependencies between domestic and global forces, which can be best appreciated through decoupling the building's form from its function in both elite and popular appraisals of the building. First, the airport rests on important continuities of planning and personnel across periods of marked rupture in Ethiopian state formation, highlighting the importance of the airport's function for that state, while more global processes have largely shaped the airport's contemporary form. Second, while expressing unease that the building's design was insufficiently 'Ethiopian', citizens also found strong reasons to consider the airport an icon of national pride, seeing in its function a home for the country's state-owned national airline – a building with an important role in taking Ethiopia out into the world. The chapter has four sections. The first deals with how global and national processes are typically understood to have framed both African state building and the built environment such as airports. The second examines the official aspirations and trade-offs underpinning the expansion of Bole Airport. The third and fourth consider citizens' appraisals of the airport's contributions to Ethiopian identity formation and the country's place in the world.

Extraverted state building and extraverted buildings

Popular approaches to understanding both the relations between national and global processes in the formation of African states and the global-local relations in modern architecture (such as airports) tend to be characterised by a one-sided emphasis. In the literature on Africa's international relations, popular ideas such as extraversion (Bayart, 2000) and the gatekeeper state (Cooper, 2001, 2002) highlight the ways in which African leaders exploit their capacity to mediate between national-level and global processes, resources and actors to perpetuate dependent relations and retain power. Through such processes, elite agendas aligned with outside interests are seen to be advanced at the expense of more sustained domestic state-building efforts. Ideas such as 'extraversion' therefore capture what is supposed to be the strategic bias of African regimes towards exploiting their (unequal) international relationships, at the exclusion of more domestic-oriented state-building efforts (Bayart, 2000). Frederick Cooper (2001, 2002) adopts a similar approach to the interplay of domestic and external forces in shaping trajectories of African statehood, based on how biases towards the maximisation of external resources (such as trade taxes on goods crossing borders, aid relations and foreign investment) which flow through 'gates' (such as ports and airports)[4] are said to distort patterns of state building and state-society relations. At the heart of Cooper's (2002) account of the impacts of these processes on African politics sits a map of railway connections in Europe and Africa, showing how Africa's linkages are chiefly oriented outwards and towards the connection of ports and mines, limiting broader connections within and between countries. This outwards – or 'extraverted' – orientation provides a striking spatial, material, and indeed infrastructural, reading of Africa's international relations, resting on the assumption that an orientation towards global actors, processes and flows in Africa comes at the expense of more domestically focused state-building efforts.

In the context of the built environment, these perspectives suggest the sorts of projects that John Kenneth Galbraith calls 'symbolic modernisation': a focus on attaining the trappings or appearances of development, in largely Western terms, at the expense of strategies which would achieve substantive economic transformations. He calls such projects a strategy for 'fooling people into believing that something was being done' (1964: 5). These are

---

4   Cooper (2018: 465–66) recently noted that in studying Africa's relations with the outside world in the context of gatekeeping '[m]uch of the focus will have to be on the sites where interaction takes place, and not just in the physical sense of a port or an airport but linkages as varied as foreign direct investment and the sending home of remittances'. Airports are thus one important site referenced by Cooper for understanding these dynamics.

exemplified by the kinds of developments a foreign visitor to a developing country may be shown to boast the country's progress, such as airports and office blocks in an ultra-modern capital city (Barsh, 1993: 143). The trade-offs implicit in the discussion of such projects are echoed in architectural discussions about homogenisation, standardisation and the dominating role of global culture and norms in reshaping the built environment in the era of so-called 'globalisation'.[5] Tellingly, Marc Augé (1995) opens and concludes his discussion of what he calls the 'non-places' of supermodernity with a series of descriptions of the experience of flying. He says buildings such as airports, driven by the logics of late capitalism, lack the identity, history or social relations which he suggests are hallmarks of 'places' or territoriality within anthropological study. Such territoriality is what bears culture, religion, nation and society – all of which, he argues, are otherwise absent from the experience of air travel and the buildings that facilitate it. Hans Ibelings (1998) builds on the idea of the non-place to argue that late-twentieth-century globalisation has produced architectural homogenisation around buildings without identity: neutral, abstract and shiny box structures, which cannot be recognised or differentiated from each other, save for the text written outside the building, declaring its location. Within such readings, therefore, airport developments are located largely within the abstract realm of the international system variously described as 'late capitalism' and 'globalisation'.

Some authors, it is worth noting here, do provide a more nuanced reading of the nature of the global processes at work in reshaping the built environment in the ways described above. For Lesley Sklair (2005, 2012, 2017), it is globalised elites, specifically, the commercial and aesthetic interests of a 'transnational capitalist class' that drives such homogenised and generic 'global architecture'. Keller Easterling (2014) finds that practices of what she calls 'extrastate-craft' are at work, through which supra-governmental institutions such as International Organization for Standardization (ISO) have reduced design to a series of repeatable formulas serving, above all, to facilitate smooth flows of global capital. However, for all their greater nuances, these authors remain focused on the central role played by global capital in driving the developments in question.

Such perspectives on architecture thus share with popular views of Africa's international relations a tendency to ascribe to buildings such as airports very 'extraverted' properties – an outwards orientation towards audiences, actors

---

[5]   Here the term globalisation is used in the way meant by these authors, which refer to the economic, social, cultural, political and technical processes, gathering pace from the 1970s onwards, through which there emerged a 'growing extensity, intensity and velocity of global interactions' (Held et al., 2003: 68).

and interests located squarely outside the nation-state. Underpinning such perspectives is thus a skewed logic, in which the external has overwhelmed, overtaken or distorted the internal. Yet, as Anthony King (2004: 42) notes, such perspectives fail to consider how such seemingly 'global' buildings may be received and redefined through their encounters with domestic actors, histories and processes, and miss the ways in which the meanings of buildings are 'de-coded and re-coded, invested with a myriad of different interpretations'. As the next sections illustrate, when applied to the study of Ethiopia's international airport, both in the decisions taken to bring the airport building into being, and in how the building has been received by residents of the country's capital, these perspectives have some serious shortcomings. Instead we find a notable interweaving of domestic and global influences in shaping both the airport's development and perceptions of it.

Imperialism encounters supermodernity

This section examines the airport through the aspirations of those responsible for its expansion. In contrast to narratives that locate developments such as airports within global processes, significant domestic and locally driven continuities can be traced within the economic and political objectives guiding Ethiopia's airport expansions over time. To trace these continuities it is worth revisiting the founding logics underpinning the move of the country's international airport from the Lidetta area of Addis to Bole in the 1960s (Zewde, 2001). The *Ethiopian Herald*, an English-language newspaper published by the Ethiopian government, discussed the construction of the airport at Bole in 1962 in the following terms when summarising a speech given the then-Minister of Public Works and Communications, Balambaras Mahteme Selassie Wolde:

> [He p]ointed out the important role played by aviation in bringing closer governments and peoples of the world in their pursuit of common political, social and economic aims. Aviation, he added, is first among the policies adopted by the governments of the world in national or international relations. (*Ethiopian Herald*, 1962)

This quote signals the importance of the airport as the frontline infrastructure of the country's international relations. Reflecting the reimaging of this vision for the present, a former senior official of the Ethiopian Airports Enterprise (EAE),[6] which was responsible for the most recent expansion at Bole, noted that 'the objective was to develop national infrastructure in line with

6   Established in 2003 to manage and expand the country's airports.

international connections'.[7] Connected with this, documents prepared for the recent expansion highlight three main goals for the expansion, the first and third of which show how important the airport is considered to be for consolidating the country's international position and reputation: to create a 'world-class African hub and gateway airport'; to be a 'cornerstone of economic development' for Ethiopia; and to 'showcase the stature of Ethiopia in African Affairs' (CPG, 2014). The second of these goals is likewise connected to a long-standing coupling of the airport with a vision for the country's development. Linkages with earlier logics can also be found here. For instance, a government document from 1967 entitled 'Patterns of Progress' (1967), published by the Ministry of Information's Foreign Languages Press Department – and thus seeking to present the country to an international audience – noted that of all the modernisation efforts under Haile Selassie's reign '[t]he most spectacular and almost revolutionary transformation in Ethiopia has perhaps been in the field of civil aviation'. This suggests that the airport has been at the vanguard of Ethiopia's efforts to present a modernising face to the world in the imperial era, and that this vision and objective has remained intact despite the country's entry into so-called 'supermodernity'.

The new international terminal project in the 1990s also rested heavily on human capacity and technical proposals developed during the imperial period, as well as those articulated even during the upheavals of the Derg regime. Project leader, Ato Hailu Gebre Mariam, was recalled by the EPRDF from retirement in 1994 to oversee the expansion, based on his experience working for the Ethiopian Civil Aviation Authority since the early 1960s when the airport at Bole was newly constructed. He later led the USAID-supported expansions to the airport in the early 1970s, and devised the World Bank-supported regional airport expansion plans under the Derg regime (*Addis Tribune*, 1997). The plans utilised by the EPRDF for the expansion in the 1990s were also updated versions of expansion documents first prepared in the 1980s during the Derg period (ICAO and UN-Habitat, 2018). This suggests that for all its globalised appearances and shiny glass façade, the driving factors shaping the airport's expansion can be located squarely inside the evolution of the Ethiopian state. Such continuities indicate a willingness of each regime to build on foundations laid by the regimes before – rather than seeking to jettison what had been developed previously in order to start again. That the airport has foundations cumulatively developed by imperial, militarist and ethnic federalist regimes signals a confidence underlying Ethiopian statehood and willingness on behalf of each regime to selectively build on what came before, despite the profound ruptures that the underlying transitions represent.

---

[7]   Interview with former EAE official, 18 February 2020.

Here it is worth noting that one other continuity between all three phases of Bole Airport's development – the 1960s construction, 1990s new terminal and 2010s expansion – was Ethiopia's dependence on foreign financing. In all three phases, the American, Kuwaiti and Chinese funding[8] was tied to the use of contractors and consultants from the lending country.[9] Yet according to one Ethiopian engineer involved in the 1990s airport expansion, the use of foreign firms also allowed for the transfer of skills for projects at a scale Ethiopia had not undertaken for a very long time. In describing working on the airport as 'like school not a job', the engineer added that 'it was not only the first mega-project [in Ethiopia] but the first good-quality project'.[10] With Ethiopia now having a reputation for its major infrastructural development projects and distinctive focus on projects such as roads, railways and dams at a time when other African countries prioritised social over material infrastructural projects, it is clear that the domestic legacies of a successful project like the airport were significant. Furthermore, when it came to the current airport's look and feel, this was also not straightforwardly a foreign import. The Singaporean consultancy firm, CPG Airport Architects, was chosen by EAE who wanted a leading international agency. One former EAE official noted that CPG was selected because 'we forced them to bring a reputable company. We didn't want to compromise ... They [the Chinese contractor, CCCC] could have gone for cost saving and compromised the quality'.[11]

The outcomes of this process were undoubtedly a fairly standard airport design. Despite CPG noting they intended to give a 'unique experience for all passengers', the vision was largely pragmatic:

A compact design which is easy to expand in the future, with minimal disturbance to operations ... A layout concept which serve [*sic.*] the efficient hub operation for an ongoing status of a regional gateway ... An airport which recognises the needs for commercial revenue, where

---

8   Contrary to narratives which posit China as uniquely constraining the states to which it lends money for major infrastructure and building projects, the airport has always been a site of construction and design constraint for the Ethiopian government (for a fuller discussion of the politics of Chinese construction projects in Africa see Innocent Batsani-Ncube, Chapter 3, this volume).

9   Respectively, American construction firm Messrs Grove, Sheppard, Wilson and Krugge and consulting engineers Amman and Whitney-Husted, New York; Kuwaiti construction firm MAA; and Chinese state-owned construction company China Communications Construction Company Ltd (CCCC).

10   Interview with engineer on airport construction project, 18 October 2019.

11   Interview with former EAE official, 18 February 2020. CPG Airport Architects is part of the bigger CPG Corporation which has designed world-renowned airport terminals such as Changi Airport, Singapore.

opportunities are maximised, from the strategic location of shops and restaurants for passengers and public. Technically straightforward design that resolves interfacing and coordination problems early, making a fast-track programme for construction feasible. (CPG, 2014)

As one former airport official noted, the extent to which the design could be indigenised was constrained by the speed with which it needed to be constructed. Practically, this meant that the chief design priorities were for the new expansion to blend seamlessly in with the existing international terminal. Thus, bar the insistence that the floor tiles and pattern should be Ethiopian marble, all materials were imported.[12] Of the 1990s original construction, one engineer involved in the project noted that indigenous touches were rather last-minute: 'there was nothing in it Ethiopian' except for when 'just before it was inaugurated some traditional cloths were added'.[13] This suggests that for the government agencies getting the building constructed in the context of limited financial room to manoeuvre rendered design a fairly low-priority concern.

Efforts were instead made to give local aesthetics a greater weight in the design of domestic airports such as Lalibela, Gondar and Axum.[14] All three airports are located near major tourist sites on Ethiopia's famous northern historic route. The airport at Lalibela, for instance, incorporates multiple references to the twelfth-century, rock-hewn churches nearby, particularly pronounced through the wooden patchwork of crosses on the ceiling. The exterior of the airport at Axum, meanwhile, features recurring motifs drawn from the fourth-century obelisks which are found in the town and reflect the glory of the ancient Axumite Empire. Here it was seen that such airports – often used by tourists visiting the country – could be important buildings through which the architectural referents of local history and specificities of regional culture could be incorporated into airport design. Domestic resources (those of the airport company and the Ethiopian state's own revenues) were sufficient to finance these buildings, so local architects were invited to find ways to incorporate these elements into their designs. As an architect responsible for one such airport design noted, they were given a largely free hand by the state agencies responsible and invited to fill in the blanks as they wished.[15] It was in this way that the some of the design trade-offs of expanding the country's airports have been managed.

This section has highlighted the significant continuities in the approach and ambitions of the Ethiopian state regarding the country's international

12   Interview with former EAE official, 1 November 2019.
13   Interview with engineer on airport construction project, 18 October 2019.
14   Interview with former EAE official, 1 November 2019.
15   Interview with architect of Ethiopian domestic airport, 31 October 2019.

airport. That these continuities exist given the marked differences between these regimes is suggestive of a strongly indigenously owned process which brought the airport at Bole into being. Thus, far from being simply oriented outwards, the foundations of the present expansion appear to lie in the long history of domestically driven Ethiopian state building. It was the particular constraints faced by the EPRDF regime that have conditioned the precise form this building has taken, with function and form decoupled through the pragmatic trade-offs needed to bring the building into being.

Tensions of tradition and modernity

Echoing this complex interplay of global and local, during the FGDs residents of the capital city revealed unease that the airport was an alien, strange and 'un-Ethiopian building' in ways that initially appear to support ideas of the airport's outwards orientation. A sense of disappointment at the building was palpable, rooted in the building's failure to incorporate references to, or somehow reflect, either the country's long history or its diverse cultural practices, norms and beliefs. A strong theme of failure therefore emerged, as discussants across all groups found the building decidedly lacking in references to what one participant described as 'the people's history and cultural beliefs and norms'.[16] On another theme, the building's deficiencies were rooted in the failure to incorporate 'cultural interpretations which symbolise the lives of the societies'.[17] Both history and culture seemed fundamental to discussants across all groups for defining 'design with Ethiopian touch'.[18] Such a concept is underpinned by an implied opposition between an indigenous, domestic building style and those originating from elsewhere. For one participant this opposition was reflected through a distinction between 'indigenous architectural works' and an 'international architectural style' that was found to be exemplified by the airport and other modern buildings.[19] The suggestion here is therefore that 'Ethiopian' and 'traditional' go hand in hand, which is suggestive of the centrality of history to understandings of the national architectural tradition. Here the discussants referred appreciatively to 'traditional knowledge'[20] and the 'commitments [of] our forefathers to their knowledge and skills of time',[21] comparing these favourably to the skills and techniques of the present.

16 FGD with government employees, 12 February 2020.
17 Ibid.
18 FGD with students, 4 February 2020.
19 FGD with youth association, 16 February 2020.
20 FGD with students, 4 February 2020.
21 Ibid.

   Discussants approached this dichotomy between 'Ethiopian' and 'modern' buildings with differing approaches, however. For some, modernity was associated with the corruptions or degradations of capitalism, which seemed to be encoded in the buildings and triggered a sense of unease. In this vein one participant noted that 'historical buildings were constructed with high commitment. They have lasting values. They show patriotic feeling of our forefathers and mothers. We today are self-centred, egoistic, making money out of architectural works'.[22] With this in mind, another noted the answer was that 'the architects should localise international standards'.[23] For others, this also spoke to a problem with the low quality of contemporary construction. Compared with the past, modern buildings were found not to stand up to the strong tests of time that Ethiopia's ancient architecture has endured, and this led to the lamentation that '[t]he quality of the materials these days is very low'.[24] Some discussants were still able to appreciate the aesthetics of the airport, despite such concerns. For instance, one discussant combined an appreciation for the airport's aesthetics and ultimate disappointment, since it was said of the airport that '[t]he buildings are beautiful but they failed under the influence of Western style'.[25] Relatedly, when describing the airport as 'attractive', another noted with a sense of disappointment that it was also 'very standardised'.[26]

   This marked discomfort with the generic feel of the airport reflects both unease about modernisation, and the distortions of the profit motive and foreign influence, as well as suggesting a more fundamental understanding of what overall purpose architecture should serve. The capacity of buildings to express what is unique and distinctive about Ethiopia – historically, culturally and socially – appeared repeatedly in the discussions as a criterion by which the buildings were judged as successes or failures. This quality that people were clearly looking for in the buildings – and which they found lacking – is rather telling. Here one participant noted that '[t]he airport buildings do not reflect the values and norms of the Ethiopian societies. You know, it is not only [the airport] but also multi-storey buildings in Addis that do not represent the cultural practices, beliefs, etc. of Ethiopia.'[27] Similarly, for another participant, architecture was thought to be a means for expressing the richness, diversity and specificity of Ethiopia, which become encoded in the buildings in the following ways:

---

[22]   Ibid.
[23]   Ibid.
[24]   FGD with construction workers, 16 February 2020.
[25]   FGD with youth association, 16 February 2020.
[26]   FGD with students, 4 February 2020.
[27]   Ibid.

[A]rchitectural designs – for example Ethiopia's famous rock-hewn churches – which are based on one's cultural knowledge, communicate the social, political, economic and religious aspects of a given society. We Ethiopians have historical buildings which somehow show the social and political lives of people in the past. They tell us about Ethiopia's magnificent history in architecture development. Modern buildings in Bole International Airport, however, say nothing about the people's culture, values, norms and beliefs.[28]

Ethiopia's historical buildings are not only thought to reflect its history, but, more interestingly, to reflect and help to constitute Ethiopia's cultural and social worlds. In this sense, one participant observed that '[w]e consider the airport as an Ethiopian asset only because it is located in our national territory, especially in Addis Ababa. Otherwise, there is nothing on the buildings and in the airline which represents all Ethiopians'.[29] Similarly the absence of an 'Ethiopian touch' within the airport meant for another that the airport buildings 'cannot represent us'.[30]

For some discussants, the airport therefore became a metaphor for the expression of anxieties connected with Ethiopia's dependence on foreign actors for the construction and financing of the building, and the implications of this in terms of the country's sovereignty. The need for foreign financing to construct the project was seen to come with some quite problematic trade-offs. As one participant noted, 'I feel that donors want to get political benefit out of their donation. I read that organisations and countries have supported the expansion of Bole International Airport. Thus, I think the interests of the donors are reflected in the buildings'.[31] They were not specific about which donors, and expressed no particular unease about China's involvement in the airport. Similarly, for others the general beautification of the Bole area around the airport suggested a tendency for Ethiopia's ruling elites to privilege international actors over domestic ones, in line with the extraversion thesis of Jean-François Bayart (2000). Asking whose interests the building serves, one participant noted it 'implicitly reveals the commitment of the government to practise in the international communities' interest'.[32] This came together for other discussants with a sense of the country's hands being tied by bodies outside the country. Here, in line with Easterling's theory of extrastatecraft, one participant noted, 'I think the buildings built in airports through the world

28 Ibid.
29 FGD with religious followers, 10 February 2020.
30 FGD with students, 4 February 2020.
31 FGD with government employees, 12 February 2020.
32 Ibid.

are under the guidance of International Civil Aviation Organization ... The building styles are authorised by aviation so that I can say that the unique cultural practices may not be allowed to be reflected on the buildings'.[33]

An icon of national pride

However, these considerable anxieties aside, popular impressions of the airport shifted considerably when conversations turned to more international and forward-looking matters which happened when they began to consider not just the building's form but also its function. These shifts began when people started talking about Ethiopian Airlines, and during the FGDs it was often difficult to separate discussions about the airport from the national airline, with many group members slipping seamlessly between references to both, even when asked to try and focus their reflections specifically on the airport. The close association between the two is even reflected in Addis Ababa's road signs, which direct people to the airport by use of the word *āyeri menigedi* which means 'airline'. The roundabout at the entrance to the airport also features a Douglas DC 3 aeroplane, emblazoned in the branding of the national airline. The symbolism of the aircraft is highly significant, since it was the first Ethiopian Airlines aircraft used for international flight, from Addis to Cairo, Egypt, on 18 April 1946, during the reign of Haile Selassie I. Its placing thus clearly signals the airport's role as a hub for one of Africa's oldest independent airlines.

During the FGDs, the shifts towards discussions of the airport's connections with the airline through its function prompted participants to look beyond the country's borders to appraise the airport's significance, sparking reflections on Ethiopia's place in the world, economically and politically. At this point the airport began to take on the character of a much more significant national building. Three specific themes emerged from within such conversations, the first concerning the importance of the airport as a means of *connecting* Ethiopia with the world, and particularly its role as an emerging continental hub. Here one discussant noted that '[t]he airport is the leading gateway to the Horn of Africa. This means a lot for Ethiopia'.[34] This sense of pride emerging from Ethiopia's growing role as an aviation powerhouse within the continent was further expressed by another participant: 'the Ethiopian airport is serving as the major centre of the Ethiopian airline i.e. an airline which is serving throughout the world. In the airport, passengers will have an opportunity of

33   FGD with youth association, 16 February 2020.
34   FGD with students, 4 February 2020.

touring/purchasing Ethiopian traditional foods, clothes, utensils … etc. that may reflect people's culture and identity marker'[35]

The second theme was the airport's role in *communicating and representing* Ethiopia to the rest of the world. Signalling the importance of the airline to performing this communicative work, one participant noted: 'In my view Ethiopian Airlines represents us on the international stage as Egypt's pyramids symbolise Egypt. You know the pyramids?'[36] Tellingly, in this quote, the airline takes on a status equivalent to some of the most famous and ancient buildings to be found within the African continent, showing the scale of the international work the airport and airline are together thought to be doing for the country. This sense that what is happening within the building is good for Ethiopia and a source of national pride also emerged in another, decidedly more quotidian but nonetheless important, sense, namely through the artefacts available to purchase, the traditional forms of food and drink to be consumed, and the visibility of Ethiopia's traditional styles of dress. All were considered by many participants to help, as one participant noted, to 'communicate Ethiopians with the rest of the world'.[37] This explanatory cultural work was described in more fleshed-out terms by another participant:

> [Ethiopia is] a multi-ethnic country. This feature can be seen in the airport. Different people wearing traditional costumes in the airport and on the airline is a good opportunity to show the world our culture and identity. We pride ourselves as a culture of hospitality, and that is what Ethiopian Airlines and the airport are doing.[38]

The sense of a unifying traditional Ethiopian hospitality being provided through the modern services within the building was also commented on by another participant who explained that '[o]ne can see our hospitality at the airport and in the aircraft. This is our identity'.[39] These visual symbols of the country's traditions are seen to be very important ways in which the airport is 'Ethiopianised' and through which a generic building is given a decisive sense of place, contrary to Augé's sense of the airport as a non-place:

> As a state-owned flag-carrier, the airport and the airline make Ethiopia known by many across the world. If someone wants to know whether the airport is Ethiopian property, it is enough for him/her to look at the

---

35   FGD with religious followers, 10 February 2020.
36   FGD with youth association representatives, 16 February 2020.
37   FGD with cleaners, 24 February 2020.
38   FGD with youth association, 16 February 2020.
39   FGD with construction workers, 16 February 2020.

aircraft, buses, employees' uniform which have the Ethiopian flag. And it is also possible to understand people's culture observing the dressing style, languages, and coffee ceremony.[40]

The sense of pride and distinctiveness which comes through here was also connected to the specificities of Ethiopia's history within the continent for one participant: 'We didn't lose our identity because of colonisation so our tradition can be observed by others in the airport. Since the national cultural identity is not spoiled by the ruins of colonisation the service the airlines provides to the passengers clearly identifies us.'[41]

The third and final theme was that rather than simply projecting Ethiopia's name internationally, several participants also observed that the airport and airline helped to *rewrite and reshape* international perceptions of the country's image. For one, this meant that the airline was important because it 'plays a decisive role in changing how the world perceives Ethiopia'.[42] Ethiopia's status and role within the wider continent was a very important touchstone here, and another described the capital as follows: 'it is the aviation capital of Africa. Addis Ababa is an African hub so that it creates a good image for the country and displays its sovereignty'.[43] For another, this good image was especially important since it was seen to be at once helping modernise international perceptions of the country and unifying an often divided domestic citizenry: 'I believe that we are lagging behind the world in every aspect except the good image we have on the international stage created by Ethiopian Airlines. No one denies the contribution of the airline to [the] country'.[44] In this regard, the airport is portrayed as an agent of transformation for the country, since its growth comes from the rapid expansion of the airline whose significance is described as follows: 'success of the airlines increases the acceptance of Ethiopia in the world'.[45] The airport building's significance then is intimately

[40]   FGD with government employees, 12 February 2020.
[41]   Ibid.
[42]   FGD with youth association, 16 February 2020.
[43]   FGD with students, 4 February 2020.
[44]   FGD with religious followers, 10 February 2020.
[45]   FGD with construction workers, 16 February 2020. Notably only one FGD participant expressed concern about the airport damaging these perceptions: 'I know that an Ethiopian airline is reliable and cheaper compared to other African airlines. It is also preferred by many passengers in Africa and the world too. Despite this, the buildings in Bole airport are below standard. I am working at the hotel and I have heard complaints from customers of Ethiopian airline about the sanitation. It has poor quality.' (FGD with religious followers, 10 February 2020).

tied to a sense of pride around how the country's reputation and place in the world is being actively rewritten thanks to its aviation success.

In this regard, its modern aspects looked considerably more appealing than first emerged in the last section, since, according to one participant 'the modern buildings in Addis in general and Bole Airport in particular are beautiful and show the level of the advancement of the country'.[46] So powerful and compelling was this sense of pride for one participant that they remarked: 'I did not visit the Bole Airport so I cannot say anything about the changes. But, it is our pride.'[47] The way in which the building is able to evoke such a strong sense of pride within someone who has never even seen it is a very strong signal of the ways in which the airport's association with the national airline helps to recode a fairly generic building with such a strong sense of national significance that it can be described with evident patriotism. This is particularly significant for the strong ethnic cleavages which dominate contemporary Ethiopian politics and which have contributed to domestic conflict since 2020. In this context, nationalist icons are likely to be particularly controversial.

Taken together, therefore, the ways that discussants inscribed the airport building with such different layers of meaning considerably complicates the skewed perspectives discussed at the start of the chapter. At first glance, shared worries about the airport's failure to embody Ethiopian design principles and concerns about international expertise and financing appear to preclude the building's emergence as an icon of national pride. However, this apparent conflict is indicative not only of the considerable nuance with which participants approached the building but also the distinctions they made between the airport's form and function. This created a separation between its capacity to reflect Ethiopia's past and its ability to rewrite its future, and differentiated the work the airport is doing for Ethiopia domestically versus that which it is doing internationally. Through consideration of the function, future and international status of the building, Bole International Airport thus emerged as a highly significant national building for projecting Ethiopia's image, reputation and standing in world affairs, anxieties about its form, historical meaning and domestic role notwithstanding. This is suggestive of the tensions and anxieties which exist over Ethiopia's modernisation, with participants simultaneously able to lament the building's lack of references to the specificities of Ethiopia's history and culture at the same time as embracing the building's ability to help forge a new international image for the country and become a major African aviation powerhouse. Furthermore, the themes of connection, communication and reshaping all reveal a strong sense of active domestic agency in terms

46   FGD with construction workers, 16 February 2020.
47   Ibid.

of what work Bole International Airport is thought to be doing for Ethiopia. Thus, rather than being considered a non-place, or a simple symptom of Ethiopia's extraversion, the airport building is thought to be helping alter the course of the country's international relationships, demonstrating considerable complexity in terms of the state-building work the airport is thought by citizens to do for Ethiopia.

Conclusion

This chapter has examined the international dimensions of Ethiopian state building through an analysis of the country's leading gateway to the world: its chief international airport. By approaching the airport through consideration of the views of two sets of actors – those involved in the design and construction as well as residents of the capital city – the chapter has found the theories commonly advanced to explain Africa's international relations and those focused on the proliferation of international design norms and principles wanting. According to such perspectives, the building's design appears to reflect extraverted buildings and state-building efforts; its orientation of the country towards global norms and actors. However, the airport reveals a considerably more complex relationship between the global and local than these perspectives allow for. Both elites and residents of Addis Ababa made an important separation between the building's form and its function, and in this decoupling resided a story of considerable nuance, not fitting easily with the rendering of the airport as a disembodied, deterritorialised or extraverted 'non-place'. While the building may not be recognised by either the elites responsible for its construction or the capital's residents as capturing Ethiopian design, culture or history, it is nonetheless deeply connected with state building and national identity formation in two critical ways. First, its founding rationales and logics, and particularly the continuities of these across major ruptures in the Ethiopian state, signal not only the confidence underlying Ethiopian state building but also that the underpinning logic of the airport's expansion has long been domestic, driven by a long and carefully articulated tradition of state planning. Second, popular perceptions of the airport's function, rendered particularly visible through its inseparability from the airline in the popular imaginary, show that the airport's function has enabled it to be firmly recognised as belonging to Ethiopia and of great significance in reimagining and rewriting its place in the world.

Thus, despite its international look and feel, both the citizens and elites interviewed found the building to be profoundly connected with Ethiopian histories of aviation success, and, as a result, strongly oriented towards the global projection of Ethiopia's national identity. The nuanced take on the interweaving of national and global influences in shaping perceptions of the building shows that an example of a global design can become strongly nationally owned, embedded within national narratives and tied to historic associations through the way it is discussed, assessed and utilised. The airport thereby speaks to a complex articulation of the global and the domestic that is missed by the skewed approaches which stress the triumph of global influences over domestic agendas and influences.

2

Building heaven on earth: Political rhetoric and ritual over Ghana's national cathedral

EMMANUEL K. OFORI-SARPONG

On 6 March 2017, Ghana's President Nana Akufo-Addo cut the sod for the construction of what he called a 'National Cathedral'.[1] The monument, he declared, would be an 'interdenominational [space for] Christians to gather on formal occasions of the state – the inauguration of presidents, the death of presidents [and] other national occasions'.[2] This watershed event ushered Ghana into a new era of church-state dynamics: one in which architecture would play a key role. Although the idea for the project was conceived earlier,[3] it was during the run-up to the 2016 national elections that it became part of the President's vision, in response to what had been a long and arduous political career. Akufo-Addo's ascendancy to the Office of the President had seen him defeated in two national elections in December 2008 and 2012 (Gyampo, et al., 2017). Therefore, when he competed again for the 2016 elections, the seventy-two-year-old took a bold step that would either see him elected or retire from four decades in politics (Brierley and Ofosu, 2016): he 'made a pledge to almighty God'[4] to build a cathedral to honour Him if he was elected. When eventually he won by an unprecedented margin of about one million votes (Yeboah, 2016), many interpreted this pledge and the prayers of the Christian community whose churches he had campaigned in (Daswani, 2019) as 'the key that unlocked his victory'.[5]

[1] Akufo-Addo speech at sod-cutting ceremony, 6 March 2017.
[2] Ibid.
[3] In 2004 when Akufo-Addo visited the Washington national cathedral (National Cathedral Update, Number 2, January–March 2020).
[4] Akufo-Addo speech at Washington Fundraising, 8 January 2019.
[5] Statement by Bishop Nicholas Duncan Williams, Member of the Cathedral Board of Trustees at a fundraising event in Washington, 8 January 2019.

Admittedly, many post-colonial nations have undertaken grand architectural projects in the recent past such as those for their legislatures (Vale, 2008; see also Innocent Batsani-Ncube, Chapter 3, this collection). Yet, a state-initiated cathedral intended for all Christians rather than a specific denomination is rare. As Lawrence Vale (2008: 3) asserts, 'grand symbolic state buildings need to be understood in terms of the political and cultural contexts that helped to bring them into being'.

To this end, the objective of the present chapter is threefold. First, it traces the modes of public persuasion adopted by the political and religious elites in the public arena. Second, it interrogates how these leaders instrumentalise the architecture – its aesthetic and embedded symbolism – in their rhetoric. Finally, it reflects on what these features around the construction process tell us about the role of religion in the quest for political dominance by the New Patriotic Party (NPP). The contention here is that the confluence of democratic politics, interdenominational Christianity and monumental architecture is not only unique in Ghana's political history but has yielded exceptional forms of rhetoric and ritual.

It is important to note here that, despite the (re)emergence within the social sciences of studies that focus on religion in contemporary politics (Bellin, 2008; Fox, 2008), those that foreground the role of architecture are few and far between (see discussion below). This study contributes to this nascent discourse by drawing out insights from the case of Ghana's cathedral to show how architecture might help to illuminate the relationship between religion and politics.

I argue, following Jonathan Fox (2018), that religious institutions are not merely instruments created and used by socio-political actors to help them pursue their own objectives, as certain functionalist theorists assert. Rather, religious organisations have 'independent agency' based on their specific metaphysical lens (Fox, 2018: 24). As I show in the case of Ghana's cathedral, while '[p]oliticians ... seek to use religious identity, institutions, ideologies, and legitimacy to serve their own ends', religious elites 'seek to use politicians to achieve the goals inspired by their religious beliefs' (Fox, 2018: 209). This acknowledges the agency of religious actors and makes the incursions of religion into politics, and vice versa, worthy of empirical inquiry (Fox, 2018).

In this chapter, I particularly focus on the rhetoric – 'speech or writing intended to persuade' (Fox, 2018: 68) – and political rituals that accompany this rhetoric. Here, a ritual is defined as 'a way of acting that specifically establishes a privileged contrast, differentiating itself as more important' than everyday actions (Bell, 1992: 90). Yet, given the critical role of framing in ritual performances (Bell, 1997), I take the position that the language that accompanies a ritual act is an inseparable part of the rite. Hence, rhetoric and ritual work together to grant political actors and their acts the needed legitimacy. As both Catherine Bell (1992) and Jonathan Fox (2018) posit, legitimacy – 'the normative belief … that a rule or institution ought to be obeyed' (Hurd, 1999: 381) – is the cornerstone of all political power. Even in non-democratic states, the leader must 'maintain legitimacy among a small number of elites' (Fox, 2018: 59). These are those 'to whom [s]he entrusts the means of coercion who will obey' (ibid.).

Relying on naturalistic data – speeches by the President, members of the Board of Trustees,[6] the architect and other channels of official communication[7] – I show how the decision to build the cathedral is influenced more by a desire to portray the nation as come of age, rather than in response to the needs of the Christian community. I furthermore demonstrate that, despite this intention to build the cathedral as a symbol of the nation's independence and maturity, the elites look to the West for both inspiration and support (see Irene Appeaning Addo, Chapter 4, this collection), which they have found in the American Christian right. I posit that for the NPP, the project represents a quest not only to thank God but also to consolidate the support of a key political constituent: the Christian elite. Finally, I show how the project reveals a deep-seated inclination to side-line minority voices and to project the values of certain groups as 'national' values.

Given my background as a Ghanaian academic and architect, this interest in religious architecture and power is shaped by my involvement in the making of churches – a privileged position that has exposed me to the ideological tensions and alliances that shape such buildings. This has led to my recognition of the limited treatment in (Ghanaian) architecture discourses of (hi)stories that foreground the 'power plays' which surround the initiation and making of the most celebrated religious monuments – despite their immense pedagogical value.

In the first section of the chapter, I discuss the question of the relationship between politics, religion and architecture, pointing out the role that rhetoric plays in this dialogue. The second section focuses on Ghana's cathedral and details the forms of rhetoric and political ritual adopted by the aristocracy in their efforts at public persuasion. In the last part, I reflect on what these tell

[6] An interdenominational group of church leaders, formed by the president and comprising two leaders each of the Methodist and Presbyterian churches, one leader each of the Roman Catholic and Anglican churches and eight leaders from Charismatic and Pentecostal Churches.
[7] These sources comprise: the first two editions of the National Cathedral Update, an online bulletin published by the cathedral secretariat on its website (www.nationalcathedralghana.org); project information mounted on the site for the cathedral and official social media handles (Facebook and Twitter).

us about the quest for dominance on Ghana's political scene and what each elite group seeks or gains in the making of this monument.

Church, state, architecture

The question of the relationship between politics and religion – which lies at the heart of Ghana's cathedral – has gained attention in recent social science scholarship, despite earlier predictions by certain secularisation theorists that the relevance of religion in politics was bound to diminish over time (Berger, 1999; Bellin, 2008). In what constitutes an extensive survey – comprising policies in 177 states – Fox (2015: 2) found that a 'majority of countries were more involved in religion in 2008 than in … 1990'. Of the many variables that such studies (Barrett et al., 2001; Norris and Inglehart, 2011) measure, the most relevant for the current study are those that involve architecture.

Studies by Lavinia Stan and Lucian Turcescu (2006) of the Cathedral of National Salvation in Bucharest and Nnamdi Elleh (2002) of Our Lady of Peace in Yamoussoukro, demonstrate specific instances of the continued relevance of religion in contemporary politics. They show how architecture created in the service of religious ideology contributes in no small way to 'sanction the leadership's exercise of power' (Vale, 2008: 8).

An important aspect of this literature is how elite rhetoric plays a role in these spatial transformations by creating the enabling environment for them to succeed. In the case of Romania, King Carol I claimed that 'the country needed a national cathedral to symbolise the victory … for Orthodoxy over the Muslim Ottomans' (Stan and Turcescu, 2006: 1123). For several decades, such political rhetoric engulfed the nation until the project became a reality in 2008 (Stan and Turcescu, 2006).

In post-colonial Ghana, the relationship between politics and religion has been a mixed bag of experiences. For example, under the military regime of Colonel I. K. Akyeampong which overthrew the Progress Party (PP),[8] the Christian Council of Ghana (CCG) and the Ghana Catholic Bishops' Conference (GCBC) found themselves on the same side of the political divide with the People's Movement for Freedom and Justice (PMFJ) (with Nana Akufo-Addo as secretary) in opposing human rights abuses (Pobee, 1987; Gyampo and Asare, 2017). During this period the PMFJ and several organisations turned to the historic churches which had gained a reputation for being 'credible reconciler[s] of warring factions' (Pobee, 1987: 59). Under the military regime of the late Jerry John Rawlings in the 1970s and 1980s the

8   Edward Akufo-Addo the father of Nana Akufo-Addo was the president of the Progress Party.

story was similar (Asante, 2017; Gifford, 1994; Gyampo and Asare, 2017). As Max Assimeng (1989) observes: 'the terror inherent in their regimes has been such that only established bodies such as the Christian Council, the Catholic Bishops' Conference and the professional bodies have been capable of ... expressing condemnation' (cited in Asante, 2017: 84).[9]

In recent history, the Christian churches have taken up roles such as civic education on issues of non-violent participation in elections (Gyampo and Asare, 2015) and have served in various capacities including on the National Peace Council (ibid.). This has led scholars such as Emmanuel Asante (member of the Board) to insist that, the CCG has never 'shirked its political responsibility' (Asante, 2017). These examples provide useful insights into the relatively favourable relationship between the NPP and the Christian elite that has culminated in the cathedral.

This question of the relationship between religious organisations and the state of Ghana continues to be a matter of debate. In their interrogation of the issue, Christopher Nyinevi and Edmund Amasah (2015) posit that Ghana's constitution 'envisages "religious pluralism" as opposed to secularism'. This, they argue, implies that 'the state equally ... accommodates all beliefs within the public space'. Accordingly, they continue, the state is free to indulge in various engagements with religious groups, 'within the confines of government's traditional welfare functions', accruing equally to the benefit of every citizen (Nyinevi and Amasah, 2015: 287). This position offers an interesting resolution, albeit an ideal that is likely to fail in the real world of interest-based politics.

Despite the active role of the church in Ghanaian politics, there had been no architectural manifestation of the cooperation between church and state –at least, not on a scale akin to Our Lady of Peace Cathedral in Yamoussoukro by Félix Houphouët-Boigny (see Julia Gallagher and Yah Ariane N'djoré, Chapter 5, this collection) – until now.

The National Cathedral of Ghana

Given the vital role that Christianity played in his electoral campaign, it is little wonder that barely eight weeks into his presidency Akufo-Addo cut the sod[10] for the Cathedral on a fourteen-acre piece of prime land that was

---

[9]   Here too, the mainline churches found themselves on the same side of the political spectrum (in fighting for democratic rule) as the Busia Danquah Tradition out of which Nana Akufo-Addo emerged.

[10]   This to my knowledge constitutes an aberration in state-initiated projects where the norm is to cut the sod immediately before construction when the design has been concluded. A ceremony to 'dedicate' the site is unusual. Subsequently, the site

donated by the state (Kwawukume, 2017). The ceremony was part of the nation's diamond jubilee celebrations and the first in a series that would be tied to Independence Day celebrations. It provided an opportunity for the clergy, all members of the Board of Trustees, to bless the site (ibid.). The President inaugurated the Board, comprising fourteen leaders from various churches, on 15 March 2017 and gave them the responsibility to 'shepherd the Cathedral project'. He also put in place a secretariat to deal with the more quotidian aspects of the project.[11]

On 6 March 2018, the President unveiled the design with its architect David Adjaye, a renowned British-Ghanaian whom the President and Board handpicked for the task (Lynch, 2018). Later that year, notwithstanding the earlier claim that the churches would fund the project by themselves, Minister of Finance Ken Ofori-Atta revealed that the government would provide seed capital for the project (Zurek, 2018). These political manoeuvres unleashed fierce debates. The Trades Union Congress (TUC) registered its opposition to the project, citing the several unmet needs of the country as the reason for their displeasure (Yeboah, 2018). The Ghana Institute of Architects (GIA) protested the decision to select the architect without a competition (Adogla-Bessa, 2018). The Concerned Clergy Association of Ghana (CCAG)[12] questioned the timing of the project and the nature of the consultations, which they believed was biased.[13] Leading members of the Muslim community – such as Sheik Aremeyaw Shaibu (spokesperson of the National Chief Imam), expressing a personal opinion – decried the project as an attempt by the Christian majority to usurp the public space (Kaku, 2018)[14]. Furthermore, the Secretary of the Convention Peoples Party (CPP), Kwabena Bomfeh, petitioned the Supreme Court seeking to put a stop to the project.[15] The court ruled unanimously that '[t]he State is free to lend support … to a religious group if it deems

---

took on greater significance as it became the grounds for various prayer meetings to seek divine aid in building the cathedral (see National Cathedral Update, Number 2, January–March 2020).

11   National Cathedral Update, Number 1, September–December 2019. Of the fourteen members of this board, there was only one woman, Reverend Joyce Aryee. This reflects the male domination of architecture – and of politics and religion.

12   This is a group of evangelical and charismatic pastors.

13   Television interview with Bishop Benny Wood, spokesperson for the CCAG, on The Pulse, Joy News TV, 27 August 2018.

14   Defenders of the project have reacted to these accusations from the Muslim community by pointing to the several years of state support for annual Hajj pilgrimages. They also indicate that the country has a national mosque (Kaku, 2018), although this was funded by the Turkish Hudai Foundation (Obeng, 2021).

15   He also prayed the court to put a stop to state funding of Hajj pilgrimages.

such beneficence to be for the good of the nation' (Ghana Legal Information Institute, 2019: 41).

These prompted several surprising developments. For one, the government indicated its willingness to build a national shrine to propitiate practitioners of traditional religions – an idea that was reportedly supported by the leadership of the CCG (Adjetey, 2019). In another example, when the president of the GCBC was questioned about the project, he indicated not only that the Church had not been briefed by the government, but also that 'the person who is there and seen visibly as representing the Catholic Conference was actually invited by the President … he was not sent by us'(Ansah, 2018). The person in question was the Vice Chairman of the Board, Metropolitan Archbishop of Accra, Charles G. Palmer-Buckle, and his statement hinted at a possible cleavage within the Catholic episcopate. In yet another unexpected turn of events, on 6 August 2021, the National Chief Imam, despite the earlier statement by his spokesperson, donated over US$8,000 to the Board in support of the project (Arhinful and Ziwu, 2021).

The President, architect and members of the Board of Trustees for their part provided several arguments to garner public support for the project. These justifications broadly flowed from two main argumentative categories (Braun and Clarke, 2006) which I call the 'sacramental' and the 'missing link'. The former refers to language and actions that seek a connection to the divine and to acknowledge God as central to politics. The latter category on the other hand makes a case for the project based on what is perceived to be a lacuna in the architectural heritage of Ghana and by extension, her quest towards 'modernity'. Hence they correspond respectively to transcendental and temporal concerns. In what follows, I describe the two categories in greater detail.

The sacramental case

The sacramental basis for the cathedral was first put forward by the President, when he announced that it signified Ghana's 'continuing and eternal gratitude' to God,[16] for a relatively smooth post-colonial era during which the nation had 'been spared civil war, famine and epidemics'.[17] He also indicated that the project was intended to make good his pledge to God.[18] Following this, members of the Board advanced arguments that similarly foregrounded the divine as an important motivation for the project: it would signify 'the fact

[16] Akufo-Addo speech at sod-cutting ceremony, 6 March 2017.
[17] Akufo-Addo speech at Washington Fundraising, 8 January 2019.
[18] Ibid.

that God is amongst' Ghanaians.[19] They constructed the project as a physical act that pointed to a transcendental reality: a sacrament (Murphy, 2015). These claims – which make of the project a thanksgiving and votive offering for the nation and her President respectively – have provided grounds for several other analogies. For example, when the choice of site – which was to involve costly demolitions[20] – was contested, the response was: 'the location is super… God deserves the best'.[21] Here, the choice of prime state land was justified on the grounds that it was part of an offering to the divine.

This framing uses ideas that are rooted in Ghanaian Christian culture – especially among Pentecostals and Charismatics – where offering money as an expression of gratitude, in fulfilment of a pledge or in anticipation of greater wealth and health, are pivotal acts of devotion (Gifford, 1994). Therefore, this rhetoric achieves its persuasive potency by using familiar concepts which are held as true in themselves. As Bell (1997: 108) points out, 'the best-known examples of religious rituals are those in which people make offerings…to praise, please, and placate divine power'. Such offerings – even when intended to express gratitude – are made 'in return for divine contributions to human well-being' (Bell, 1997: 108).

In the cathedral's case, what it offers is architecture – but in return for what? The question of what the making of the cathedral is expected to do for the nation brings us to the second reason often given for the project within the sacramental category – national unity. From this point of view, 'over 71 percent of the Ghanaian people adhere to the Christian religion'[22] and yet are 'almost paralyzed by excessive denominationalism'.[23] Therefore, it is argued, '[t]he inter-denominational cathedral will help unify the Christian community'.[24] As Reverend Eric Nyamekye, the chairman of the Church of Pentecost, suggested: 'Fancy that the National Cathedral has been built and Ghanaians come together, and God is pleased with us and his eyes and ears are here … What do you think will happen in this nation?'[25] Based on such expectations, the President and his acolytes enacted certain political rituals. The first (as indicated earlier) was the constitution of the Board of Trustees, meant to signify 'the emergence

[19]   National Cathedral Update, Number 2, January–March 2020.
[20]   These included several politically noteworthy buildings: The Malian Embassy, the Passport Office, bungalows for Supreme Court judges and some colonial-era buildings.
[21]   Reverend Paul Frimpong Manso, Head of the Assemblies of God Church and member of the Board of Trustees, interview on The Pulse, Joy News TV, 27 August 2018.
[22]   Akufo-Addo at Washington Fundraising, 8 January 2019.
[23]   National Cathedral Update, Number 2, January–March 2020.
[24]   73Akufo-Addo at Washington Fundraising, 8 January 2019.
[25]   National Cathedral Update, Number 2, January–March 2020.

of a united Christian coalition'.[26] Another was the initiation of a calendrical rite (Bell, 1997), such that events associated with the cathedral coincided with Ghana's Independence Day celebrations. For example, the unveiling of the site and later of the design and its architect took place on 6 March 2017 and 6 March 2018 respectively. More importantly, the announcement that – despite delays to its commencement caused by the Covid-19 pandemic – the US$250m project[27] would be completed and dedicated on 6 March 2024 (Jacobs, 2021) was meant to signify 'the spirit of national unity [and] cohesion'.[28] It was to this same end that selected members of the Board visited the two former presidents of the opposition National Democratic Congress (NDC) – Rawlings and John Dramani Mahama – to 'brief [them] on the progress on the cathedral [and] listen to their views'.[29]

Therefore, the cathedral occupies a special position, as a sacred symbol, with a potential to act as 'a channel of God's presence'[30] and engender national *unity*. The language used here mirrors religious rituals in which offerings to a deity are followed by a unifying communal sharing in the object of the offering (Bell, 1997). Admittedly, this idea is more latent than explicit, but the association of the entire process with a meal, by the late Reverend Asante Antwi (then Chairperson of the Board), provides much-needed insight: '[m] ay I say this is the first course … it is going to be a great dinner for all of us in this nation'.[31] The most puzzling facet of this – and a glaring attempt to ensure 'the continued quiescence of those who are excluded' (Vale, 2008: 8) – is the belief that the resultant unity among Christians will bring about 'national unity and social cohesion',[32] by bringing 'Christians, Muslims and whatever sort of belief [system] … under an umbrella that unifies everyone'.[33] This argument that Christian symbols will hold persuasive power over the cultural imaginaries of all Ghanaians, regardless of creed, demonstrates how far those involved would go to gain popular support for the project.

---

[26]   Akufo-Addo at launch of Cathedral Design, 6 March 2018.
[27]   Speech by chairperson of the Board of Trustees, Apostle Opoku Onyinah at Accra Fundraising, 5 September 2021.
[28]   National Cathedral Update, Number 1, September–December 2019.
[29]   National Cathedral Update, Number 2, January–March 2020.
[30]   Ibid.
[31]   Reverend Asante Antwi, former Head of the Board of Trustees, at the Cathedral launch, 6 March 2018. He died on 13 September 2020 and his position as Chairperson of the Board was taken over by Apostle Opoku Onyinah (*Myjoyonline*, 2021).
[32]   Akufo-Addo at Washington Fundraising, 8 January 2019.
[33]   David Adjaye, interview on Executive Lounge, Joy News TV, 19 April 2018.

The 'missing link' argument

When he cut the sod for the project, the President declared that he 'believed…
there was a missing link' in the architectural heritage of Ghana: a Cathedral
for national purposes.[34] Subsequently, it was revealed that the Episcopalian
Cathedral in Washington inspired the President when in 2004 (as Foreign
Minister) he visited it for the funeral of President Ronald Reagan.[35] To drive
home this point, the National Cathedral Update published an article which
offered an exegesis of how the church in Washington acts 'as inspiration for
the National Cathedral of Ghana'.[36] This understanding paved the way for
rhetoric that foregrounded Western (and as I show later, Jewish) precedents
as a means of legitimation. As the architect put it:

> When St. Paul's was built in London, it was a Tudor village, bad
> sanitation, terror … and half the people said … 'we don't need a big
> church'. Well, it became the embodiment of the ambition of the nation
> and … the manifestation of the DNA of the place.[37]

These point to language that seeks legitimacy for the project based on historical
actions of the West: a sign of the nation's march to 'modernity';[38] and provides
a useful framing for praise of the President as following the example of 'all
great nations'.[39] These are all despite the stated intention to create a building
that 'physicalizes the moment when the Ghanaian and African church, by
sidestepping the Gothic cathedrals, broke the umbilical cord, architecturally,
from the European "messengers" who brought the historical faith'.[40]

This paradox is aggravated by the fact that the President and the Board
also look to the West, especially the US and some of its Christian-right
figures, for technical and financial support. For example, in February 2020
the Board of the Cathedral honoured Republican Senator Jim Inhofe for his
role in 'facilitating the National Cathedral's relations with … the Washington
National Cathedral and the Museum of the Bible'.[41] This relationship resulted
in the appointment of Cary Summers, former president of the museum, to
the Board in the role of advisor.[42] Subsequently, the Secretariat's website

---

34   Akufo-Addo speech at sod-cutting ceremony, 6 March 2017.
35   National Cathedral Update, Number 2, January–March 2020.
36   Ibid.
37   David Adjaye interview on Executive Lounge, Joy News TV, 17 April 2018.
38   Ibid.
39   Reverend Asante Antwi, at sod-cutting ceremony, 6 March 2017.
40   National Cathedral Update Number 2, January–March 2020.
41   Ibid.
42   Ibid.

showed Summers and Anthony J. Lynch (of the Lynch Pinnacle Group)[43] as 'US Representatives'. Of greater significance, the Jerusalem Prayer Breakfast (JPB) with its chairman Robert Ilatov (a member of the Knesset) and co-chair Michele Bachmann (former Republican Congresswoman and presidential aspirant) visited the offices of the Secretariat.[44] The visit of the JPB[45] signified a momentous turn in the Cathedral's story – the 'official' entry of Israel and Christian Zionism,[46] for which the evangelical base of the Republican Party is well known (Zonszein, 2020).

It is important to note that, from the earliest speeches, the leaders cited Jewish history as providing legitimate grounds for believing there to be a missing link. This quest underpins the President's and the members of the Board's incessant references to the 'temple and tabernacle'[47] and the comparison of Akufo-Addo's actions to those of the historical Jewish kings. Subsequently, when Ken Ofori-Atta spoke at the Knesset – as part of the 2019 meeting of the JPB – he invited his audience into a partnership 'to build the National Cathedral … to mobilise Africa … to look East and pray for the peace of Jerusalem' (Rahman, 2019).

The most significant ritual ceremony (see figure 2.1) in this regard occurred on 5 March 2020 when a piece of stone slab – imported from Israel and delivered by its ambassador[48] – was laid in the position where the altar for the Cathedral is to be built (Dapatem, 2020): a symbol of the cathedral's connection with Israel.[49] These ideas were buttressed by the architect in the images he put out as part of his sources of inspiration – a matter to which I shall return.[50]

---

[43]   According to its website the Lynch Pinnacle Group specialises in helping business and political leaders to 'build intelligence, credibility, and success for high-profile, iconic capital campaigns, national initiatives, and special projects in both the public and private sectors' (Lynch Pinnacle Group, 2021).

[44]   National Cathedral Update Number 1, September–December 2020.

[45]   The JPB is an initiative of the Knesset to gather mainly evangelical politicians and influential business people to 'pray for the peace of Jerusalem' (Jerusalem Prayer Breakfast, 2020). This visit coincided with the first meeting of the organisation in Africa, which was held in Accra.

[46]   Some evangelical Christians believe that the establishment of an Israeli nation that controls the entire territory of the Holy Land from a capital in Jerusalem is in line with God's will. The political implication of this is unflinching support for Israeli policies in the region (Sizer, 2004).

[47]   Akufo-Addo at launch of Cathedral Design, 6 March 2018.

[48]   Several observers have taken note of Israeli attempts to court African nations in order to garner support at the UN for its policies in the Middle East (Gidron, 2020; Holmes, 2018).

[49]   Reverend Victor Kusi Boateng interview with Joy News TV, 4 March 2020.

[50]   Ibid.

The rhetoric and rituals just discussed – based on the idea of a missing link – make a case for the project rooted in the perception that all 'great nations' have built such monuments. Taken together, these ideas maintain that the torch of religion and 'progress', passed on from the Jews to the West, will pass to Ghana if the nation follows in those footsteps. The editorial of the National Cathedral Update alluded to this in citing the Kenyan theologian John Mbiti: 'Europe and America Westernized Christianity ... Now it is our turn to Africanize it.'[51] Although indigenous variants of Christianity are well established, the Cathedral is seen as an act that 'consolidates this movement towards an Africanisation'[52] of the religion: a process of inventing symbols that are decidedly grounded in the perceived histories and cultures of the African continent.

Architecture in the rhetoric

In interrogating the role of architecture in the rhetoric and ritual just discussed, I distinguish between the quest to persuade the public about the need for the Cathedral and the legitimacy that elites seek for the design. This section deals with the latter.

In general, references to the building's aesthetic have been limited to discussions by the architect, with brief remarks by other political figures. These remarks have been dominated by references to its ancillary facilities: the Bible museum, music school and restaurants.[53] These seek to legitimise the design by indicating that it is 'not just another church building'.[54] Nevertheless, this paucity of verbal rhetoric about the propriety of the building's design for the Ghanaian cultural context, is compensated for by spectacle: colourful ritual ceremonies (see figure 2.1), the dissemination of computer-generated architectural images and photographs in the polity. These constitute visual rhetoric: 'image[s] rhetors generate, when they use visual symbols for the purpose of communicating' (Foss, 2005: 143).

Here, the large format images displayed on the construction site provide the primary source for my analysis, since they are the most prominently displayed and have become a part of the visual culture of the city. The most relevant of these images can be categorised into two: those that depict the Cathedral and those that depict the sources of inspiration for the design. While the former is

51   National Cathedral Update, Number 2, January–March 2020.
52   Ibid.
53   Reverend Kusi Boateng interview with the AM Show on Joy News TV, 4 March 2020.
54   David Adjaye interview on Citi TV, 18 September 2018.

Figure 2.1 Ceremony to lay the foundation stone imported from Israel on 5 March 2020. The image shows the ritualistic use of traditional umbrellas that inspired the design of the cathedral (Emmanuel K. Ofori-Sarpong, March 2020).

useful for appreciating the aesthetics of the building, the latter is more significant for understanding its cultural framing. They depict the project as rooted in Ghanaian 'community', 'tradition', 'identity' and 'history' (see figure 2.2). These are shown in inscriptions and depictions of crafts, festivals and funerals. Nevertheless, the cultural artefacts (architecture, umbrellas, stools, symbols) and history of the Akan ethnic group[55] – particularly the Asante[56] subgroup (see Tony Yeboah, Chapter 10, this collection) – are the most referenced by far. The images portray the history and traditions of this group as 'national', much like the framing of Christianity discussed earlier. Here too, there is the assumption that the stool will hold persuasive power, for example, over indigenes of northern Ghana whose chiefs use hides instead of stools as their symbol of power.

[55]   The majority ethnic group in Ghana: 47.5 per cent according to the Ghana Statistical Services (www.statsghana.gov.gh).
[56]   Although the history and culture of Asante has popular appeal both within and outside Ghana, they are the stronghold of the NPP.

Figure 2.2 Images of the sources of inspiration mounted on site hoarding: 'history', 'community', 'tradition' and 'identity' (Emmanuel K. Ofori-Sarpong, October 2021).

Figure 2.3 Board depicting the connection of the Jewish tabernacle to royal umbrellas and the design of the cathedral (Emmanuel K. Ofori-Sarpong, October 2021).

Furthermore, these depictions reinforce the idea – within the missing link category – of the project as a continuation of history. According to one of the inscriptions, '[t]he main architectural form references the tabernacle, one of the earliest structures of western religion'. It points out that 'the tabernacle and Ghanaian umbrella are types of canopy – a prototypical architectural form that has been used throughout history to ... create community'. The accompanying drawings show a conceptual progression from the Jewish tabernacle to the umbrella and their culmination in the cathedral's form (see figure 2.3). This analogy reinforces the idea that the nation's progression from 'communal' umbrellas to a cathedral is consistent with historical progression from the Jewish tabernacle to Western cathedrals. There is therefore an effort to show a direct lineage from the Jewish tabernacle to Ghana's culture and the National Cathedral. This is buttressed by rhetoric about the various features of the Cathedral: 'the garden of gethsemane ... [a] wailing wall ... [and] every fruit and vegetable in the Bible', and a restaurant that will serve Israeli food. These underlie claims that the cathedral will provide an alternative tourist site for Africans who cannot afford a trip to the Holy Land.[57]

The design has also been legitimated by references to the architect's accomplishments. At the unveiling of the design, the President indicated:

> [W]e have commissioned one of the most iconic of global architects, and a son of Ghana, David Adjaye as the main architect ... his iconic works include the National Museum of African American History and Culture in Washington DC and ... the museum of the Nobel Peace awards in Oslo.[58]

When a journalist questioned the Secretary of the Board of Trustees about the practicability of some of the flamboyant ideas, he declared 'we are bringing experts ... our architect is ... the most expensive and sought-after architect in the world'.[59] As Adjaye himself revealed,[60] this thinking contributed to his selection as the architect without an open competition. Like other actions, this desire for a 'starchitect'[61] has *also* been defended to be in continuity with (Western) history: 'behind every great cathedral is a great architect ... [t]he

---

[57] Reverend Kusi Boateng interview with the AM Show on Joy News TV, 4 March 2020.

[58] Akufo-Addo at the unveiling of the Cathedral design, 6 March 2018.

[59] Reverend Kusi Boateng interview with the AM Show on Joy News TV, 4 March 2020.

[60] David Adjaye interview on Executive Lounge, Joy News TV, April 2018.

[61] A portmanteau neologism from the words 'star' and 'architect'. It has become common in global architecture for architects who travel the world undertaking prestigious projects and commanding a lot of media attention.

national cathedral ... follows in this tradition'.[62] It is however interesting that neither the Board members nor the architect mention the extensive history of open competitions that have accompanied these historical projects.

Ghanaian politics through the lens of the cathedral

Based on these rituals and rhetoric, I posit here that one cannot describe the cathedral as based on the *needs* of the nation. That notwithstanding, the project serves various purposes. In what follows, I explore these purposes and what they reveal about the role of religion in the politics of the NPP and the role of politics in the theology of the religious elite.

Far from arguing that the President and the Board of Trustees are *only* weaponising faith and making claims they do not hold as true, I argue that the rhetoric here is grounded in a theological worldview that sees active engagement in the polity as fundamental part of faith. That is, while other observers – such as Nana Ama Agyemang Asante (2018) – dismiss their religious motivations, I take them seriously. In this case genuine religious motivations and political machinations are not mutually exclusive. The NPP seeks to fortify its position as a friend of religion, especially the evangelical Christian wing whose legitimation of Akufo-Addo has been critical to his politics. The role of these leaders as people with 'spiritual' insights,[63] grants legitimacy to the ideas underpinning the sacramental arguments and recasts the electoral victory and rule of the President as one that transcends random political events. As the primary agent and 'initiator of the National Cathedral'[64] – framed as an offering to the divine – he assumes the role of a divinely ordained spiritual leader. One that is 'like ... the Old Testament kings'.[65] Statements such as '[w]e welcome you to perform your *sacred* responsibility ... because ... you were *chosen* by God ... [e]verything is clear to us',[66] are an enterprise in which the role of the church leaders is indispensable. This transmutation of the President from a political to a divinely ordained leader and of the project from a wilful annexation of civic space by the political class to a divinely mandated cathedral – with a unifying 'unction' – is critical for understanding the success of the project so far. It is a primary part of how Akufo-Addo has been able to initiate a monumental project based on a personal promise,

62   National Cathedral Update, Number 1, September–December 2019.
63   Bishop Duncan Williams, for example, claimed that he could tell the enterprise was a 'noble course' because he looked into the eyes of the President and saw a 'spiritual man' (Statement at Washington Fundraising, 8 January 2019).
64   National Cathedral Update, Number 1, September–December 2019.
65   Reverend Asante Antwi speech at sod-cutting, 6 March 2017.
66   Reverend Asante Antwi, at Cathedral launch, 6 March 2018.

handpick an architect, create an interdenominational board, donate prime state land, and 'provide seed money' from the state's coffers[67] for a project that so many believe to be needless, extravagant, or sited wrongly.

For the Christian elite, their appointment by the President was the first act of their legitimation, a move that is not out of step with the theological positions of these church leaders. It is what Asante (2017) alluded to when he cited the retired Archbishop, Peter Kwasi Sarpong: 'Christ wants his church not to be meaningless in society or to be pushed to the periphery [but] to be right at the centre of things, right where the action is' (Sarpong, cited in Asante, 2017: 80). While Christian leaders have played various roles in the politics of post-colonial Ghana, this act symbolises a decisive shift in their positionality to the centre of power. For the CCG and the GCBC, this is a crowning achievement after many years of struggle in which they found an ally in the NPP. For the new Charismatic and Pentecostal Churches, this represents a resounding recognition of their new-found political significance.

Additionally, the enterprise could provide the religious elite useful resources to spread their versions of Christianity and to exert greater societal influence. A significant pointer to this is the partnership with the American Museum of the Bible. The 'half-billion-dollar museum is part of a broad effort ... to promote an evangelical view of the Bible's history, importance, and influence' not only in America but the entire globe (Baden and Moss, 2016). Being the largest supporter of evangelical ministries in the US (Moss and Baden, 2017), the opportunity this provides to promote evangelical Christianity, especially through the Cathedral's Bible museum, could be enormous and the political fruits immense. The Executive Director alluded to this when he said that the laying of the foundation stone was a signal to the project's donors 'elsewhere'. While indicating that they were not expecting the project to be funded mainly by Christians in Ghana[68], he stated that the American representative(s) were going to 'report back' for the commencement of 'major donations ... [of] substantive amounts of money'.[69]

Finally, this collaboration between the Board and American evangelical Christians, and by extension Israel, is responsible for how the process of building the Cathedral has become entangled in an emerging global evangelical movement – operating through the groups such as the JPB – to support the political interests

---

[67] National Cathedral Update Number 2, January–March 2020.

[68] Equivalent to US$16.70 or GBP £12.74 in 2021. Despite this rhetoric, the Minister of Finance announced on the floor of parliament on 29 July 2021 a campaign asking one million Christians to commit to a donation of 100 Ghana cedis every month for a three-year period (Agyemang, 2021).

[69] Dr Paul Opoku-Mensah, interview with *Citinewsroom*, 5 March 2020.

of Israel in the Middle East (Dadoo, 2020).[70] Given this situation, any offer of help from the JPB, the Knesset or American evangelicals cannot be seen as a benign act of kindness. The resultant centring of evangelical ideology could have a profound impact on the nation's foreign policy.

Conclusion

The proposed National Cathedral of Ghana occupies a unique position in the history of religious monuments: it is an interdenominational Christian cathedral for national purposes, initiated by a democratically elected president. This confluence of democratic politics, plural religiosity and monumental architecture has yielded the elaborate forms of verbal and visual rhetoric that have been interrogated in this chapter. I have argued that the rhetoric and associated political rituals can be put into two categories of ideas that I called 'sacramental' and 'missing link'. I showed how, despite the stated intention to create a building that signifies a severing of Ghanaian Christian architecture from that of the West, the leaders rely heavily (for its justification and realisation) on Jewish and Euro-American antecedents and partnerships.

In the process, both the political and religious elites achieve greater legitimacy and dominance as they utilise each other's resources and social networks. The religious elite provides the resources necessary to recast Akufo-Addo as a divinely appointed President, whose actions are consistent with the great leaders of the past. Akufo-Addo provides the resources for the religious elite to amplify its theological perspectives; and while he does not highlight the fact in his speeches, the new National Cathedral is a way of showing gratitude to the church not only for its role in his election, but also in attaining the democracy that the nation enjoys.

---

[70]   Brouwer et al. (1996) offer useful insights about how American evangelical ideology – that includes a tendency to view Israel's desire for dominance in the Middle East as divinely mandated – has become global and especially relevant in the many post-colonial states.

3

China's 'parliament building gift' to Malawi: Exploring its rationale, tensions and asymmetrical gains

INNOCENT BATSANI-NCUBE

On 26 May 2010 at 2.05 pm, Members of Parliament in Malawi sat down on blue decked seats in their oval-shaped debate chamber resplendent with shiny lights on its dome – the largest in Lilongwe. Visitors looked down from the gallery located just above the members' sitting area. These guests would have cleared security at the imposing reception checkpoint facing the Presidential Way, walked through the semi-circular amphitheatre, jogged up the steep steps of the Roman-style colonnade, passed through security scans at the main building entrance, waited for directions in the large foyer, registered and then taken the steps to the gallery located on the first floor accompanied by smartly dressed protocol officers. On the day, the First Deputy Speaker was presiding and sat in the Speaker's throne facing ruling party members to his right and opposition his left. Behind him, the Malawi coat of arms grafted on the wall augmented the Speaker's presiding authority. Parliament was congregating to debate President Bingu wa Mutharika's State of the Nation Address which had been delivered the previous Friday to coincide with the inauguration of the Chinese government-aided, sprawling new parliament building complex.

In preambles to their floor speeches, parliamentarians from across the political divide, and displaying rare unanimity, were gushing in their appraisal of the building. For example, the ruling Democratic Progressive Party's (DPP) Hon Munthali (Karonga South) started the ball rolling when he congratulated President Mutharika 'for making it possible that the New Parliament Building is really built and I am among the first Members of Parliament to occupy it. This will always keep my memories fresh in future'.[1] Not to be outdone, Hon Chitete (Mchinji North East) from the official opposition Malawi Congress

---

[1]   Parliament of Malawi, *Hansard*, 26 May 2010.

Party (MCP) also weighed in: 'Thank you Mr First Deputy Speaker, Sir, for recognizing me to make my contributions to this unique, unforgettable, and remarkable meeting of Parliament ... this magnificent Parliament building reminds me of that of King Solomon in the Bible which was built for the Lord. But this one is constructed for Honourable Members like you and me. Glory be to God'.[2]

This Chinese-funded and constructed parliament building which so enchanted the Malawi parliamentarians was not an isolated act of benevolence by China, but part of a larger phenomenon across Africa. By the mid-2010s, the People's Republic of China (PRC) had financed the construction and refurbishment of fifteen parliament complexes for African countries (Wang and Wang, 2015). These landmark buildings are delivered in complete aid project form (Cheng and Taylor, 2017) and have reshaped the outlook of African capital cities and restructured how legislatures function and are perceived. The involvement of the PRC and Chinese construction firms in these parliament buildings includes design, construction, furnishing and maintenance. In other words, China is engaged in an enterprise of donating complete parliament buildings to African countries. Upon completion, the PRC sends a senior official to symbolically hand over the building to the beneficiary government.

However, this handover does not mark the total exit of the Chinese in the building. They usually continue to maintain it through subsequent three-year cycle bilateral agreements. This marked interest by China in African parliaments read together with recipient states' unbridled enthusiasm for receiving such symbolic buildings with a central role in national identity formation and articulation as gifts raises new questions critical in understanding contemporary China-Africa relations and the development of representative political institutions in Africa. Within academic literature there is scant reference to Chinese-funded parliament buildings save for their inclusion in the totalising characterisation of 'vanity' construction projects being undertaken by the PRC in the continent (Mohan and Power, 2008; Will, 2012). This scholarship focuses on the motivations of China in dispensing such aid to African countries. Examples include Ali Askouri (2007), Robert Rotberg (2008) and Gernot Pehnelt (2007). While David Shinn (2009) highlights the similarities between US and Chinese interests in aid architecture, Giles Mohan and Marcus Power (2008: 7) contend that China seemed 'happy to work on projects that were effectively inessential monuments to the glory of the African regimes they worked with, reflecting the political or psychological needs of African leaders'. Examples of the 'monuments' they refer to are parliament buildings

2   Ibid.

in the Republic of Congo, Lesotho, Sierra Leone, Mozambique and Malawi. Their argument centres on African leaders' penchant for commissioning large infrastructural projects for political expediency. A poignant illustration of this profligacy is the construction of mega-sports stadia which Rachel Will argues remain more as white elephants than active symbols of soft power (Will, 2012).

While I agree with their general point that China often funds vanity projects in Africa, this characterisation does not hold for parliament buildings – in three ways. First, parliament buildings, from a conceptual standpoint, are key-point state structures which cannot be reduced to vanity structures as they symbolise the state, the people and the political system (for more on state buildings and statehood see Julia Gallagher et al., 2021). The size and scale of the Chinese-built parliament buildings conform to the standard of structures of this magnitude.[3] Second, the buildings are ongoing political concerns as evidenced by their functionality and the direct participation of the PRC in their maintenance. Third, from an institutional angle, the buildings embody a political institution that in theory and performatively imposes restrictions on, rather than embellishes executive authority,[4] hence, their functioning cannot be attributed merely to the whims of the so-called 'authoritarian' ruling elites (Emmanuel K. Ofori-Sarpong makes a similar argument in Chapter 2 of this collection).

At the time of writing, China was constructing new parliamentary complexes for the Republic of the Congo and Zimbabwe, and also renovating the Gabon building which had been ravaged by fire during anti-government demonstrations in 2016.[5] I seek to understand the PRC motivation, the rationale for acceptance of such aid by the recipient African states and the implications of this specific type of aid. In this chapter I contribute to this endeavour by drawing on an ethnographic study of the Chinese-funded Malawi parliamentary building in Lilongwe. In it, I conducted participant observation in the parliament for forty-five days where I observed quotidian practices and took pictures in and around the building. I also use data collected in July to August 2019 from interviews with political elites, parliamentary staff bureaucrats, civic society leaders and scholars. Finally, I draw on data from the parliament building press reports, speeches by political elites and parliamentary Hansards.[6]

---

3   See Hicks (2006); PRC (2019).
4   In the separation of powers doctrine, one of the functions of the Legislature (parliament) is to scrutinise the work done by the executive (government).
5   I am exploring this further through my PhD research, which looks at two other Chinese-funded and -constructed parliament building projects – in Lesotho and Zimbabwe (Batsani-Ncube, forthcoming).
6   Hansards are the verbatim reports of parliamentary proceedings.

In the chapter I argue that China's decision to finance and construct Malawi's parliament building was directly a function of its foreign policy strategy of promoting its One-China principle by severing Taiwan-Malawi relations. As a corollary to the above, the choice of fully financing the construction of the parliament building was also informed by earlier Taiwanese involvement in the project. However, the intense desire by Malawian ruling elites for a purpose-built parliament building was an albatross that weakened Malawi's bargaining power. Specifically, I find that the manner in which the building project was carried out gave disproportionate power to the Chinese side, undermined key in-country institutional arrangements, disregarded in-country skills and sowed seeds of distrust of China's intentions in Malawi.

Evidence from this research puts into context this puzzling Chinese investment in multi-party parliament buildings. I show that this development is actually in line with the PRC's evolving technique of expanding its political outreach by engaging opposition political elites in addition to ruling parties. My findings also lend credence to Mohan and Power's (2008) rumination about the extent of Chinese involvement in internal African politics. This is because its investment in parliament buildings such as the one in Lilongwe has the 'echoes of earlier merchants and imperialists, who insisted their interests were largely commercial, but who ended up becoming more and more mired in internal institutional building and policing' (Mohan and Power, 2008: 37).

I have divided the chapter into four mutually reinforcing sections. First, I foreground the parliament building complex, showing where it is located in Lilongwe, describing its components and weaving in user experience. Second, I show Chinese Government involvement in the parliament building project by tracing the negotiations and consummation of Malawi-China diplomatic relations. Third, I demonstrate the tensions in the construction process. I show how China and its nominated construction firm had carte blanche powers in the execution of the project, laying the ground for asymmetrical gains in the relationship. Fourth, I explain factors that led to Malawi political elites to allow China a free hand in the construction of the parliament building. I also discuss its implications in the context of the building's user experience.

'The house that Bingu built': A tour of the parliament building

The new parliament building is strategically located near the Lilongwe City centre area, foregrounding the Government complex (Capital Hill) and adjacent to the Dr Hastings Kamuzu Banda Mausoleum and also (since 2015) the President's Hotel and Bingu wa Mutharika Convention Centre (BICC). This location places parliament at the epicentre of Lilongwe. The complex

Figure 3.1   Entrance of the Malawi Parliament building in Lilongwe (Innocent Batsani-Ncube, July 2019).

consists of three constituent parts, namely the reception checkpoint (figure 3.1), the amphitheatre and the main building that houses the debate chamber and offices. The most visible part to the ordinary citizens is the reception checkpoint manned by soldiers and other security personnel to regulate entry and exit. The checkpoint is in front of a well-manicured lawn and flower beds and faces the busy Presidential Way, Lilongwe's main boulevard which takes one to the Kamuzu Presidential Palace to the east and into the residential areas to the west. It is in the form of a flat-roofed structure clad in shiny Chinese grey tiles, with the centre that marks the high point of the roof inscribed with the words 'Parliament Building' in gold and with pillars on each side.

Most ordinary people I engaged in Lilongwe's townships have a mental picture of this reception checkpoint when they speak of the Parliament building's aesthetics because this is what they have seen when passing by the complex. The reception checkpoint point acts as an enabling gate for those with privilege and courage to enter. However, others see it as an inhibiting palisade for most citizens. Conspicuously, the China aid logo is emblazoned outside this entrance wall, signifying in-country acquiescence to the PRC's branding of the parliament building gift for all and sundry to see.

The next constituent part of this complex is the amphitheatre which is designed to host petitions, deputations and public gatherings during important events such as the official opening of parliament. To capture this representative component, as one walks past the reception checkpoint into the compound, the amphitheatre is heralded by a ground map of Malawi on the left. This map shows that Malawi is divided into three regions (North, Central and South); that the regions are further divided into twenty-eight districts; and that the districts are demarcated into 193 constituencies. Each of these 193 constituencies is represented on the map by one stone brought by the sitting MP at the time of inaugurating the complex. At the centre of the arena stands a bust of Mutharika that was designed and sculpted in China. The amphitheatre stands are decorated with Roman-style colonnades and there is a permanently mounted public address system installed by the Chinese contractors to facilitate the projection of speeches from the main building for people listening outside. This central point also leads one to the pick-up and drop-off zone for members and up a few steps to the security-manned entrance of the main building. This is where the plaque showing that the building was inaugurated by the Malawian President on 21 May 2010 has been placed.

From the colonnades, the next part of the complex is the main building. It is a double-storey structure (plus basement) that houses the debate chamber, members' lounges, offices and printing press. The debate chamber is the centre-piece of the main building. It is a carpeted, oval-shaped auditorium with a dome and has 243 blue-draped members' seats arranged in a horse shoe format, a visitors' gallery on the first floor, and media booths.[7] The dome is revered in Malawi's political circles and represents an 'inverted calabash'[8] or a pot[9] which denotes Malawian hospitality. While the dome gives the chamber a striking aesthetic quality, it is a source of consternation for sitting MPs because of its propensity to leak during the rainy season (Khamula, 2020). The Chinese contractors who still hover around the complex as part of the maintenance agreement between China and Malawi have been mending the dome for the past ten years with no durable success. Abutting the debate chamber are two lounges, one for ordinary Members of Parliament and the other for cabinet ministers.

Apart from the debate chamber, the bulk of functional spaces in the building are reserved for offices. The allocation of office space provides a window to partly understand users' experience. For example, part of the basement with

---

[7] The colour of the seats caused friction during the early days of the building because blue is the colour of the ruling DPP. The opposition felt the colours were chosen by the Chinese to glorify the DPP. However, they were not successful in changing the colours as the government would not budge.

[8] Interview with a former Speaker of Parliament, Lilongwe, 10 July 2019.

[9] Interview with an architect, Lilongwe, 11 July 2019.

limited aeration inappropriately houses the printing unit. The staffers there contend with health-threatening fumes produced by their heavy-duty printing machines. In mitigation, the parliament provides milk to the printing press staffers. However, their colleagues in the Hansard department with whom they share the basement have not yet benefited from this amelioration.[10] The locus of power in the building is on the second floor. This floor has offices of the presiding officers and senior parliament administrators. The red-carpeted foyer and mini reception manned by security officials is an indicator of the special status of this floor. However, the construction flaws in the building are felt by those in the basement and senior officials alike. For instance, the ceramic floor tiles occasionally become dislodged because of the Chinese contractors' favoured use of cement as opposed to durable tile adhesive mixture. The building is also intermittently enveloped by a foul smell which a presiding officer I spoke to diplomatically referred to as a 'plumbing challenge'.[11] According to a parliament technician, the plumbing problem is due to the 'initial poor workmanship' by the Chinese contractor.[12]

Flashback: basis for the shift, the negotiations and China's motivations

The new parliament building was a product of the shift in Malawi's relations from Taiwan to the PRC and a powerful representation of this transition. The shift was a result of two forces: political realism driven by a desire to extract economic benefits from mainland China and President Mutharika's idiosyncratic preferences. The stupendous growth of the PRC as a global player made the switch from Taiwan attractive and inevitable.[13] President Mutharika coveted the switch because it enabled him to obtain a powerful patron.

Clearly China's rise and political realism played an important role in shaping the shift from Taiwan to the PRC. However, beyond this truism, I also found some localised factors such as Taiwan's association with the previous one-party regime. In Malawi, Taiwan was heavily tainted by its long association with the dictatorial Hastings Banda regime and the prevailing sentiment at the resumption of multi-party politics was in favour of abandoning relations with Taiwan. For example, one civil society leader complained that:

Taiwan was part of supporting the repressive regime. Some of the paramilitary wing of [Banda's] MCP was being trained in Taiwan. So,

10   Interview with a senior parliament officer, Lilongwe, 8 August 2019.
11   Interview with a parliament presiding officer, Lilongwe, 28 August 2019.
12   Multiple conversations with parliament technicians, Lilongwe, 5 August 2019.
13   Interview with a senior academic, Zomba, 20 August 2019.

it was a country that was associated with negative aspects which defeated the values of democracy that Malawians had strived for.[14]

In addition, the feeling of antipathy towards Taiwan in Malawi had gained currency partly due to their low aid levels. For example, Taiwan's support of irrigation projects such as rice in selected parts of the country, constructing a medical facility and providing a handful of educational scholarships, seemed scanty when compared to what the PRC was offering their allies. Some felt that 'even if those were put together [Malawi was] just being manipulated for nothing'.[15] It is within this context that the relations between the PRC and Malawi were mooted, negotiated and consummated.

The initiation of discussions between Malawi and the PRC was a mutual exercise. While the PRC was covertly making approaches to Malawi through back channels, the Government of Malawi itself started seriously considering the switch around 2006, in the middle of Mutharika's first term.[16]

The PRC approach in Malawi was in synch with its documented strategy of enticing African countries with huge financial packages in exchange for recognising its One-China principle. Timothy Rich (2009), notes that in 2004, 'China offered Angola an aid package nearly matching an assistance package from the International Monetary Fund (IMF) but with no constraints and followed this with a US$9 billion loan in 2006' (Rich, 2009: 16). Rich correctly concludes that this kind of support that he dubs 'the Chinese Marshall Plan' had the effect of transforming the diplomatic battle by raising the cost for recognition. This seemed the case for Malawi's ruling elites who were palpably enchanted by the PRC's manoeuvres, as a former Malawi cabinet minister reminisces:

> It began not to make sense to me why we were still having a relationship with Taiwan versus forty-eight countries having relations with Mainland China ... As it turned out I discovered that [in] the relationship before up until that time the presidents before benefited a lot from the relationship with Taiwan personally, not the country.[17]

It is in this context that President Mutharika assembled a team of senior government officials led by the then-Minister of Foreign Affairs, Joyce Banda to engage the PRC and weigh the offers being made.[18]

---

14   Interview with a veteran civic society leader, Lilongwe, 16 July 2019.
15   Ibid.
16   Interview with a former Foreign Minister, Lilongwe, 16 July 2019.
17   Interview with a former Foreign Affairs minister, Lilongwe, 12 July 2019.
18   Ibid.

One of the items on the negotiation table was Malawi's request for funding for a new parliament building. This project was at that time being funded by Taiwan and, from 2005 to 2007, Taiwan had only disbursed US$5 million towards the project.[19] Progress was slow, the political elites were not happy and the parliament operations were in limbo. This background provided the opportunity for the PRC to practically show Malawi that it would not only take over the previous Taiwan-backed project, but better it. In this instance, the PRC tabled a US$50 million grant which would construct the parliament building within eighteen months. In addition, the PRC indicated to the Malawi authorities its desire to improve the plans, enlarging the building and ensuring that an iconic parliament would be constructed.[20] Here a former cabinet minister noted that:

> When a decision was made to switch to mainland China, our condition too as Malawi Government was to ask the Chinese Government to take over this project (Parliament Building) which had the initial funding of US$5 million from Taiwan. The Chinese Government readily accepted and they agreed to look at our drawings, improve on them and construct in the aspect of a grant. So, there was a good amount of grant in that year and we also somehow changed our drawings because now there was money enough to cater for the project.[21]

However, the Taiwanese were not willing to give up their sphere of influence without a fight. At that time, Malawi was their biggest diplomatic partner in Africa and they made sure the PRC efforts were, according to one official, 'all frustrated'.[22] This is because 'Taiwan [got] to know and [threw] all sorts of spanners including interfering with the efforts'.[23] This influenced the nature of the discussions between Malawi and the PRC. They were held secretly, centrally controlled and took a conspiratorial character. For example, in the negotiations held in China, members of the Malawi delegation did not travel together but flew to different locations first and found their way to the appointed rendezvous.[24] One such incident occurred in December 2007. Mutharika dispatched a delegation of two ministers and Foreign Affairs officials to Beijing to sign a memorandum of understanding as a precursor to the establishment of diplomatic relations.

---

[19]   Interview with a former Speaker of Parliament, Lilongwe, 10 July 2019.
[20]   Ibid.
[21]   Interview with a former Foreign Affairs minister, Lilongwe, 12 July 2019.
[22]   Interview with a Foreign Affairs Ministry official, Lilongwe, 16 July 2019.
[23]   Ibid.
[24]   Ibid.

When the Taiwanese authorities gathered information about the PRC-Malawi engagement, then Foreign Minister James Huang summoned Malawi's ambassador to Taiwan, Thengo Maloya, who provided a diplomatic double-speak refutation that 'the relationship between Taiwan and Malawi is stable, and I think it's stronger' (Hsiu-chuan, 2007). He further pointed out that 'he was not sure if the two senior ministers were planning to go to Beijing, but he knew for sure that they had not been instructed by Mutharika to do so' (Hsiu-chuan, 2007). However, by the 2008 new year the die was cast. Huang initially made overtures to Malawi by dangling a US$6 billion package but no response was forthcoming (Wines, 2008). He then made a last-ditch effort of flying to Lilongwe on 2 January to meet Banda and Mutharika in a bid to shore up the relations.

However, Malawi's authorities rebuffed his overtures and refused to meet, forcing him to re-route on 4 January to Swaziland,[25] one of Taiwan's longest-standing allies. This left Banda to announce that: 'We have decided to switch from Taiwan to mainland China after careful consideration on the benefits that we will be getting from mainland China' (BBC, 2008). The nature of these negotiations and the agreement thereof has had a legacy in Malawi. In particular, the actual agreement establishing diplomatic relations between Malawi and the PRC remains a secret, not recorded and kept at the Treaty office in the Ministry of Foreign and International Cooperation like other diplomatic agreements. A senior official in the Ministry only recalls seeing the Chinese language version of the agreement in Beijing.[26]

Upon reflection, the concession to take over the construction of the parliament building provided China with an opportunity to project its influence in Malawi through its parliament. In contemporary Malawian politics, parliament is multi-party in membership and character. This means that one finds the dominant political factions in parliament, making it an important arena to exert influence. Specifically, all four political parties that have alter-nately governed Malawi, namely the DPP, the MCP, the People's Party (PP) and the United Democratic Front (UDF) have a presence in the Legislature. This is the only place where one can find these political factions together. Having built the country's parliament, China has created a congenial place to meet and cultivate good relations across a range of parties, in the knowledge that future elections may deliver a change of party in charge.[27] This reasoning

25 Swaziland is now known as Eswatini.
26 Interview with a Foreign Affairs official, Lilongwe, 16 July 2019.
27 In June 2020, government changed hands from the DPP to an MCP-led coalition government. The Chinese Ambassador was the first to pay a courtesy call on the new President.

is described in broader Chinese-Africa political engagement scholarship. In a study on the Communist Party of China's International Department (CPC-ID)[28] David Shinn and Joshua Eisenman (2012) note that the CPC-ID engages both the ruling (*guozhengdang*) and opposition (*fanduidang*) parties. Part of this engagement corresponds with work of the foreign committee of the PRC's Parliament, called the National People's Congress (NPC).[29]

At least part of the rationale behind Malawi's Chinese-funded parliament building can be understood from the perspective of this work of the NPC. This is given more credence by the fact that at the commissioning of the new parliament building, China deployed as chief guest Li Zhaoxing, the then-chairman of the Foreign Affairs Committee of the Standing Committee of the National People's Congress of China (Zhaoxing, 2010). When viewed from this angle, the PRC through the NPC is engaged in forging far-reaching political relationships with diverse Malawian political elites. This strategy protects Chinese interests in Malawi in the long run because it hedges against changes of government or party turnover.

The construction phase:
carte blanche powers to Chinese contractors

When China took over the parliament building project, they not only displaced Taiwan, but fundamentally changed the project's local implementation modalities. Malawi's extant institutional framework for public construction projects was truncated, or in some cases blatantly flouted. In particular, China varied the original plan with limited input from the Public Works department, unilaterally appointed a Chinese construction firm and exclusively sourced building materials and key artisans from China. The Chinese side had full control of the labour recruitment, contractor supervision and post-construction maintenance planning.

Their first act was to push out local architects who had designed the building and the local contractors who were at the construction site. The MNA consortium[30] of architects who were project consultants, and Terrastone and Deco, the contractors, were all asked to cease operations. The architects were requested to 'hand over every document pertaining to construction of

[28] The CPC-ID is an organ that was set up in 1978 to lead the charge of conducting the CPC's political and diplomatic work.
[29] The NPC Foreign committee works at 'strengthening and improving the mechanism for regular exchanges with other parliaments and congresses' (see Eisenmann, 2008: 241).
[30] The MNA consortium comprised three architectural firms namely MD Initiative, Norman & Dawbarn and ABC Design Associates.

parliament building'.[31] This included 'the construction drawings and specification [that] the government passed on to the Chinese Government for them to proceed with the construction'.[32] When I interviewed players in Malawi's construction industry, I got a sense that as much as they welcomed the Chinese funding, they would have preferred a situation where the original Malawian contractors and consultants were retained in the project.[33]

The implication of this approach was that local companies were deprived of the opportunity to participate in the subsequent development of the parliament building project. More regrettably, their initial contribution was expunged from the official Malawi Government literature on the project. This revised history of the parliament building project that emphasises China's role is inconsistent with photographs taken of the site before the Chinese arrived.[34]

This hostile takeover, ostensibly supported by the government, is still a sore point for concerned parties in Malawi. More importantly it provides a concrete example of Chinese modus operandi in delivering their aid. This government support for the removal of Malawian companies from the construction site was a decision that came from the very top echelons of the Malawi Government.[35]

Civil servants involved in the project welcomed Chinese support but would have preferred to continue with the original guidelines. However, they allege that their advice was not taken on board.[36] This led to an acrimonious settlement between the government and the original Malawian contractors. To cap this ignominious exit, the contractors were paid via promissory notes instead of legal tender. One senior architect, who was following the developments, sums up the Chinese takeover:

> The sad part is the fact that after the takeover of the Chinese Government, Malawians had very, very minimal participation in the project ... All the architects and engineers, they all came from China. The contractor was also a Chinese company. Materials they came also from China including even the part of the labours or unskilled labour came from China.[37]

31 Interview with original architect and designer, Lilongwe, 11 July 2019.
32 Ibid.
33 FGD with officials from Malawi Building and Allied Industries, Lilongwe, 12 August 2019.
34 See Victor Ndagha Kaonga's blog of 30 August 2007: http://ndagha.blogspot.com/2007/08/new-malawis-parliament-building.html [Accessed 31 January 2022].
35 Interview with former Public Works ministry official, Lilongwe, 25 July 2019.
36 Ibid.
37 Interview with senior architect, Lilongwe, 11 July 2019.

This displacement of local skills and competence, and the use of imported materials, contradicts China's win-win cooperation rhetoric which is deployed to portray its support as different from Western counterparts. The Chinese funding of the parliament building might have been a victory for diplomatic strategy, but it displaced Malawian architects and contractors from the project, causing a direct loss of jobs and the opportunity to be part of shaping an important state building.

The Chinese Government was exclusively in charge of appointing a contractor who in turn procured construction materials and recruited requisite labour. Once the Chinese contractor was appointed, he undertook a complete consolidation of the character of the project as China-driven. The initial plan by the earlier designers to give the parliament a façade which depicted Malawian traditions by integrating locally available materials was abandoned. For example, plans to use local Dedza tiles gave way to Chinese vinyl tiles on the facade. The Chinese-supplied building materials for the project enjoyed duty-free status. This was considered as Malawi's contribution since the financial support was being given as complete grant-aid.

However, the quantification, transportation and accounting of the materials left a lot to be desired and created opportunities for leakages. Speaking to officials in the Customs section of the Malawi Revenue Authority (MRA), I found out that bills of quantities were sometimes written in Chinese so could not be read by Malawian officials. In addition to this complexity, the building material was brought into Malawi in batches and through more than three different ports of entry. This made it challenging to reconcile the submitted bills of quantities, amounts of materials imported and what was actually needed at the construction site. The mid-ranking officers at the MRA told me that, in the absence of a bonded warehouse, it was difficult not to rule out the possibility of leakages in the form of more materials brought into the country under the duty-free dispensation.

Moreover, the contractor-controlled labour recruitment and as a result most of the skilled workers came from China. I spoke to informants working in relevant offices in Public Works[38] and Finance ministries[39] to get an overview of the process of obtaining authorisation to work in Malawi under this project. The contractor would produce a protocol labour requirement and a list of names of Chinese nationals who needed work visas. These lists were supposed to clearly show the skillset brought by expatriate workers and the duration of their stay. However, it was practically difficult to enforce this provision because over and above the project's 'special status', the protocols and lists were written in

---

[38]   Interview with a former Public Works ministry official, Lilongwe, 25 July 2019.
[39]   Interview with debt and aid official, Lilongwe, 18 July 2019.

Chinese and there was no capacity in the Public Works Office to interpret the documents. The documents would then be sent to the Treasury, a department in the Ministry of Finance, so that a cover note could be appended for final submission to the immigration department which issues work permits. This process did not take place as described since the Public Works Ministry resorted to only asking the contractor to submit estimated numbers of employees they would bring. This loophole resulted in semi-skilled labour being brought from China. An informant who was actively involved in the project pointed out that some of the personnel brought from China were deployed to do menial tasks such as being night watchmen.[40] Moreover, a conversation I had with local artisans in two different settings, as well as officers from the Public Works Ministry, showed that the Malawian artisans who were recruited for the project were rated as semi-skilled workers and received work and remuneration which they considered as less than their worth.[41]

Contrary to China's rhetoric of mutual partnership and sharing expertise with African countries, this scenario provided credence to how this Chinese Government-aided project failed the skills transfer test. A former Public Works official reflecting on some of the problems associated with labour recruitment and morale told me that:

> The other problem which we had was because all workers were from China. Here it was only labourers. Sometimes they wanted to suppress them but our Ministry of Labour used to visit the place to make sure that they were happy. But there was no transfer of anything or skills, there was no skills transfer because they were mostly using labourers.[42]

This approach possibly planted seeds for animosity as the Malawians I spoke with, especially those involved in the construction sector, were distraught at how locals had been muscled out of the building project. While the parliament building has beautified Lilongwe and provides residents with a sense of pride, it is equally a constant reminder of the ill-treatment endured by local companies, artisans and semi-skilled workers.

Implications of the blank-cheque approach to Malawi

Having shown how China had free rein in implementing the parliament building project, in this section I explain the reasons for and implications of Malawi ruling elites' blank-cheque approach. In the first place, Malawi's government

40   Interview with a former Public Works ministry official, 25 July 2019.
41   FGD with artisans, Lilongwe, 5 August 2019.
42   Interview with a former Public Works ministry official, Lilongwe, 25 July 2019.

accepted China's financial and material support because it desperately needed
a purpose-built parliament building. Since the capital moved from Zomba to
Lilongwe in 1975 (Potts, 1985), the Legislature had lacked a permanent home.
Initially, Malawi's parliament had remained in Zomba when the other arms
of the state moved. The Zomba parliament building, inaugurated in 1957, was
meant for not more than thirty members. With the increase in membership to
193, and the resumption of multi-party politics in 1994, parliament needed a
bigger meeting facility. In 2001, then President Bakili Muluzi suggested that
parliament move to the new State House in Lilongwe (now called the Kamuzu
Palace) a 300-room presidential palace built during the Kamuzu Banda era.

At the new State House, the banqueting hall was transformed into a parliamentary chamber and tea rooms were converted into committee rooms. This
adaptation was not without difficulty. For instance, the banqueting hall was
not suitable for plenary sittings because:

> The guest and the Member were only separated by a very small barrier
> ... You have gone there to watch but, in the end, you are not very far
> from the Member who is sitting in front of you. So, you were all like
> Members because they couldn't do much about it and it became very
> inconvenient to Members and yet the rules of the House have in their
> thinking that these barriers should be clear.[43]

The State House tea rooms were not suitable for use as committee rooms
especially for the larger portfolio and oversight committees such as the Public
Accounts and Public Appointment Committees, so parliament incurred further
costs by using hotels for some of its business.

Alongside these practical reasons, Mutharika had political reasons for
leveraging Chinese Government support to construct the parliament building.
Politically, Mutharika was a 'big ideas President' who was keen on monument
building,[44] like other African presidents such as Félix Houphouët-Boigny
in Côte d'Ivoire (see Gallagher and Yah Ariane N'djoré in Chapter 5, this
collection, and Nana Akufo-Addo in Ghana (see Ofori-Sarpong in Chapter 2,
this collection). In retrospect, this explains a plethora of signature construction
projects done during his tenure. When I spoke to elites and ordinary people
in Lilongwe, Mutharika was described by his admirers as 'a visionary', a
man keen on development who 'built' many important landmarks in Malawi
which include the Kamuzu Mausoleum, the Parliament Building and a new

---

[43]   Interview with a former Clerk of Parliament, Lilongwe, 4 July 2019.
[44]   Speaking to Malawians, they are most likely to point out a number of Mutharika's
construction projects which include state buildings, tobacco processing factories and
housing units.

university. Architects who were tasked with designing these buildings report that he was actively involved in the initial design process and followed all the subsequent steps with keen interest.[45] Extrapolating from this interest, it is understandable why the funding of the parliament building was a central condition put forward by the Malawian negotiation team with Beijing.

Mutharika gave prominence to this issue by repeatedly mentioning this promise to deliver a new parliament building at rallies.[46] The construction phase took place during the 2009 electoral season where it was an important reference point for Mutharika and his newly formed DPP.

Delivering the parliament building in record time enhanced Mutharika's political capital especially in the context of delivering physical symbols of 'development'. This is because the parliament building project, as Malawi-China's first and biggest undertaking, provided a backdrop during the elections on what the relationship could potentially produce. Mutharika received two-thirds of the vote, making his the largest victory in the era of Malawi's multi-party politics. Some of the major reasons that have been attributed to this success include this physical Chinese support and the President's handling of the food security situation during the first term.[47] Moreover, Mutharika's speech at the official commissioning of the building shows that he was personally and politically invested in the project. He said: 'I am delighted that my dream has come true. The construction of this parliament [building] is an extremely important milestone for the Malawi Government and I am glad that China has delivered its promises in time' (Xinhua, 2010).

Notwithstanding the President's gushing praise, the construction of the parliament building project produced a series of negative impacts on Malawian agency. The exclusive manner in which China controlled the design, funding construction and subsequently the maintenance of the building suggests the side-lining of Malawian expertise and internal public works processes. Such Chinese dominance in Malawi's public works arena undermined the country's control of its parliamentary habitat. A Malawian senior academic reasoned that, 'if you have the Chinese building your parliament, you are basically surrendering a huge degree of your sovereignty'.[48] This perspective is based on the fact that the building does not yet fully belong to the country due to the continued presence and involvement of China in it. The management contract between the two governments still centres the Chinese companies

45   Interview with a senior architect, Lilongwe, 11 July 2019.
46   Interview with civic society leaders, Lilongwe, 23 July 2019; FGD with traditional leaders, Biwi, 14 August 2019.
47   Interview with a civic society leader, Lilongwe, 16 July 2019.
48   Interview with a senior academic, Zomba, 20 August 2019.

in maintaining the building.[49] This reality is also a legacy of the manner in which the project was carried out. For example, in the maintenance works carried out since 2010, most materials were Chinese, as were the contractors.[50] This situation undercuts the state public works bureaucracy and limits the extent which Malawi and Malawians can have a say in the maintenance of the building.

One very practical legacy – and headache for the current users – is the fact that some of the building's signage is written in Chinese. This has made it difficult for local engineers employed by government to fully understand the nooks and crannies of the building – an important attribute which would help in domesticating the maintenance its in the long run.[51] While the replacement materials continue to be sourced from China by the contractor, opportunities for the construction industry in Malawi are limited.[52]

With regard to the user experience, I found out that, while people appreciated and celebrated having a purpose-built structure, their non-involvement in the earlier phases of the project had a negative impact. Most of my informants who were present in 2010 when the building was commissioned mentioned that their first experience in the building was when it had been completed. Their initial reaction was that it was a magnificent building,[53] looked 'stunning'[54] from outside and they were looking forward to working from it. However, once they moved in they 'realised that it had so many shortfalls'.[55] For example, commenting on the lack of a security screen between the visitors' gallery and the members' seating area, a senior parliamentary staffer regretted that:

> The people who constructed this building never thought about the fact that when you are seated up there even a small book … which weighs about 500 grams can be a potential danger to a Member of Parliament seated down there. There is an open space between the Members sitting down in the chamber and members of the public such that if somebody were to throw this book on the head of somebody, it can have disastrous effects.[56]

---

[49]   Interview with a Foreign Affairs official, 16 July 2019.
[50]   Multiple conversations with Parliament maintenance staff, Lilongwe, 5 August 2019.
[51]   Ibid.
[52]   Focus group discussion with Malawi contractors, 12 August 2019.
[53]   Interview with a senior parliament officer, Lilongwe, 29 August 2019.
[54]   Interview with a parliament officer, Lilongwe, 12 August 2019.
[55]   Interview with a parliament officer, Lilongwe, 5 August 2019.
[56]   Interview with a senior parliament officer, Lilongwe, 8 August 2019.

This anxiety over the security limitations in the chamber has an indirect impact on making the chamber truly accessible to members of the public. For instance, in February 2020, parliamentary proceedings were halted after some MPs objected to the presence of prominent activists, Timothy Mtambo and Gift Trapence of the Human Rights Defenders Coalition (Kadzanja, 2020). Apart from the security dimension, other users feel constrained by the building. Staff in the printing press are stuck in the basement and, as indicated above, grapple with toxic fumes from the heavy-duty machines.

A senior official rationalised this anomaly by highlighting that the Chinese-built structure is the first phase and the second will house the printing press and other auxiliary offices.[57] Until that comes to pass, the user experience of the printing section remains clouded in smoke. Others also pointed out that the way the library was designed is not suitable for a parliamentary library.[58] This is because it was allocated one 'large' room too small to partition. This scenario has forced parliament management and officers and large stacks of books to share space with their clients. This shortage of space occurs in the context of a building that is designed with vast corridors which could have been reduced to optimise work areas. These are examples of the experiences of working in the building. The positive feelings of a separate and friendly work environment for the Legislature are tempered by uneasiness due to its limitations.

Conclusion

In this chapter, I leveraged the Chinese-funded parliament building in Malawi to explore China-Africa relations, Chinese foreign aid delivery in Africa and the extent of African state agency in engagements with big powers. I have shown that the implementation of this building project highlights the asymmetrical power between the donor and the recipient. Whereas the motivation for the building implies a mutually beneficial arrangement, the same cannot be said about the method of executing the project. The disproportionate power that China had in project management through exclusively determining the contractor, materials procurement and labour recruitment brings to the fore the larger question of the position of African states in determining the course of their development. Here, this is brought to bear through the ways in which Malawian companies were pushed out of the project to make exclusive way for those from China. In the chapter I have shown that, whereas the mind that conceived and initially designed the parliament building was Malawian, Chinese foreign aid had the effect of expunging this fact from history. This is

57 Interview with a senior parliament official, 26 July 2019.
58 Interview with a parliament official, Lilongwe, 5 July 2019.

why the extant materials related to the parliament building project incorrectly suggest the idea as Chinese – a version found even within official Malawi Government literature. I have also shown that the limited participation of Malawians in shaping the final product has had far-reaching implications. While it is a positive development that at least Malawi now has a purpose-built Parliament building that looks stunning from the outside, the users grapple with a dysfunctional structure that impacts their work. From the leaking chamber, the poorly designed library, the peeling tiles and the foul smell from the plumbing system, to the fume-filled printing section in the basement, the building simply is not as functional as the exterior veneer suggests.

Regarding the study of African states in their relation to China and other global players I have shown that the Malawi Parliament building project is a microcosm of China's new strategy of concrete investment in African governance architecture. There are already fifteen parliament buildings constructed and refurbished by the Chinese Government across the continent. Each has its own nuanced story, but I contend that the rudiments remain similar. This finding ignites an important discourse on the character of the ruling elites and the malleability of African states' institutional architecture. I have shown that the bureaucrats and attendant structures in Malawi were given less room to exercise their functions in a project whose conception was secret, and implementation laced by high politics. From this perspective, this chapter has modestly contributed to the age-old debate of the presence, utility and effectiveness of institutions in African states.

4

New homes for a new state: Foreign ideas in Ghana's public housing programmes

IRENE APPEANING ADDO

All sorts of plans have been introduced since the so called crusade to Holland but one stubborn fact remains. The houses intended to ease the sufferings of our people have yet to be built. (*Daily Graphic*, 1954: 5)

This was the criticism Kwame Nkrumah, the leader of the Convention People's Party (CPP) and later first President of Ghana, received for his unsuccessful attempt at addressing the country's housing situation and for his decision to adopt the prefabricated Dutch housing method. Prefabricated housing had been touted as a quick way of producing housing for the teeming masses who were daily trooping to the urban centres for employment opportunities as the development of industries, mines, railways and harbours gathered momentum. As well as failing to meet growing needs, the Dutch-constructed houses did not reflect the cultural living arrangements of the people and they did not feel Ghanaian enough.

Public house-building became an important objective during the transitional and early independence years of Ghana due to three political agendas; Africanisation, industrialisation and modernisation. The Africanisation agenda required that African senior civil servants eventually occupy the management positions of government businesses as the Europeans departed the then-Gold Coast. Thus, there was the need to provide living accommodation for the African officials, public sector workers, and formal and informal sector workers. Next, the industrialisation agenda resulted in the establishment of pioneer industries and businesses in urban centres across the country, leading to mass migration of workers from the rural areas.[1] Meanwhile, the housing

---

[1]   The urban population which was estimated at 570,597 in 1948 (13.9 per cent of the total population) increased to 1,547,700 in 1960 (about 23.1 per cent of the national population) (Songsore, 2020: 6; GSS, 2014: 6, 19).

dynamics in the urban centres – high rents, poor quality housing and limited rental units – were inadequate for such large numbers of migrant workers. The third agenda, which was the new government policy to modernise and improve the standards of housing, propelled massive house-building projects across the country. All three agendas combined to introduce a situation where public housing demand outstripped supply in the urban centres of the new state.

The demand for 'adequate' public housing was so compelling that foreign assistance in terms of loans, technical assistance, construction materials and technology, and housing policies had to be incorporated into the development plan, thus creating a disconnect between 'dependent' house-building and 'independent' state building during the transition to independence. It is also noteworthy that the transitional years had foreign expatriate technocrats at the helm of the building industry.

In this chapter, I argue that the new state's sense of responsibility for housing the growing urban population made it dependent in new ways on foreign actors, recreating and reimagining its dependency and showcasing the tension of the independence state-building project. Using existing literature and information collected from the archives and newspapers, I discuss the state of public housing and the housing-building agenda during the transitional and early independence years, and draw out the challenges, contradictions and new kinds of dependencies to which it gave rise. I discuss the formation of foreign partnerships to address the housing situation by citing two examples – the Schokbeton and the Ghana National Construction Corporation housing programmes. The chapter concludes with a discussion on the ubiquitous architecture produced as a result of these engagements. In order to set the scene, I begin by describing state building and the modernist planning approach adopted by African states as a vehicle for industrial growth and development.

Modernist planning, post-colonial state-led projects and ambitious state building

Core to the project of state building is the aspiration to make independent decisions about managing internal institutions without external interference, and the construction of identity through international recognition and access to international resources. This statement is in line with Julia Gallagher's (2018: 883–84) definition that statehood or state-subjectivity is analogous to selfhood or self-consciousness, a situation where both 'a sense of self – the degree to which the state can embody the identity and aspirations of its population – and its ability to act, its agency ... beyond itself, on the international level'. According to Freek Colombijn (2011), public housing involves highly political choices where the high expectations of a young nation are realised. Thus, house-building is an expression of the pride and product of state building.

So modernist planning by post-colonial governments, optimistic about the possibilities for the comprehensive planning of human settlement and production, was expected to act as a flagship of state building, and house-building was a core part of this project. According to Sibel Bozdogan (2001), the modern movement ideology, referred to as a 'revolution in architecture', was closely linked to house-building. Otherwise referred to as 'architecture in revolution', house-building projects conveyed a political message that legitimated new states and defined their identity. The ambitious post-colonial developments and optimistic state-led projects created a 'false' belief in the transformative potentials of state-led massive modernist projects. This was because post-colonial modernist planning was based on grand plans and programmes developed by experts and implemented using top-down approaches often leading to a hegemonic planning mentality that excluded the role of local knowledge and tradition (Abubakar and Doan, 2017). Furthermore, the size of these programmes undermined core aspects of independence as new states' sovereignty was inevitably challenged when they attempted to engage external actors in state building (Chandler, 2010). James Scott (1998: 22) explains that 'miscarried or thwarted' projects of the new state resulted in 'miniaturisation' and 'controlled micro-order in model cities'.

Nkrumah argued that Ghana needed a technological and scientific great leap forward to create a new and thoroughly modern state and escape the grip of colonialism. Thus, professionals from Eastern Europe and America were contracted to assist in Ghana's state building. The foreign countries introduced Western modernist planning ideology to Ghanaian dwelling cultures thereby stagnating the traditional forms of architecture in the country (d'Auria, 2014). For example, Constantinos A. Doxiadis's reconceptualisation of the Tema master plan and his model city of Akosombo presented visions of high modernist planning and state building and were seen as a guarantee of emancipation, although they could also be described as a form of neo-colonialism, based as they were on a very generalised, Western model which took little account of local aesthetics, norms and needs (Bromley, 2003; d'Auria, 2010; Miescher, 2012; Jackson et al., 2019). In terms of architecture, foreign modernist architects such as James Cubbit, Jane Drew, Maxwell Fry, Leo De Syllas and Otto Koenigsberger served as advisors in Ghana's town planning and designed many modernist buildings (Uduku, 2006). By hybridising traditional dwelling practices and context-sensitive neighbourhood layouts in housing design, colonised territories were posited as sites for experimentation as the ambivalent modernist tenets of the late-colonial and post-independence architectural production were re-articulated (d'Auria, 2014). This led to a major contradiction between 'the idea of a national style based on tradition' and 'the revolutionary principles of the new nationbuilding' (Bozdogan, 2001: 61). For Paul Collier and Anthony Venables (2014), governments in Anglophone Africa, on independence, inherited building standards that were inappropriate for their level of income since the British Government was experimenting with the principles of tropical architecture in its colonies. Yet the new African political elite had no African alternative with which to compare it. Modernism offered the kind of abstraction and formal novelty devoid of historical associations that matched nation-building ideological aspirations (Bozdogan, 2001: 61).

Formation of a new state

The transitional and post-independence years (1950–1966)

The period leading to 1950 was regarded as one of urbanisation in the Gold Coast as people migrated, especially to the mining towns and agricultural producing areas. This was driven by Ghana's post-Second World War economic boom, which led to the establishment of state-owned enterprises and the introduction of pioneer companies as government sought to promote industrialisation. Public health policies coupled with taxation, urban slum clearance and rehousing programmes were used to address the 'insanitary' conditions that prevailed as a result of overcrowding and high densities in Accra (Patterson, 1979). Information at the Ghana Public Records and Archives Administration Department (GH/PRAAD) in Accra indicates that a meeting held on 5 January 1950 to discuss sites for new government and quasi-government bungalows in the Cantonments area noted the 'grave shortage of houses in Accra between 1950 and 1951', and advocated housing construction to address the situation, particularly the use of prefabricated building components.[2]

As part of the preparations towards self-government from 1951, the CPP government undertook massive development of economic and social infrastructure in the country. Under Nkrumah's leadership, between 1951 and 1957 it introduced measures for internal self-government and the establishment of administrative ministries (Biney, 2011), including Nkrumah's Africanisation agenda, a 'tactical action' to work with the colonial administration and other countries to firmly establish the new state.

Nkrumah in 1951 decided to implement a development plan to promote massive industrialisation, previously formulated by the British colonial

[2] GH/PRAAD/RG 5/1/50. Notes of a meeting held in the Secretariat on Thursday, February 23 1950 to decide on the question of sites in the Accra government residential area for government requirements and those of quasi-government building.

administration. The war years had made it impossible to export raw materials or import building materials and other basic supplies. This gave rise to plans to set up manufacturing industries to produce the country's needed commodities. So-called 'pioneer' companies were established to produce everyday needs such as liquor, cigarettes and clothing. The brick and tile roofing industry was set up in part to address the shortage of roofing sheets. Railways were constructed to enable the transportation of goods between urban centres. Marine transport was developed for import and export activities as well as to promote goods transfer from Akosombo and Accra to Takoradi and vice versa. These developments occurred in tandem with the spread of the modernist urban planning agenda from Europe to the Global South. The development of these industries drove the need for further housing development schemes.

By 1951, a sharp rise in cocoa prices led to an increase in private housing building among wealthy cocoa farmers (Seers and Ross, 1952). This, along with the government's industrialisation agenda, the housing shortage and increased rents, induced further private building activity and speculative building, driving up demand for building material imports. Dudley Seers and Claud Ross (1952) have stated that cement imports rose from 53,000 tonnes to 117,000 tonnes between 1938 and 1950, but by 1951 they had risen to 240,000 tonnes. Within the same period the demand for corrugated roofing sheets increased from 1,600 tonnes to 8,300 tonnes. The economy of the Gold Coast was described at this time as 'fragile', with material and labour shortages posing inflationary risks (Seers and Ross, 1952: 1). One initiative to offset these risks and ensure local production of goods and services involved the establishment of a cement grinding plant, the Tunnel Portland Company Limited at Takoradi in 1957. The company was co-owned by a private British firm and the government of Ghana.

A second Five-year Development Plan (1958–63) was formulated during the post-independence period. The plan proposed to spend about £20 million annually. However, there was a drop of £28,410 in the budgetary allocation for the housing sector after independence in 1957 (from about £800,000 the previous year). The plan also sought to pursue an Africanisation agenda; however, the government acknowledged that 'efficient government administrative and technical personnel will be recruited from abroad if the need arises' (*Ghana Today*, 1958a). This decision created leeway for foreign participation in Ghana's development agenda. While providing housing was not specifically addressed in the new plan, several committees were set up to deal with Ghana's housing effort and issues of building techniques, cheap forms of construction, building costs and design (*Ghana Today*, 1958b). In 1958, Nkrumah personally

introduced a new housing policy to address increasing public dissatisfaction
with regards to housing allocation in the new state.[3]

Traditional housing and Ghana's housing system

Prior to the provision of public housing in Ghana, the main housing source
was self-built traditional family houses, otherwise known as compound houses.
These houses were usually large and belonged to families instead of individuals
(Amole et al., 1993). They were rent-free and they provided accommodation
for less privileged members of the extended family (Korboe, 1992). In the rural
areas, most family houses were constructed with locally accessed building
materials such as earth, stones, sticks and thatch, using traditional building
techniques such as wattle and daub and rammed earth, which were tailor-
made to address the climatic conditions of a locality (Addo, 2016). However,
as Ghana became urbanised in the 1950s and wealthy cocoa farmers and elite
members of society built themselves European-style houses, the traditional
family houses also metamorphosed. Now cement-based materials were used
for wall-construction while metal roofing sheets were introduced. European
architectural ornamentation – such as columns – was incorporated into the
design of building frontages. Traditional family houses became more stately,
although continuing to have the attributes of shared housing.

With the steady migration into the urban centres after the Second World War
and Ghana's preparation for self-governance, the housing stress experienced
in the urban centres increased. The grave shortage of houses in Accra between
1950 and 1951 remained a big subject in the discussion of political and social
policies in the Gold Coast.[4] Ministers of state, African senior civil servants
and workers of quasi-government organisations – for example, those of the
West African Airways Corporation and Air Services, the Gold Coast Industrial
Development Corporation and the Gold Coast Agricultural Development
Board – had to be housed.[5] So in January 1950 a meeting was held in Accra
to discuss government bungalow requirements for the 1950–51 fiscal years.
They included six houses for the new ministers, eight T2[6] bungalows for the

[3]   The dissatisfaction was caused by perceived malpractice and nepotism (Werlin,
1972; Agyapong, 1990).
[4]   GH/PRAAD/RG 5/1/50. Notes of a meeting held in the Secretariat on 23 February
1950 to decide on the question of sites in the Accra government residential area for
government requirements and those of quasi-government building.
[5]   GH/PRAAD/RG 5/1/50. Residence for Ministers C/50-Type Bungalows. File no.
BC. 228.
[6]   T2 bungalows are public houses built specifically for ministers and under secre-
taries of state.

new under-secretaries and twenty-five A49[7] bungalows for officers paying less than £150 per annum in rents.[8] The initial cost of the T2 bungalows was approximately £3,500 in 1949.

However, the T2 buildings' cost increased to £5,000 by 1950. Some parliamentarians in the Gold Coast expressed great dissatisfaction when the government decided to build ministers' bungalows at a cost of £10,000 as against the initial ceiling of £5,000. Their objections were based on the fact that other social services had not been met. The MPs questioned the whole principle of providing official residences for ministers at the public expense.[9] Still others questioned why a £10,000 building for ministers was considered extravagant noting that the Cocoa Marketing Board was constructing junior overseas officers' houses with two bedrooms for £5,950. The T2 buildings were described as houses that 'appear to provide accommodation which is likely to be required by a minister and his family'.[10] The house type titled 'Houses for the Ministers of Gold Coast Government' went on display at the 1952 Royal Academy Summer Exhibition in London (Hughes and Lomax, 1952). It was adapted from the British Council house type designs. Comments from unofficial African advisers[11] led to revisions in the design. The T2 bungalow was further revised to include a room for storing boxes and baggage, an additional stoep on top of the garage, a laundry room and a 'boys' (staff) quarters with a wide verandah and kitchen facilities. The additions portrayed a form of elitist living where the quarters of the assistants to the African officials were separated from the main bungalow, as they had been in colonial officials' bungalows. In the end, a revised T2 building costing £71,903 for the construction of eight ministers' bungalows were approved and awarded to British Firm Messrs George Watson and Company in December 1950. By

7   A49 bungalows are public houses built for African senior staff working in the colonial administration.
8   Ibid.
9   GH/PRAAD/RG 5/1/50. Secretary of State. Telegram No. 693. Parliamentary Question. 2 May 1950. Residence for Ministers C/50 – Type Bungalows. File No. BC.228 – 6/11/53: 23.
10   GH/PRAAD/RG 5/1/50. Parliamentary question. Dissatisfaction in the Gold Coast over the decision of the government to build a bungalow at a cost of £80,000 and why the ceiling of £5,000 per bungalow agreed on last year, in view of the need for expanding social services, has not been maintained. Telegram No. 693. Secretary of State, 2 May 1950.
11   GH/PRAAD/RG 5/1/62. Note of a meeting held in the secretariat on Thursday 23 February 1950 to decide on the question of sites in the Accra government residential area for government requirements and those of quasi-government building.

22 September 1951 only 124 housing units had been constructed, without any electricity supply, while one-hundred units were yet to be constructed.

Other discussions in cabinet meetings dealt with acquiring appropriate sites and suitable lands for new government, non-government and quasi-government bungalows in the Cantonments area.[12] Some of the considerations for a suitable location were easy accessibility to a main road and bus route, proximity to the new Cantonments restaurant[13] and distance from the centre of Accra.[14] Several housing programmes including the introduction of prefabricated housing construction methods were considered options necessary to address the critical housing situation in the new state.

The Development Plan of 1951 for the Economic and Social Development of the Gold Coast provided an outline of what the country hoped to achieve in all fields of development (Government Printing Department, 1951: 1). The objective was 'to ensure that the progress of development proceeds in an orderly manner on a firm economic basis and also to ensure that effort is directed towards the attainment of a higher standard of living for all' (ibid.). The inadequate and substandard public housing situation in the new state was considered to be a result of (i) high costs of building materials and labour, (ii) shortage of skilled building craftsmen, (iii) lack of mechanisation in the building industry, and (iv) the steady drift to the towns (migration) leading to a severe shortage and overcrowding of available accommodation in these. According to the Development Plan, both experts and unskilled manpower were needed to achieve the plan's objectives. In addition, 'a proportion of the materials required for development projects must be imported and this meant a dependence on world conditions of supply' (ibid.). This meant that both the availability and conditions of importation were likely to impact supplies and cause delays. Finance was also a critical issue. Financing of the projects were projected to be from Ghana's reserves, taxation and loans. Objective six stated that '[i]f men and materials are available, there remains the question of finance. This must be found from reserves, future taxation and loans' (ibid.). The sum of £2.5 million was earmarked for the development of housing programmes (Government Printing Department, 1951: 20–21).

To improve the standard of housing in the Gold Coast in 1951, and to appear modern, Kojo Botsio, then-Minister of Education and Social Welfare, requested

---

[12]   GH/PRAAD/RG 5/1/50. Notes of a discussion regarding sites for new government and non-and quasi-government bungalows in the Cantonments Area. Meeting held in the Secretariat on 5 January 1950.

[13]   GH/PRAAD/RG 5/1/50. Notes of a meeting held in the Secretariat on 23 February 1950 to decide on the question of sites in the Accra government residential area for government requirements and those of quasi-government building.

[14]   The city centre of Accra was regarded as having insanitary conditions.

the Colonial Secretary of State to supply him with housing documents from the UK to guide him in the standards being adopted in public housing, the methods by which the provision of housing was allocated, the proportion for letting or sale and the relative cost of different types. It was anticipated that the information provided would guide the formulation of the country's national housing policy. The Colonial Secretary, E. G. G. Hanrott[15] in his response, gave the minister a series of documents on UK housing conditions and policy, noting, however, that they might not be suitable for low-cost housing in the tropics.

These documents formed the basis for the formulation of Ghana's first building regulations which were thus premised on foreign design guide-lines.[16] Housing programmes including (i) the Accra rehousing schemes, (ii) the subsidised housing scheme, (iii) village improvement and rural housing, (iv) rehousing in connection with slum clearance, (v) plant and experimental work, community centres on housing estates, (vi) railway housing estate (in Takoradi), and (vii) the housing loans scheme were implemented in the new state. The total cost for all the programmes was estimated at £6 million (Government Printing Department, 1951). In addition, a broad range of approaches was used in constructing the houses (Owusu-Addo and Bond, 1966). They included swish buildings which were constructed from earth rammed into a wooden formwork to form bricks as shown in figure 4.1, and prefabricated post-tensioned structures. The construction of the experimental swish buildings increased during the early years due to the introduction of a rotary hydraulic block moulding machine which could produce up to 140 swish blocks per hour (Nartey, 1954: 1). The Gold Coast Women's Federation also submitted a three-point resolution to the government in 1954 advocating that the lack of adequate housing was the 'cause of broken homes and juvenile delinquency' (Akua, 1954: 1). The CPP government responded by tasking the Department of Housing to develop experimental 'scale models of moderately furnished prefabricated houses' which would be shown to the public in an exhibition to be transported from 'place to place' (ibid.).

The housing situation remained critical for the new state. Inadequate housing conditions continued to feature prominently in the newspapers and several editorials were written on the subject. The *Daily Graphic* in July

---

15   Letter dated 10 July 1951 in response to Kojo Botsio's request.
16   A new Ghana Code was recently released in 2018. The Building Code GS1207 of 2018, is a 1,700-page and thirty-eight-section document comprising requirements, recommendations, planning, management and practices of construction in Ghana. It incorporates the use of traditional local materials in building construction. It is also Ghana's first-ever building code.

Figure 4.1   An experimental swish building for the Forestry Commission at
Kibi, built in the 1950s (Iain Jackson, 2018; reproduced with the permission
of Prof. Jackson).

1954 cautioned the government that 'time was being wasted on planning
and talking' and that this had resulted in a worse housing situation where
over 500 persons had been rendered homeless in Cape Coast and Takoradi
following flooding. Meanwhile, the Department of Rural Housing had
completed designs and models for twenty types of house to be constructed
in the rural areas under the Self-help Housing System with the first batch
of housing under this system to be built in the Akim-Akuapem district
while preliminary work for the construction of sixty-four different types
in the Akoroso New Township were underway (Peregrino-Peters, 1954:
5). A housing grant proposed by the Salaries and Wages Commission in
1957 for all pensionable African officers and civil servants to assist them
build and own houses was rejected by parliament because 'it was not the
Government's policy to confer preferential treatment on Civil Servants' in
the matter of housing (*Ghana Today*, 1957c: 2). The cost of undertaking
such a project was going to have serious implications for the economy.
Instead, deductions were to be taken from the salaries of civil servants and
deposited in a building society. An article by Kwabena Mensah appearing
in the *Evening News* newspaper in 1965 complained about 'the systemic

concentration of almost all the nation's industries in big cities, especially Accra'. The resulting migration had led to severe social problems, of which the '[h]ousing problem is the most acute' (Mensah, 1965a: 3).

Even after Nkrumah was ousted in 1966 the housing problems in urban centres in Ghana remained a major social problem. Tenants complained about 'sky-high rents' that could be as much as one-third of a worker's salary while describing the landlords as 'Shylocks'.[17] Tenants and landlords were constantly at loggerheads and the Rent Control Office,[18] always flooded with litigations, was perceived to be more sympathetic towards the cause of the landlord and landlady (Mensah, 1965b). There were calls for a comprehensive housing project to address workers' acute housing issues (Olympio, 1966: 2). Cilly Olympio went further to ask the government 'to fight [shyness and] to ask for long term foreign aid for housing project' (ibid.).

Foreign relations in Ghana's housing development

Ghana's foreign policy outlined by Nkrumah on the eve of independence in 1957 was premised on the fact that the government did not intend to follow a neutral policy but to preserve its independence (*Ghana Today*, 1957a), working with others to achieve an African personality in international affairs, in line with Nkrumah's pan-Africanist agenda. This view was articulated by Nkrumah when he decided to welcome foreign investment and private capital for the development of the country (*Ghana Today*, 1957b). For Nkrumah, maintaining foreign relations meant that the government would be able to mobilise resources to develop the country including the housing sector but would avoid the need of seeking 'free gifts of aid' from other countries in the Commonwealth.

A bilateral agreement with Czechoslovakia on agricultural development and industrialisation was established in 1957. Yugoslavia also offered fifty-seven scholarships to Ghana to support economic development and progress (*Evening News*, 1966a: 6). Ghana also established financial ties with Germany, America and Canada. The Americans and the Canadians were first involved in the establishment of an aluminium smelting plant at Kpone as part of the Volta River Project. Nkrumah's tactical action propelled him to maintain ties

17   Shylock was the Jewish usurer and antagonist of Antonio in Shakespeare's *The Merchant of Venice*. Here the term is colloquially used to describe a landlord or landlady who is regarded as relentless, hard-hearted and taking advantage of desperate tenants who needed accommodation in the urban centres.
18   The Rent Control Department was established in 1963 to work with landlords and tenants to promote optimum peaceful coexistence through education, reconciliation and economic development in the country (Rent Control Department, 2020).

with Britain during the early transitional years of self-government (Biney, 2011). Being in West Africa, the Gold Coast's relative geographical proximity to the UK meant that mail boats could make the trip in around two weeks. Thus, the nation benefited from relatively fast access to British products, design expertise, and building contractors (Jackson et al., 2019). As the British ties waned, the government extended invitations to Dutch and West German financiers (Biney, 2011).

Foreign involvement in achieving the housing needs of public workers was part of this consideration. On 27 July 1966 the front page of the *Evening News* (1966b: 1) reported that the Germans were going to build houses in Accra because they had confidence in Ghana's economy. The newspaper mentioned that contracts between the Ghana Housing Corporation (GHC) and the German Trade Union Confederation had been signed and they were to build 820 moderately priced houses for workers in Accra. Four prototype houses comprising one-storey and two-storey 'luxurious' buildings were built in Kaneshie, a suburb of Accra. This was after the first contract of the scheme known as 'satellite city' signed in 1964 was abandoned after the overthrow of Nkrumah in 1966.[19]

The Schokbeton housing programme

As part of the economic and social development of the Gold Coast, the need for an improved and high standard of housing featured prominently in the policy as the government's vision was to 'see every family living in its own comfortable home' (Government Printing Department, 1951: 20). Hence, individuals were to be offered personal loans in a maximum amount of £1,600, to be repaid over thirty years (ibid.: 21). Improved rural housing conditions were regarded as reward to the farmers and miners who were thought of as drivers of Gold Coast revenue generation, and such a policy was designed to prevent rural-urban drift of the youth as services improved in the villages. Hence, the government proposed to introduce power machines and experimental housing that would enable mass-housing production. Schokbeton prefabricated housing was part of this strategy. So in a meeting held on 23 February 1950, the Acting Director of the Public Works Department (PWD) and part of the colonial administration,

---

[19]   *Evening News* (1966b: 1). The initial contract was abandoned due to hostilities that developed between Ghana and the German Trade Union Confederation, and attacks from the *Spark* newspaper. The ongoing Cold War tensions between American capitalism and the expansion of socialism as well as the decolonisation agenda and the politics of non-alignment strained relations between Ghana's trade union confederation and the international trade union organisations (Sackeyfio-Lenoch, 2017).

W. Dempster,[20] announced that 'he was hoping to arrange for prefabricated bungalows to be built by contractors from 1950–1951'.[21]

The Schokbeton method of construction in Ghana and globally was mainly championed by the Dutch. During the 1950s it was described as having superior structural strength, rapid erection, insulating value, fire resistance and affordability. After introducing this 'superior' technology to the Gold Coast, a proposal was made to establish a prefabricated construction firm in the country in 1952 which would start local production in four years. Tools and building materials were to be imported from the Netherlands. The Gold Coast Government was required to provide £4 million to build the factories. According to the *Daily Graphic* (1952: 1), the first of four prototype factories to be built by N. V. Schokbeton was to be sited in Kumase. The newspaper records that the firm had received serious criticisms of the initial house designs because up to thirty-two different prefabricated components were to be used in their construction. However, the design had been modified to comprise only twelve prefabricated components and also to incorporate the climatic and cultural traditions of the users. Hence, the new design 'would be extendable, have a mosquito proof mesh, allow for sufficient ventilation, and could stand tropical humidity'. Above all, they would be about 15 per cent cheaper. The new extendable type would comprise two bedrooms, a living room, verandah, kitchen, store and garage. On 9 July 1952, Nkrumah, accompanied by the Minister for Housing, Ansah Koi, laid the first slab of eighteen units at Kaneshie in the Greater Accra Region. Present was the general manager of N. V. Schokbeton, Mr N. F. Wilmar who mentioned that ten houses had been completed and were awaiting occupation (*Daily Graphic*, 1952: 3).

What is interesting is that Daniel Chapman mentioned that the designs would be sent to Holland for approval and if given, component parts would be made there and shipped to the Gold Coast where an experimental building would be constructed. In Chapman's opinion the new design was 'more suitable and also superior' to the earlier designs (*Daily Graphic*, 1952: 1). With industrialisation, a real attempt was made to encourage foreign firms to operate in the country through the provision of sites, buildings and utilities (Ghana Information Services Department, 1960). The desire to adopt international architectural styles by seeking approval from Holland was in contradiction to Ghana's state realisation and recognition agenda. On one hand the country

20   W. Dempster was an assistant director who was promoted to the position of deputy director of Public Works, Gold Coast in 1951.
21   GH/PRAAD/RG 5/1/50. Note of a meeting held in the secretariat on 23 February 1950 to decide on the question of sites in the Accra government residential area for government requirements and those of quasi-government building.

wanted to boldly proclaim its independence and self-identity yet it was quick
to imbibe foreign ideas and build foreign relationships to address the 'infant-
state' in which the country found itself (Gallagher, 2018).

The Schokbeton prefabricated housing programme was suspended following
a visit to the Gold Coast by experts from the United Nations Technical
Assistance team on housing (*Daily Graphic*, 1954a: 1). They asserted that it
was more costly to build a prefabricated house in Ghana than to construct a
self-built house because almost all the components were imported and such
an action would negatively impact the traditional self-help methods practised
throughout the territory (Jackson et al., 2019). Instead, the experts suggested
that the £2 million grant be split between two programmes: £890,000 invested
in a mortgage bank, and the rest to start a 'roof loan program' (Arku, 2009).
They proposed a four-level restructuring of Ghana's housing provision system,
encouraging those who could afford it to build their own homes, and providing
loans and subsidies for those who could not.

The Schokbeton housing programme was generally considered a failure:
it did not promote existing traditional housing, required a lot of importation
and did not provide jobs for African labourers; moreover, only sixty-four of
the estimated 1,698 housing units were completed by 1954. Its failure was
partly attributed to the fact that it was planned by the colonial government
and did not fit Nkrumah's state-building and identity-formation agenda of
Gold Coast's early years.

Ghana National Construction Corporation /Ghana Housing Corporation building projects

Even after independence in 1957, house-building was incredibly difficult
and politically contentious. The government ventured into new foreign
partnerships to assist it address the housing demand. The Ghana National
Construction Corporation (GNCC), which was established in 1956, was later
renamed Ghana Housing Corporation (GHC) and went into a joint venture
with an Israeli Construction Company – Solel Boneh in 1958 (Stanek, 2015).
The Corporation was the main government organisation responsible for
the construction and maintenance of public houses and government official
buildings. It was required to build about 800 housing units for both government
and non-governmental organisations by September 1958, at a cost of about
£1 million (*Ghana Today*, 1957c). In addition, a Housing Research Bureau
was established for the purposes of researching low-cost housing (*Ghana
Today*, 1958c). The Corporation experimented with landcrete, where propor-
tions of one part cement to five parts earth were mixed to construct low-cost
buildings. By November 1957 the Corporation had completed a sample
prototype landcrete dwelling in Accra costing only £300. According to the

then-Minister of Housing, Ashford Emmanuel Inkumsah, the buildings, which were designed for nuclear families, were to be rented out at low rates to poor households. The building cost could be further reduced if ten parts of earth was used (*Ghana Today*, 1957d).

According to *Ghana Today* (1957c), the government housing measures resulted in a total expenditure of £4 million, providing housing for about 50,000 people staying in industrial urban areas and in larger towns such as Accra, Kumase, Takoradi, Tamale and Oda. In all, 450 houses of different sizes and more than 2,000 single-room units for industrial and labouring workers were completed. By 1958, a year after Ghana's independence, the GHC and the PWD had embarked on massive housing development by constructing variations of the DH 121 type houses costing between £3,950 and £4,025 in North Osu and South Ring Road in Accra (figures 4.2 and 4.3). The GNCC depended heavily on a foreign workforce, especially British architects based in Accra or overseas, and only occasionally involving the African workforce in the PWD. Most of the construction materials were shipped from Britain due to shortages in the Gold Coast (Stanek, 2015). Such dependence influenced the kind of architecture produced. For example, Modesto Apaloo commented that the various 'foreign expert advice' on housing did not incorporate the use of local building materials and local builders, which often led to expensive construction. This resulted in A. K. Conduah (the State Construction Corporation Engineer), strongly advocating the use of bricks and roofing tiles in construction because of the ability of burnt bricks and tiles to resist dampness and heat in the tropical weather, their aesthetic appeal and the affordable cost of construction because the earth could be accessed locally (Conduah 1966a, 1966b).

Conclusion: ubiquitous architecture, hybrid foreign styles, a form of statehood

Having gained independence, the leaders of the country wanted to showcase the new and modern Ghana and demonstrate to the population that it could support itself and solve its own problems. The development agenda was based on economic and social development for state building and higher standards as the country strode towards modernity, in line with an approach then trending in the West. The Ghana Information Services Department (1960) intimated that the trend in architecture so familiar during the first ten years of self-government was only perceived through the pages of 'magazines'. So Ghana, in its preference for modernism and its reconceptualisation of urban development under the Nkrumah administration, implemented a distinctive worldview that was consistent with colonial priorities and a worldview that

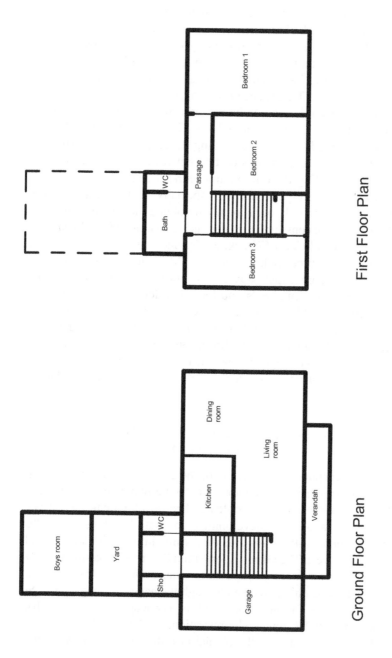

Ground Floor Plan

First Floor Plan

Figure 4.2 House Type DH 121E. Built by Ghana Housing Corporation; Architect: E.G.D. (April 1958). (Archival records GH/PRAAD/RG 5/1/120. BC 393; Staff Housing Ghana National Construction Corporation, 3 July 1958; reproduced with permission of the Archive).

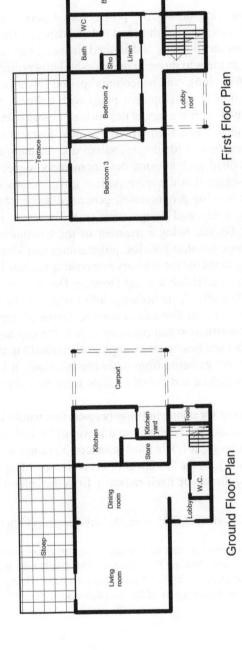

Figure 4.3 House Type 3 (DH 121). Built by Ghana National Construction Corporation; Architect: R.D. Norwood, 13 November 1958. (Archival records GH/PRAAD/RG 5/1/120. BC 393; Staff Housing Ghana National Construction Corporation, 13 November 1958; reproduced with permission of the Archive).

laid emphasis upon a new architectural style of construction with a suburban ideal (Hess, 2000: 53). Nkrumah's response to the colonial regulation of architectural space also reflected a distinctive 'imagining' of modernism, a vision which was allied to his heroicised vision of a culturally homogeneous 'nation' (ibid.).

Ghana's house-building during the post-colonial period also exposed broader tensions between state building and independence.[22] The new nation, with very few African technocrats, and limited financial capital, created an opportunity for foreign ideas to thrive in the state-building project. According to Anthony King (2015: 366), 'the neocolonial period [after 1951 in Africa] saw the implementation of development plans with cultural, political and economic links situated within a larger network of global communications and economic dependence and such an environment fostered the means to continue the transplantation of ideologies, values and planning models from the West'. King described such housing development as 'dependent urbanisation' (ibid.: 367) stating that the metropolitan governments in Africa, in developing low-cost housing programmes, generated and exchanged information on standards, costs, and design with other European powers with interests in Africa.[23] Ghana, being a member of the Commonwealth, was encouraged to exchange housing policies, programmes and ideas with other member states. Again, to enable the ministry responsible for housing and town and country planning to establish a Rural Housing Department and to fulfil its mandate in providing affordable housing, information on the 'methods of financing the scheme, terms of disposal of houses, degree of standardisation, systems of building construction and plans, as well as the composition of the self-help housing teams and headquarters organisation' (ibid.) in the provision of low-cost housing were gathered from other organisations. It is interesting to note that similar modernist and colonial ideals were circulated throughout the European colonies.

Nkrumah was looking for public housing projects that would lead to rapid industrialisation for his nascent country, but this was of limited importance to his foreign partners (Boakye, 2017). In most instances, Nkrumah was not able to expressly exercise agency, to the detriment of his nation-building agenda. His government wanted to dissociate itself radically from the colonial legacy yet

---

[22]   See, for example, Colombijn (2011) on similar developments in Indonesia in the 1950s.

[23]   For example, housing programmes such as the self-help housing concept adopted from the Jamaican Hurricane Housing Organisation Aided Self-help Rural Housing Scheme received a lot of attention in the 'New Commonwealth'. Telegram from the Governor of Gold Coast to the Governor of Jamaica dated September 1953, 'Self-Help Housing'.

was heavily dependent on foreign loans. The involvement of foreign partners and the introduction of new ideas in the architectures of public housing led to the near collapse of Ghana's indigenous architecture.

Ghana's continuous engagement with international partners has introduced influential and ubiquitous architectures, rooted in a complex hybrid of foreign ideas and styles. Unfortunately, new African societies have not been able to recreate or reimagine their own shape and spirit and have been unable to claim their own birthright and independence in architecture and housing development because of the continents' continuous engagement with the Global North.[24] This observation is contrary to the expectations of the Europeans and John Lloyd's (1966: 40) conviction that although there was a strong influence of colonialism on Africa architectural development, 'there has also been a reaction to the challenge of alien pressure, thus this new society will have its own shape and spirit. It will be African and not in Europe's or America's or even Asia's image'.[25] Ghana's foreign policy and dependence on international relations for independent state building introduced neo-colonialism and defined a particular form of statehood that is evident in post-colonial architecture and housing development.

[24] Tony Yeboah, Chapter 10 in this volume, discusses a similar problem with the rebuilding of a traditional chief's palace after the original was destroyed by the British.
[25] Lloyd was a lecturer at the Faculty of Architecture in Kumase who became the principal of the Architectural Association in London in 1966.

PART 2

LIVING

5

Beautiful state/ugly state: Architecture and political authority in Côte d'Ivoire

JULIA GALLAGHER AND
YAH ARIANE BERNADETTE N'DJORÉ

This chapter is about the state in Côte d'Ivoire. In it we explore the state through its buildings – the presidential palaces, national assembly, government departments, hospitals and police stations – objects which embody, enable and symbolise statehood. These buildings are the places where the state is located and in which state functions are enacted; laws are made and enforced, services are provided. They might be said to be the places through which statehood is made.[1]

The ways in which buildings make the state are not simply through elite plans and projections. True, they are conceived and built by elites who decide where they sit in cities, what happens in them, what they look like and who is allowed inside them.[2] But state buildings are also the scenery for citizens' lives, and in many contexts they encapsulate identity and wellbeing through their enaction and representation of state activities that can restrict or enable the way people live their lives. Citizens' encounters with state buildings – including attempts to obtain services from them, experiences of visiting them, the visual familiarity of their presence in the city, through the

---

[1]   The chapter draws on research from a project about statehood in five African countries, all explored through state buildings. Here we describe some of the broader project's theoretical and methodological approaches, but also the particularities of the findings in Côte d'Ivoire which, like all the countries explored in the research, has a unique character.

[2]   Much existing literature focuses on how buildings embody elite projections of power, or conceptions of political culture. On how buildings project political power, see Milne, 1981; Edelman, 1985; Elleh, 2002; on how they carry collective memory and culture, see Elleh, 1997; Bevan, 2007; Kusno, 2010; and on how they reflect or even reproduce political ideology, see Goodsell, 1988; Buchli, 2014; Minkenberg, 2014.

media or in national symbols, and from circulating stories about what goes
on inside – make them particularly tangible representatives of the state, on
both a day-to-day level and in the ways they stimulate people to contribute
to the wider political project. Thus, in living with, using and thinking about
state buildings, citizens participate in state-making (Gallagher, 2022).

Our particular interest is in the way citizens described their state buildings
in a series of interviews, and we draw on such descriptions to build an understanding of what statehood means in Côte d'Ivoire.[3] The descriptions unfold
the state through seeing, feeling and imagining, from glimpses of the Cité
Administrative towers from around the Plateau district, through the smells
and sounds inside a hospital or police station, to stories about what happens in
the cellars and crocodile lakes of the presidential palace. From these emerge
popular conceptions of what the state means, including its significance, shape
and health. These are not mere observations: citizens, we argue, don't just
watch the state, but bring it into being in the ways they engage with it.

The work draws on aesthetic theory from architecture and art to interpret
citizens' descriptions of state buildings. In particular, we focus on citizens'
accounts of beauty and ugliness in their state buildings. We see how beauty
emerges through seeing buildings from a distance, very idealised and almost
mythological. Ugliness, meanwhile, lurks beneath the surface and is felt
through the skin, nose and ears, and imagined with the help of memory and
myth. Taking this aesthetic approach to reading the state in Côte d'Ivoire we
find a state whose beauty is extraordinary but ephemeral, and whose ugliness,
which is visceral, disgusting and at first glance deeply buried, threatens to
overwhelm it. The Ivoirian state, experienced through its buildings, is idealised,
distant, threatening and fragile.

Ivoirians' views of their state buildings provide a new starting point to
understand statehood in Africa, as a juxtaposition of order and disorder, a
compelling aesthetic of struggle that lays the basis for state authority. This
challenges two influential 'aesthetic' accounts of the African state, those of
Achille Mbembe (2001) and Jean-François Bayart (2009), which explore order,
disorder and authority in the state in rather different ways. Mbembe's account
of state-society relations sees both partners locked into an 'illicit cohabi-
tation' leading to a 'mutual zombification' (Mbembe, 2001). His descriptions
of political power, sticky with disgusting smells and sounds, are dominated
by impotence and disorder, which citizens and states are unable to escape.

---

[3]   The relationships described, between the buildings and the state they embody and
represent, emerged within and from the interviews. We did not make the connection
during interviews, but our interlocutors did so, moving easily between descriptions
of buildings and of state functions and activities.

It is less an account of state authority, than of the impossibility of escape from a dysfunctional state farce. Bayart's account of the state allows for some beauty, but purely as a façade designed for external donor consumption. Bayart's 'rhizome state' is split between a smooth, rationalised veneer and a substantive, convoluted reality (Bayart, 2009).[4] Here, citizens are equally entrapped within a state logic that is devoid of order; the best they can do is to see and to understand an artificial beauty that is projected away, towards a different set of relationships. In contrast, we find a more complex state-aesthetic in Côte d'Ivoire in which state and society cohabit, but move together across registers of order and disorder, seeing, feeling and thinking their way through struggles between the two. If ugliness can feel like Mbembe's 'zombi-fication' or Bayart's '*pays réel*', it is complemented by strong perceptions of beauty, order and potency in the state that are as aesthetically compelling as its uglinesses. Our account suggests that although Ivoirians understand their state on different levels – even, at times, as a beautiful surface and an ugly core – these are an intrinsic part of domestic political authority.

We base our argument on empirical material drawn from two sources. The first is an ethnographic study of key buildings in Abidjan and Yamoussoukro (the de facto and nominal capital cities). During fieldwork in 2019 we explored both cities to build a sense of what state buildings look and feel like, where they sit in relation to their cities and who goes in and out.[5] We documented our findings in fieldnotes and photographs. The second source is a series of nine focus group discussions (FGDs) carried out with citizens living and working in and near Abidjan. These included people drawn from different ethnic, social, religious and age groups. Each group contained between six and ten people.[6] The groups were approached through and assembled by

4   Bayart uses 'rhizome' to capture how the state forms complex, interconnected connections within itself that are invisible from a surface view. In another analogy he describes this as a '*pays réel*', contrasting it with the '*pays legal*' which is presented to the outside world.

5   Not all state buildings are in cities, of course. Local municipal buildings, as well as police stations, courts, schools and medical facilities exist throughout the country. They often take rather different shapes to those in the capital city; FGDs often drew comparisons between prestigious facilities in Abidjan and the very small and shabby counterparts in rural areas.

6   We do not suggest that our focus groups are comprehensively representative of citizens in Abidjan, let alone Côte d'Ivoire. They are instead a collection of reflec-tions from a variety of citizens who live in the capital. All discussants participated under assurances of anonymity. We have not identified any of the groups and have given each a simple descriptor to allow the reader to contextualise the discussions being described.

a gatekeeper – a religious leader or local community group, or school – so that groups were reasonably homogenous. This helped us establish relaxed conditions where people already knew each other or could identify each other as coming from the same community. We found this a good way to establish trust and create the conditions for people to discuss and think together. We started discussions by asking members of the group to list 'Côte d'Ivoire's most important public buildings'. Once a list had been agreed, we asked them to describe the buildings. Most groups found the topic peculiar and many people were anxious that they 'didn't know much about it'. But once we explained that we were not interested in facts, but in their observations, conversations flowed.

The rest of the chapter proceeds as follows. First, we establish our theoretical approach, beginning with aesthetic theory from art and architecture, and explain how we understand and use the terms 'beautiful' and 'ugly'. Next, we describe Côte d'Ivoire's state buildings, concentrating on how Ivoirians read their beauty and ugliness. Finally, we discuss how these ideas of beauty and ugliness found in buildings can be read politically and what they reveal about citizens' understanding of their state.

Beauty, ugliness and aesthetics

'Beautiful' and 'ugly' are subjective terms. Although there might be a consensus within a community about what deserves such descriptions (Bourdieu, 1993), it is usually accepted that individuals may deviate from the norm (since 'beauty is in the eye of the beholder'); and that, on the whole, standard-making varies between societies (Abiodun, 2001; Dewey, 2005; Nuttall, 2006; Njiofor, 2018, although see Ruskin, 1989 for an argument in support of objective standards). Following this approach, we are therefore not looking for specific definitions or examples of beauty and ugliness, but the possibility of a framework to read how individuals and communities make aesthetic judgements.

We find two helpful approaches – drawn from philosophy and psychoanalytic theory respectively – that explore common human origins of aesthetic engagement. These attempt to describe the building blocks that lead to socially constructed aesthetic judgements. The first comes from philosopher John Dewey's analysis, which he builds on a biological foundation (Dewey, 2005). He takes a sensory approach to aesthetics, describing the way in which our lives are shaped by stressful interactions with nature – our strivings for survival and our ability to overcome or resolve impediments to it. Life, he argues, is an ongoing engagement between experiences of chaos around us (which people *undergo*) and attempts to create order (in which people *do*). The dynamics between chaos and order are reflected in art, which itself is an attempt to create meaning in the face of chaos – a form of order out of disorder. The second approach is that of psychoanalyst Hanna Segal, which similarly explores the human tussle with chaos and order, which she explicitly relates to 'ugliness' and 'beauty'. She suggests that '[u]gliness is what expresses the state of the internal world in depression ... the chaos of fragmentation and destruction' (Segal, 1986: 200) and beauty is 'the whole, the complete, and the rhythmical ... An undisturbed rhythm in a composed whole seems to correspond to the state in which our inner world is at peace' (ibid.: 201). For Segal, 'ugliness – destruction – is the expression of the death instinct; beauty – the desire to unite into rhythms and wholes – is that of the life instinct' (ibid.: 203). In Segal's reading, therefore, ugly objects are fragmented and chaotic while beautiful objects are harmonious and complete. Each corresponds to our internal objects (the 'internal working models' we create to help us explain and navigate the world),[7] respectively depressive (an expression of death) and peaceful (an expression of life).

These similar definitions give us a sensory and emotional approach to aesthetics, more in line with a traditional Greek understanding of the term (as 'sense perception') than the Platonic one that informed the European enlightenment prioritisation of intellectual judgement and a hierarchy of taste.[8] Dewey's idea of 'doing' as a way of confronting 'undergoing' is a far more nuanced approach to understanding how humans deal with the world around them. Intellectualisation tends to deny dependency, pretending that emotional, or purely sensory reactions, can be overcome. Dewey and Segal depict a far more vulnerable human being whose sense of mastery over the world is contingent and partial. While understandings of what constitute fragmentation and destruction, and rhythm and harmony, may vary between and within societies, it is reasonable to assert that most people can relate to such terms, even if they experience them in different ways, because both correspond ultimately to human experience.

Dewey and Segal use this foundation to reach similar conclusions about how powerful art is made and appreciated. Dewey argues that aesthetically powerful art both reproduces and represents the engagement between chaos and order. It reproduces it in the act of creation, as the artist undergoes a struggle with her objects and materials, trying to bring order, by doing, to

---

7   The term 'internal working models' is John Bowlby's (1973: 203). He describes how they work: 'Each individual builds working models of the world and of himself in it, with the aid of which he perceives events, forecasts the future, and constructs his plans'.

8   Dewey (2005: 32) believes that the intellectualisation of art makes it 'pallid and bloodless'. Daniel Mulugeta (2021) develops a fascinating and rather different way to show how affective engagement with built forms links to ideology.

her work. The resulting work also represents through its own ambiguity which, while including elements of order, must also contain suggestions of the struggle of creation so that the viewer is left with their own struggles to understand and appreciate the work. 'Man whittles, carves, sings, dances, gestures, molds, draws and paints. The doing or making is artistic when the perceived result is of such a nature that *its* qualities *as perceived* have controlled the question of production' (Dewey, 2005: 50 emphasis original). An overly ordered work of art is rigid and aesthetically vacuous, according to Dewey, because it has erased all signs of the struggle to produce it. In turn, Segal writes that profound art expresses both beauty and ugliness. One without the other would not speak fully to the human condition. She writes that a 'satisfactory work of art is achieved by a realization and sublimation of the depressive position ... The achievement of the artist is in giving the fullest expression to the conflict and the union between these two' (Segal, 1986: 203).

Other accounts of aesthetics agree with this idea that artistic power stems from an unresolved struggle between beauty and ugliness. Robert Venturi argues, for example, that powerful architecture contains ambiguity, expressing tension between 'irrational parts' and a 'rational whole' (Venturi, 1966: 25); and Mbembe argues that the power of Congolese music lies in its 'declaration of the most radical and the most immediate faith in a life which is necessarily contradictory and paradoxical' (Mbembe, 2006: 63). From each of these perspectives, aesthetic power is contained within an unresolved relationship between beauty and ugliness. Either one without the other is banal and superficial: references to both and an exploration of the relationship between the two are essential.

But we can take this idea of aesthetic power further if we draw on West African ideas about art described in Susan Vogel's work on Côte d'Ivoire. Vogel argues that the power of Baule artistic objects rests on metaphysical rather than physical dimensions. These are not visible in the objects, which are 'incompletely seen', but given to them through an 'active collaboration between artists and observer[s]' (Vogel, 1997: 72). Baule people have strong attachments to such objects 'finding in them something that helps to define their lives; what the artist contributes, however, is not the object's powerful essence but simply its locus, a shell that is its physical exterior' (ibid.). Vogel's approach suggests that the 'observer' is not merely tracing the artist's struggle between chaos and order, but working through her own, and it this working through that lends the work of art its real power.[9]

---

9   Sasha Newell makes a similar argument in his work on masking ceremonies in Côte d'Ivoire. 'The village audience does not differentiate between the theatrical

To sum up: we have a definition that links beauty to rhythm and harmony, and ugliness to fragmentation and destruction. We have argued that these are not objective qualities, and that they have little to do with pure intellect but speak to us as humans about how we make sense of our physical and emotional experiences. We have thought about how a compelling aesthetic engagement relies on a relationship between beauty and ugliness. Art or objects that have the power to move us are those that represent struggles between the two, because they reflect the human condition of being caught between order and chaos; life and death. Finally, we have suggested that the viewer is at least as creative an agent as the artist in the process of making a powerful aesthetic.

We now apply this framework to descriptions of state buildings in Côte d'Ivoire. We think about how beauty and ugliness are experienced and how they are related to each other.[10] Before we begin, we want to emphasise that the views expressed in discussions – and indeed those found our own observations – are not 'expert'; neither the authors nor the discussants that contributed their thoughts to this paper are architects or critics. The descriptions tend to be associational, reflecting Amos Rapoport's (1982: 19, emphasis original) point that '[d]esigners tend to react to environments in perceptual terms (which are *their* meanings), whereas the lay public, the users, react to environments in associational terms'. Some even tend to anthropomorphise the buildings, supporting Rasmussen's (1964: 38–39) argument that 'animation of a building makes it easier to experience its architecture as a whole rather than as the addition of many separate technological details'.

Beautiful buildings

On the face of it, Côte d'Ivoire's state buildings easily lend themselves to notions of an ideal beauty in that so many of them are breathtakingly splendid. The country's first President Félix Houphouët-Boigny undertook an ambitious building programme, first in Abidjan, the capital he inherited at independence in 1960, and then in Yamoussoukro, the capital he created in 1983. The main

representation and the actual presence of these terrifying creatures in their midst; they are not meant to recognize that these creatures are human fabrications… Everyone acts as though the masks were real creatures, even though everyone knows it is a human production, and by virtue of that, the mask takes on real, non-human powers' (Newell, 2013: 143). We have explored how visibility and invisibility inform aesthetic appreciation in a comparison of state architecture in Côte d'Ivoire and Ghana (Gallagher et al., 2021)

10   For different accounts of how buildings are experienced as objects of imagination, see Daniel Mulugeta, Chapter 9, and Tony Yeboah, Chapter 10, this collection.

Figure 5.1   Basilique Notre-Dame de la Paix, Yamoussoukro (Julia Gallagher, March 2019).

administrative and business centre of Abidjan, Plateau, showcases a collection of stunning modernist buildings, including the dramatic international-style Cité Administrative (the offices of most of the country's civil service), a daringly abstract cathedral, the tropical modernist City Hall (Kultermann, 1969: 43), the mysteriously hidden presidential complex with its green concave roof designed to represent a stool (Massire, 2018) and the iconic Pyramide covered market (Ciarkowski, 2015). Most of this can be viewed from the President's luxury modernist Hôtel Ivoire[11] which faces Plateau across the lagoon (Hertz et al., 2015). The celebrated view encompasses a small but apparently perfect high-rise city, full of architectural wonders.

   Houphouët-Boigny pushed his love of extravagant architecture even further when he moved the capital to his home-town in the centre of the country: Yamoussoukro became the site of a handsome new presidential palace, erected on the banks of a crocodile lake, a gigantic marble-lined Peace Foundation, another hyper-modernist luxury hotel, a chain of large new administrative and parliamentary facilities and the baroque-style Basilique Notre-Dame de la Paix (figure 5.1). Modelled on St Peter's in Rome, the Basilique is reputedly the largest Catholic church in the world and its construction is said to have doubled the country's external debt (McGovern, 2011: 17). Nnamdi Elleh (2002: 159) writes of the Basilique that 'it exceeds all built, colonial-inspired chauvinist

[11]   Hôtel Ivoire was renamed the Le Sofitel Abidjan Hôtel Ivoire in 2012.

Figure 5.2   Cité Administrative, Abidjan, seen from the steps of Cathédrale Saint-Paul (Julia Gallagher, March 2019).

projects on the continent'. These monuments to modern statehood sit incongruously within a modest African village.[12]

Iconic architecture has become a defining feature of the Ivoirian state, mixed up with the myth of its first President, and providing a particular description of state-society relations that is at once dramatically visible and virtually opaque. Abidjan's Cité Administrative (figure 5.2) gives a good flavour of this. The original two towers were built in the 1970s and three more were added in 1984, financed with foreign loans as the economy faltered (Bamba, 2016). Although the complex of five skyscrapers is signposted, and visible, from most angles of the Plateau district, and although it is known to house most of Abidjan's government departments, there are no external indications of which departments live there, or how they are arranged. It is visible to everyone, but actually closed to most people who can only gaze through the compound railings, down into a car park busy with suited officials and security guards. The buildings themselves, sticking up into the sky like five cuboid, gilded fingers, are impenetrable, covered with an opaque metallic surface only broken up by a thin geometric grid.

12   The Basilique was part of Houphouët-Boigny's attempt to fuse state and spiritual authority. Emmanuel Ofori-Sarpong discusses a more recent use of religion in Ghana's political story, Chapter 2 in this collection.

In focus groups, the towers were described as 'works of art',[13] always 'seen from the outside'.[14] In this they are a good example of an approach to 'state as spectacle', found throughout our discussions: the state was to be looked at from outside, usually from far away, and, as we shall see, these characteristics were essential parts of the way its beauty was defined.

Group discussions on Côte d'Ivoire's 'most important public buildings' yielded descriptions of 'jewels', 'icons', 'masterpiece', 'chic', 'works of art', 'perfect' and 'shining'. Most of these terms were applied to flagship buildings such as the presidential palaces, the Yamoussoukro Basilique and Peace Institute, the Assembly of Deputies and the University as well as the Cité Administrative. In a discussion between public sector workers about the Basilique, the pinnacle of Houphouët-Boigny's architectural monumentalism, one woman said: 'I am always struck, fascinated by the quality of the work and then, it is an architectural masterpiece ... it is impressive for an African country to achieve such a work', while a colleague commented: 'We still wonder how all this could have been possible'.[15]

The praise often focused on exceptionalism. The buildings were 'famous and respected' throughout the region. The Basilique was 'the largest in the world', and 'one of the most visited in the world';[16] the Pyramide was 'one of the most beautiful buildings in history'.[17] The buildings represent the superiority of Côte d'Ivoire. Some said that Abidjan was more like a European capital than an African one, others spoke with pity or wonderment at seeing inferior buildings in neighbouring countries. Much was said about what visitors make of these buildings; they were thought to be awed, impressed and envious. For many people across the groups, the buildings projected superiority and were a great source of pride. A group of students described how they saw their state buildings in relation to the rest of the world. One spoke of being 'blown away' when he visited the Hotel le Parlementaire in Yamoussoukro. 'I thought maybe I was in London or in other countries... We don't know how important our country is to the outside world because we are here, we do not value it... when you look at the whole, in West Africa, Côte d'Ivoire is a beautiful country.' Another agreed: 'When we find ourselves in Burkina Faso, Cameroon, we beat our breasts and say, we have jewels, we can compete with others.'[18]

13   FGD with university students, Abidjan, 29 March 2019 (FGD1).
14   FGD with teachers, Abidjan, 8 August 2019 (FGD4).
15   FGD with junior civil servants, Abidjan, 20 June 2019 (FGD2).
16   FGD1 – students.
17   FGD with elders, Abidjan, 21 January 2020 (FGD8).
18   FGD1 – students.

In most groups, people were not interested in giving precise details of what made these buildings so beautiful. The students talked of 'rigour' and 'seriousness', of the presidential palace as one that 'concentrates power [and] attracts attention'[19] – impressionistic terms that express ideas about the symbolic weight of the buildings. Some buildings were said to possess miraculous properties. A teacher said of one room in the Peace Foundation in Yamoussoukro that 'the colours, and the light, even when you're angry, when you walk into that room it calms you down'.[20] One state official said of the Mother-Child Hospital at Bingerville that 'as soon as you come back I think that 50 per cent you're already cured because of the level of architecture'.[21]

When pushed for detail, some people mentioned painting and tiles, modern furnishing including computers, air conditioning, tarred roads and cleanliness. This was a beauty associated with order – regularity, efficiency and most of all, a cleaning up of dirt. For example, one Treichville[22] resident said: 'I like the renovation of public buildings, whether it's the computers or the air conditioning.'[23] And a woman from Bingerville[24] said: 'Bingerville City Hall has changed: it's not like before. It used to be old stuff but now it's changed, it's become clean.'[25]

But these more prosaic forms of beauty were far less interesting to the people we spoke to, who were more inclined to dwell on the remarkable and even other-worldly features of their state buildings. Such a focus reinforced people's sense of distance from the state.

Expressions of distance were a particularly striking feature of FGDs. Many times people mentioned the fact that they had not been inside, that, as one man said of the National Assembly, 'from the outside yes, but from the inside no … from afar, I see'.[26] On a few occasions one person in a group had been to visit the Presidential Palace or the Assembly of Deputies, but the descriptions were similarly distant: the visitors were 'honoured' and 'awed'; the buildings were still 'miraculous' and 'wonderful'. They found it difficult to convey more intimate or complicated impressions as though going inside yielded no further insight on the workings of the buildings.

An even more extreme version of distance came through descriptions of the origins of the buildings which people frequently described as other-worldly.

19   FGD1 – students.
20   FGD4 – teachers.
21   FGD with self-employed workers, Abidjan, 19 June 2019 (FGD3).
22   Treichville was the area of Abidjan reserved for black families in the colonial era.
23   FGD of Treichville residents, Abidjan, 19 January 2020 (FGD7).
24   Bingerville is a city on the periphery of Abidjan.
25   FGD of traders, Bingerville, 8 January 2020 (FGD6).
26   FGD2 – civil servants.

This other-worldliness sometimes emerged in accounts of buildings that were designed and constructed by foreign architects and builders; 'the whites', or 'the French'. This theme was explored by the students. One talked of buildings that were 'built by Italians, with a know-how not possible'. A colleague replied that some of the buildings were so miraculous they could only have been 'built by masks, by geniuses'. A third described the buildings being further elevated by their association with President Félix Houphouët-Boigny, described as an almost mythical founding father. Houphouët-Boigny was 'a genius. Seriously, he was not normal'.[27]

In short, the beauty found in Côte d'Ivoire's state buildings was ideal, abstract and ordered. The terms of description maintained the sense of an ideal through their abstraction – after all, who can argue over definitions of terms like 'jewel' and 'icon'? Such terms float high above thick description. When pushed for more precise terms, people arrived at 'painted', 'clean', 'tiled', and described modern fittings that made the buildings function in an ordered way. Yet all the descriptions of beauty emphasised distance. State buildings were appreciated from afar, and by sight. This was taken to an even deeper level when people began to express thoughts about the miraculous provenance of their state buildings. Perhaps they didn't even belong here, seeming to emerge (in unexplained ways) from foreign ideas and technologies, or from other worlds.

Ugly buildings

Descriptions move properly from beauty to ugliness as people begin to describe the insides of real buildings – buildings where the state must be navigated up close. A teacher described what his visit within the Regional Directorate of Education felt like:

> Well, there are buildings you're looking for, there aren't even signs, that is, you can pass without knowing you've passed the building … And then when you find the building too, you come in, no one tells you, you have to ask. I've come to withdraw my certificate, where should I go? They say good, take the elevator and you go to the 6th. But you arrive in front of the elevator, elevator number two, it's closed: broken down. Elevator number three, broken down. Only one elevator is here, it's drunk, no you can't use it, you have to take the stairs … You get to the sixth, it's not organised. The offices are there, you don't know which one … this, that, nothing. It's up to you to inquire and you are told: Sir, go straight, you take the left, you will find the third door, it is there … You lose yourself. Nothing is indicated.[28]

[27]   FGD1 – students.
[28]   FGD4 – teachers.

If beauty is discussed in ideal, abstract terms, ugliness is found in what is bewildering. There are two areas where ugliness is encountered. The first is in buildings that people go into – service-providing buildings like hospitals and schools, and law enforcement buildings like police stations, law courts and prisons. The second is in the iconic buildings that few go into, but whose insides can be imagined and mythologised.

These uglinesses are usually visceral because they are felt within the bewildering explorations of the insides rather than seen from the distant outside.[29] The courts are 'too small, squashed', where 'you hear but you cannot see'.[30] A conversation of private sector workers focused on schools, which one member described as 'not hard buildings' but made with wood and straw, and where, 'with even a small wind, everything flies away'. Another remarked on the lack of space, so that students are 'stuck, tight, and when it's like that, it's complicated'.[31] The teachers described the hospitals[32] which are dirty and 'make you feel sick'; 'when you go in there you feel you're going to die, even if you're not ill'.[33] The prison is 'humiliating, it's not pretty at all to see', police stations are 'degraded, lacking hygiene and order' and the Maison d'Arrêt et de Correction d'Abidjan[34] needs to be 'unclogged'.[35] The most common feature of such buildings is the toilets which are variously locked, absent or disgusting. In one discussion within a group of women the conclusion was reached that 'toilets are the evil of public buildings'.[36]

Even the idealised public buildings reveal an ugly underside. In a group of elders there was a discussion about how often beautiful façades are a cover for ugliness. In the example of the Cité Administrative, 'the outside, you can see, but when you get in there, it's just bullshit'.[37] The toilets are broken, the building is crumbling, the lifts are stuck. Other icons were worryingly neglected. The Institut National Polytechnique Félix Houphouët-Boigny is 'dying, well, falling apart'.[38] The awe-inspiring Basilica was described as increasingly shabby, with cracks in the walls now host to weeds. One group of civil servants talked of 'slackening [and] areas that oozed', one man describing a recent visit where: 'there was brush all over the place, the paint was gone,

---

29 For a fuller discussion of sensory engagement with buildings see Gallagher (2022).
30 FGD with private sector workers, Abidjan, 9 August 2019 (FGD5).
31 FGD5 – private sector workers.
32 Public hospitals.
33 FGD4 – teachers.
34 Abidjan Detention and Correction House
35 FGD4 – teachers.
36 FGD6 – traders.
37 FGD8 – elders.
38 FGD1 – students.

Figure 5.3 Palais Présidentiel, Yamoussoukro, with man watching a crocodile (Julia Gallagher, March 2019).

frankly there was no more shine'.[39] The ugliness of public buildings was therefore often associated with neglect. There were further, more sinister hints of decay and ugliness gathered through hearsay, which, too, was visceral, described in hauntings and the dead bodies of migrant labourers buried in the foundations. There were also rumours about tunnels, secrets, places where you can't go within and between these buildings.

The glittering presidential palace in Yamoussoukro (figure 5.3) had its submerged ugliness inbuilt: its crocodiles. Houphouët-Boigny's sinister guards, had been, since his death, able to break through the fence and wander the town. They are a source of constant fascination: sightings attract observers to the banks of the lake that flanks the palace. The building itself is not used now but appeared (again from a distance; no approaching the gate, no photography) to be in immaculate condition, like a shrine. But the crocodiles were

---

[39]   FGD2 – civil servants.

a grisly and dangerous legacy from Côte d'Ivoire's founding President. One woman said: '[Houphouët-Boigny] had to make human sacrifices and he had to throw people into the Caiman Island, albino people … History has really terrorised us. When you see the caimans, you think they're man-eaters, so it's really scary. Well, we don't know if it's true, but [she paused] it's still true.'[40]

In short, ugliness is disordered – found in neglect, ruin, lack of discipline and terror. It also gets inside people, in that it comes through the senses of sound, touch and smell, felt in sensations of dampness, being squashed or of buildings that blow away in the wind; and disturbing noises, disgusting smells and in terrifying rumours. The ugliness of buildings is not encountered from a distance, through sight, because people report descriptions from their insides, where the ugliness invades them through skin, noses, ears and imagination.

The ugly side of the mysterious origins of the state emerge through a story that is commonly related about the presidential palace in Abidjan being rented, probably from the French, and not Ivoirian at all. This story came up in nearly all the discussions and always in a particular way; it was reported as a rumour for which the interlocutor did not want to vouch, but only as something they had heard. One man said: 'The presidency, it seems, I don't know if it is from a reliable source, but they say that the presidency is rented. Well now, I don't know how it goes.'[41] It appeared shameful to suggest that the presidency was only borrowed; the rumour was ubiquitous but disavowed. Its status as rumour rather than a fact gave it the flavour of a 'public secret', something everybody 'knows' but nobody explicitly acknowledges.

Most powerful of all, is the idea of abandonment. All the stories of neglect and of false façades led to this powerful and disturbing idea that the state's buildings had been left to rot away. This idea is poignantly encapsulated in the fate of Houphouët-Boigny's capital Yamoussoukro, where many of his grandest buildings are left empty. According to a teacher: 'The streets of Yamoussoukro, every one, is 99 per cent degraded. Yet we continue to tell our children that it is the political capital.'[42] In a group discussion of private sector workers, a man pointed out that Yamoussoukro was 'abandoned on all levels' – the roads, the schools, the House of Members, the parliament.[43] Several people pointed to a disturbing precedent: the original colonial capital of Grand Bassam whose elegant buildings have been left to decay in a dramatically visible manner.

---

40   FGD5 – private sector.
41   FGD3 – self-employed.
42   FGD4 – teachers.
43   FGD5 – private sector.

An aesthetic reading of the state

We have given two accounts of Côte d'Ivoire's state buildings, one focusing on
their beauty and one on their ugliness. Beauty, as our FGDs suggest, tends to
be *seen*. It is described in ways that emphasise a separation from mundane life:
jewel-like, exceptional and miraculous; and it is also associated with order:
cleanliness, modernity, solidity. Ugliness, in contrast, is usually experienced
through the haptic senses of *touch, smell and sound* – being squashed, getting
lost, invaded by the smells of broken toilets. Citizens described experiences
of disorder, confusion, fear and nausea.

These descriptions of buildings are on the one hand disembodied and intel-
lectualised, and on the other hand, embodied and emotional. The buildings
were provocative: people were often excited by what they saw, and they were
usually depressed by what they felt. Furthermore, accounts encompassed far
more than an assessment of materiality. They dwelt on the history of the
buildings, stories about who built them, who owned them, how others saw
them, how they performed and how they were cared for. It seemed to us at
times that the buildings were being examined for signs of health, very much
in line with Rasmussen's argument about animation – the buildings were
treated like a person.

The differences between *seeing* beauty and *feeling* ugliness throw up
further reflections about the ways that different sensory experiences position
people in relation to objects. In his work on people's sensory engagement
with buildings, Juhani Pallasmaa (2012) argues that sight emphasises distance,
spanning separation between an object and its viewer. He describes the eye
as narcissistic, nihilistic and hegemonic: seeing lends the viewer a feeling
of control. In contrast, sound is about interiority and incorporation, empha-
sising proximity, even implication in the object. 'I regard an object, but sound
approaches me; the eye reaches, but the ear receives' (Pallasmaa, 2012: 53).
We suggest that this point is equally valid for touch, smell and taste, all of
which involve more proximate engagements than sight. People cannot control
the haptic senses in the way they can choose what to look at; the distance
established by looking is absent with touching, smelling and hearing as objects
enter the body uninvited.

Given this reading of how people experience buildings, we suggest that the
qualities of relationship established by the different senses can be understood
as a manifestation of Dewey's doing and undergoing. The control lent by
seeing beauty speaks to his idea of doing – making order and sense of the
world; and the disempowerment experienced by the haptic senses, which
tend to dwell on ugliness, speaks to his idea of undergoing – muddling
through a bewildering array of objects. There is something assertive about the
Ivoirian state's identity expressed through iconic buildings that express great

confidence, even bravura. The people who took part in our FGDs appeared to identify with this confidence, expressing it in the pride and attachment they felt about these buildings. When it came to anxiety about vulnerability, the attachment was as strong. Buildings that appeared neglected and falling apart represented disturbing evidence of decay, confusion and abandonment. All of this points to the idea that state buildings provide Ivoirian citizens with a powerful aesthetic along the lines suggested by Segal and by Dewey. They draw them into a profound representation of, and engagement with, struggles between chaos and order; anxiety and peace.

There are two levels on which this relationship might be understood, suggesting different levels of implication between the state and its citizens. The first is that the state is an external object that urban residents frequently encounter. Its aesthetic power lies, following Segal, in the correspondence between its own struggle between chaos and order and the struggle citizens face, in the world and reflected in their internal objects. In this reading, the state is an aesthetic object, like a work of art, that provides an illustration of the human condition. State elites' own attempts to exert order over a chaotic world (pace Scott's 'seeing state', 1998) are akin to the artist who tries to create beauty through struggles with her objects and materials.[44] Citizens – in this scenario the audience – perceive the struggles in the ambiguity of the work, for, as Dewey suggests, the process is similar for artist and audience.

However, the state is more than a powerful work of art. Its struggles are important and intense, not just in themselves but because of the profound impacts they have. The aesthetic is not detached but embedded in the lives of citizens. This observation leads us to our second understanding of the relationship between state and society, which posits it as one of mutual implication and co-constitution. The state is produced through the community, not alongside it. We observe this particularly in the stories and fantasies people have about their state buildings, from their miraculous origins to their dangerous dungeons and tunnels. As with Vogel's work on Baule art, observers lend the work real power. Through their aesthetic engagement citizens invest in their state and become co-makers of it.

So what is this Ivoirian state? There is something apparently assertive about the Ivoirian state's identity conveyed by iconic buildings that express great confidence, even bravura. The people who took part in our FGDs appeared to identify with this confidence, expressing it in the pride they felt about

---

44   We find it interesting that Scott's state is 'seeing'. His reading of the state's attempts to bring regularity and uniformity to complex, diverse social systems is all about imposing order on chaos. He links his use of the word 'seeing' to notions of distance and control, very much in line with Pallasmaa's approach.

their buildings. But beneath was considerable anxiety about vulnerability. Buildings that appeared neglected and falling apart represented disturbing evidence of decay, confusion and abandonment. All of this points to the idea that state buildings draw Ivoirian citizens into a profound representation of, and engagement with, chaos and order; anxiety and peace. But, separate as they are, it is more difficult to comprehend the possibility of a struggle between them. For Ivoirians, the descriptions and analysis paint a picture of a highly idealised but fragile state. The idealisation is found in the extreme elevation of the beauty, its abstraction and other-worldliness taking it well outside the realm of normal life; the deep burying of the ugliness and its revolting, othered qualities; and the extreme separation between the two. A strong quality of both beauty and ugliness is therefore their separation from normality and the avoidance of their integration with each other. It appears as though, in imagination, our interlocutors try to keep the two apart. Beauty is too ideal to question, as though its perfections are not robust enough for close examination. It is unclear where it comes from, and the whole edifice might collapse if poked into. Ugliness can appear as too terrible to confront. It emerges reluctantly through whispered stories and horrifying images. Its beauty and ugliness describe a fantastical but highly fragile state whose foundations are unknown, suspect and potentially overwhelming.

Conclusion

There has been a tendency in the history of architecture in Africa to focus on the power of monumental colonial buildings that impose order on African wildernesses.[45] This approach represents a dichotomy between the colonial state and colonial subjects. But, at least in this post-colonial context, order and disorder are not separated, with state buildings reserving the order and leaving disorder to the citizens. Instead, our discussion has suggested that in Côte d'Ivoire state buildings are powerful because they contain within themselves both beauty *and* ugliness. They reflect and embody the state as a complex project, engaged in a constant struggle between order and disorder. Their power lies in the ways in which citizens read these struggles in them.

We have argued for a meta-approach to notions of beauty and ugliness, rooted in people's senses and imagination. We have used Dewey's and Segal's work to describe aesthetic power based on representations of struggles between

---

[45] Colonial architects have described this juxtaposition (for example see Herbert Baker quoted in Metcalf, 1989: 193 or Maxwell Fry and Jane Drew, 1956), and post-colonial scholars have critiqued it (for example, Elleh, 1997; Demissie, 2004; Amutabi, 2012).

beauty and ugliness, and we have found such struggles in Côte d'Ivoire's state buildings, which are aesthetically compelling and suggestive of the power of the state in popular imagination. The aesthetic leads us to a picture of the Ivoirian state of extreme beauty and ugliness.[46] These extremes suggest a fragility to the state, as beauty can barely be explained, coming from elsewhere, possibly of miraculous origins, and ugliness is often too fearful to examine. They appear to be necessarily kept apart in case one might overcome the other.

Finally, we have attempted to show that public buildings as aesthetic objects are powerful, and powerfully illustrative and productive of political structures and processes. As one of our interlocutors suggested, 'when we talk about architecture, we talk about the way we think'.[47] Such thinking, we argue, is part of state-making.

[46]   We do not suggest that this Ivoirian state aesthetic is typical of all states – our broader project, which is comparative, suggests that, while the aesthetic approach to statehood is generally useful in describing state authority, qualities of and relationships between beauty and ugliness are read in different ways in different contexts. For a comparison between Côte d'Ivoire and Ghana, see Gallagher et al., 2021.

[47]   FGD1 – students.

6

Colonial legacies in architectures of consumption: The case of Sam Levy's Village in Harare

TONDERAI KOSCHKE

Like most sub-Saharan colonial cities,[1] the spatial system in Harare, the capital of Zimbabwe, was made to facilitate a racial divide which has today partially evolved into a class divide (Brown, 2001). The Urban Plan of Harare (called Salisbury under British colonial rule until two years after Zimbabwe's independence in 1980) divided the city along the central-east-west axes demarcated by Samora Machel Avenue. The industrial sites and high-density native residential areas were relegated to the south of the city, while the wind-sheltered northern suburbs were designated settler residential areas. Today, this area known as 'North of Samora',[2] is inhabited by Harare's wealthy residents, including the greater part of the city's white population.

As colonial urban planning promoted a dichotomous society, little care was given to the inclusion of infrastructure and spaces for social interaction between different parts of Harare's society. Most parks with public access are located in the northern half of the city,[3] and are not known for drawing visitors from other areas. However, one type of semi-public space which does so is the shopping mall. The most well known shopping mall North of Samora is Sam Levy's Village in the prominent suburb of Borrowdale. Strategically

---

[1]   Daniel Immerwahr (2007) summarises different explorations of the archetype of the 'colonial city', which is fundamentally different from the metropolitan city, suggesting that it is always depicted as a 'dual city'. His observations are of Lagos, a city also shaped by British colonialism.

[2]   The term 'North of Samora' has come to refer to more than just a geographic area, but to the people and culture of the wealthy part of Harare's population that lives in the northern suburbs.

[3]   Examples include the Harare Gardens, Greystone Park Nature Reserve, Kingfisher Park – all North of Samora.

situated along Borrowdale Road, which connects the northern suburbs to the city centre, Sam Levy's Village is a landmark to residents of the surrounding suburbs, travellers through the city and workers from southern high-density areas who work in the wealthy northern ones, reaching them by commuter omnibus mainly along this route. The large property features different kinds of retail establishments and spaces for recreational purposes. Considering the way in which consumption is intrinsic to everyday life in the city, the mall has the potential to be a space for interaction for people from different parts of the city and different groups of Harare's society.

However, rather than fulfilling this vacant role, Sam Levy's Village stands out as an asylum for those seeking racial and class exclusivity. The architectural design of the mall which originally opened with a 'Little England' theme, mimics an English Cottage architectural style. The cross between functioning structure and monument to consumption reflects the post-independence aspirations of parts of local society.

This chapter examines how the design and conception of the mall produced a space which resonates with only a small part of the city's population. The lack of integration between different social groups in the mall illustrates the perpetuation of social separation in Harare's urban fabric. The chapter discusses the racial and class hierarchies and power dynamics observable in the mall and relates them to the shifting power dynamics in Harare's society. The mall was built ten years after independence, and has survived the succession of severe political and economic crises that Zimbabwe has experienced since. By linking architectural developments at the site and public perception of and engagement with the structure, the chapter illustrates how the architecture of the mall continues to uphold colonial legacies and solidify their place in the city's social space.[4]

An in-depth analysis of the architecture of the mall provides the basis for the arguments in this chapter. Qualitative and quantitative on-site observations are supplemented by the analysis of newspaper articles about the mall to reveal public perceptions of and interaction with the mall. In addition, the analysis draws on five semi-structured interviews with a mall user, two shop managers, one senior security employee of Sam Levy's Village and another of the adjoining Village Walk. Several attempts at interviewing the Sam Levy administration itself were not fruitful, an experience which this chapter shares with a number of journalistic accounts about the now-late founder of the mall, Sam Levy. The secretive nature of the Levy family is commonly attributed to its close political ties and extreme wealth.

---

[4]   Such a legacy stands in stark contrast to the opening up of formerly colonial spaces to urban residents through public libraries in Nairobi, discussed by Marie Gibert in Chapter 7, this volume.

The obstacles encountered during research reveal some of the political tensions in Harare today and how deeply intertwined Sam Levy's Village are with them. One interview was held at the adjoining Village Walk, a new addition to the Village shopping area, which I use as a comparison to the Village. It was bought from the Sam Levy family by the Innscor group and opened in 2017.[5] There was a strongly negative reaction by the guards at the Village Walk to the presence of a camera, and I was later informed that several lawsuits against journalists who wrote about the Village Walk in connection with political parties are currently underway. Permission to take pictures and hold further interviews for research purposes was not obtained. It is also notable that Emmerson Mnangagwa, the current President of Zimbabwe, a business-oriented strategist who is known for the catchphrase 'Zimbabwe is open for business', was present at the opening of the Village Walk (NewsdzeZimbabwe, 2018). The control of wealth is central to Zimbabwe's political landscape, which is why developments at places like the Village, where wealth exchanges hands, can reveal much about political affairs, and why they are so tightly controlled.

An analysis of the architecture of the mall sheds light on the aspirations and secondary objectives that accompanied the integration of consumption into the daily lives of Zimbabweans when the mall was planned. Literary sources from architectural theory on commercial architecture as well as on consumption and development in the Global South and Zimbabwe specifically, allow me to describe how the mall emerges as a place in which consumption, social interaction and politics come together. By exploring how the mall functions as an asylum for those seeking race and class exclusivity, I argue that the architecture of the Village cements and reproduces the stark divisions that characterise Harare's socio-political landscape.

Consumption and public space

Since the early days of markets and bazaars, society has had a need for a place to purchase a variety of goods, for social contact and for entertainment. A variety of temporary and permanent building types have fulfilled this requirement. In the twentieth century, conditions of capitalist modernity gave rise to a new architectural structure for this purpose: the shopping mall (Lepik, 2016). Malls are an effective tool for the decongestion of city centres and suburbanisation of cities, as they decentralise the function of retail. Since its

---

[5]   Innscor is a large manufacturing and production company of consumer staple goods founded by prominent businessmen Zed Koudounaris and Michael Fowlers, best-known for their chains of fast-food companies, also involved in several scandals such as the Panama Papers tax evasion investigation (Choto, 2016).

ascension to popularity in the US in the 1950s, the shopping mall has gained global traction. The tradition of open-air malls was established by Jon Jerde, an architect from Los Angeles, with his design of the Horton Plaza Mall in San Diego in 1985. His design was based on a positive spatial experience he had while visiting Italy, which inspired him to design a mall which recreates the atmosphere of an Italian town centre. He considered the idea of Italy, with its connotations of style and luxury, as fitting to accommodate 'a new type of social life permeated by consumption' (Lepik and Bader, 2016: 17).

The themed open-air mall makes use of many of the elements categorised as features of commercial vernacular architecture by Robert Venturi et al. (1977) in their seminal text on architectural symbolism, *Learning from Las Vegas*. One such element is 'the quality of being an oasis in a perhaps hostile context, heightened symbolism and the ability to engulf the visitor in a new role' which are each considered 'essential to the imagery of pleasure-zone architecture' (Venturi et al., 1977: 53), a term which groups malls with architectures of leisure such as theme parks. Indeed, one notable difference between the mall and previously more popular retail streets is that much of the produced space in the latter is dedicated to leisure activities. In this way, malls encourage the public to spend large amounts of time within them, while creating a co-dependence between leisure and consumption.

Dietrich Erben in *World of Malls* (Lepik and Bader, 2016) points out that malls developed from a consumer culture which caters foremost to the leisured class with the time and money to consume. To demonstrate this, Thorstein Veblen (as cited by Erben, 2016: 25) illustrates the 'conspicuous consumption' of the affluent classes in North America, in which the value of acquired goods lies primarily in their 'publicly visible, prestigious appropriation'. Erben (2016: 25) describes 'buildings designed for consumption' as 'stages' on which consumers can flaunt their means. Malls, therefore, have their origins in this tradition of buildings for consumption being used as a means to affirm the existence and power of certain social classes. Today, they still reveal much about the aspirations of societies that continue to rely on them to fulfil the requirements of infrastructure for retail, leisure and social interactions and, importantly, to enable and emphasise social hierarchies.

Malls in the Global South

These aspirations are a source of tension, particularly in the post-colonial context of countries in the Global South where questions of class are more commonly conflated with questions of race. Mehita Iqani (2016), similarly to Erben, characterises consumption as motivated by power, aspiration and communication. To demonstrate consumption as communication, she uses the example of pop-culture consumption by youth groups who position themselves against dominant cultures via styling. Consumption is used to distinguish different groups of society on the individual, personal level, as well as on a larger scale. Iqani (2016: 34) illustrates how 'consumption, or the retail economy more broadly, is deployed for political reasons in order to make claims about stability, governance and quality of life at both the national and the global levels', particularly in the geographical areas where consumption is viewed as part of a 'system designed to "save" Global South economies from persistent underdevelopment'. Infrastructure for consumption can therefore be used to paint a specific picture of a country's social and economic condition.

This may be one reason why consumption in the Global South is an established field of research. Similarly, studies on the importance of public space in the Global South have been on the rise since the end of colonialism (see Laura Routley Chapter 11, this volume). In Zimbabwe, the importance of accessible public space has been established by many scholars as imperative for sustainable development (Munzwa and Jonga, 2010: 11). Public space is also seen as particularly important for low-income households which are more likely to source their livelihood in public spaces (Brown, 2001). Yet this emphasis on low-income social groups in the context of research on public space in the developing world has seen the architectural form of the mall itself largely neglected, despite the fact that malls are spaces of consumption that fulfil the most common functions of public spaces. This is particularly true in the African context, which is excluded even inworks such as *World of Malls* (Lepik and Bader, 2016) which endeavours to give a global overview.

Yet, malls have established themselves as an integral part of consumer-driven life in cities such as Harare, since the time period following the formalisation in 1989 of 'the colonization of the International Monetary Fund (IMF) and the World Bank by the Chicago School' (Iqani, 2016). This was when Zimbabwe made the switch to the free market economic model, which was then a pre-condition for aid and investment. The change of economic policy was marked by a period of growth in the city (Brown, 2001),[6] during which Sam Levy's Village was built.

The failure of Sam Levy's Village to function as an inclusive public space, as I shall show, draws attention to the serious class and race divides in post-colonial Zimbabwe. The study of the mall as an architectural form which reproduces these divisions is therefore imperative as a first step towards finding alternative spatial solutions which would help to bridge the divides in this society.

---

[6] The Economic Structural Adjustment Programme (ESAP) for example, which ran from 1991 to 1995, encouraged investment and created a property boom despite a recession induced by the 1992 drought.

Sam Levy's Village

A large billboard on Borrowdale Road just outside the Village informs any newcomer to this part of town that the tall fence and vast parking lot visible from the street belong to the landmark shopping mall. Unlike the durawalls[7] surrounding the typical private household or gated community in the suburb, the fence allows the passer-by to gaze through, although only up to the shops which are all turned inward towards the central walkway. The neglected back façades are completely closed off, featuring only a few posters and store logos, in addition to piping and air conditioners. The main entrance is sheltered from view by an offset shophouse, and one passes through a decorative wrought-iron gate to access the main walkway. The original structure, built in 1990, consists of a Y-shaped assembly of buildings on both sides of this pedestrian street. The 'Little England' theme of Sam Levy's Village, similarly to the previously mentioned Horton Plaza Mall in San Diego, uses elements loosely translated from what a small town or village centre in a European setting might look like – rows of individual houses that open onto a cobbled street. The red-brick terraced houses with gabled roofs are marketed as being designed in an 'English Cottage' style (Kangondo, 2014). The wide walkway is paved with bricks in a herringbone pattern and features low, brick-walled islands of green lawn, the occasional fountain and many rose bushes.[8] Only the occasional palm tree breaks the mould by adding a Mediterranean touch, or a resort holiday atmosphere.

The ground floor shops have glass shopfronts which are sometimes separated into squares, with glazing bars reminiscent of British sash windows. This square pattern is echoed by small, opaque, square windows that embellish the second floor façade of the shops. This second floor is accessed by a stairway shared between two upper-floor terraced housing units, which can be entered through a high, arched doorway – one such entrance is partially visible in figure 6.1. Decorative brick patterns dot the shops and walkways. The warm red brick contributes to an inviting ambiance, and the small scale of the buildings creates an atmosphere that is intimate enough to encourage social encounters. Six different entrances and shops on both sides mean that people walk in both directions and often back and forth, making it easy to bump into acquaintances. The plan is clearly meant to encourage communication and establish an air of familiarity. By encouraging social interaction, it attempts to fulfil the function of public places in the city centre such as town squares.

---

7   A type of prefabricated perimeter wall popularised by a company called Durawall.
8   The national flower of England, closely associated with British culture and a popular cultivar in the more manicured suburban gardens in Harare.

Figure 6.1   Sam Levy's Village in Harare (Tonderai Koschke, October 2019).

The occasional bench lining the islands in the street and the four cafés in the main structure invite visitors to linger.

To fully realise the character of a 'village', the occasional shop breaks the mould of the terraced houses and the 300-metre-long walkway widens into areas with additional space in which to linger, as is offered by village squares. The most prominent one accents the corner where the walkway splits into two to form a Y-shape. The Zim Bank building which faces onto this square is adorned by white columns complete with abstracted capitals.

This abstraction is one indication of the mall's very surface-level architectural motifs. In the context of the American, open-air, themed mall design concept, the amalgamation of different elements that echo Western architecture, from gabled roofs that are intended to look like quaint English houses, to grand white pillars squashed into a façade whose scale is entirely unsuitable for a double colonnade, sell a Britishness that is only symbolic. Outside the Zim Bank building, a small replica of Big Ben brings the entire concept to the verge of caricature. In its early years, the mall was guarded at the gate by a man dressed in the historical uniform of a London Metropolitan Police officer: a blue tail coat and top hat (Kangondo, 2014).[9] The British theme is packaged for consumption within the mall in a manner which is reminiscent of amusement parks.

While the architectural concept of the outdoor shopping mall lends itself well to the temperate climate in Harare, symbolism, as Venturi et. al. (1977) describe, takes on specific meanings according to context. At the Village, one cannot escape the irony of the British theme of the mall, which invites visitors to imagine themselves strolling through an English haven in a structure built in such contrast to the surrounding city, only ten years after independence. This theme being used to make claims about 'stability, governance and quality of life' countered the narrative of the anti-British Zimbabwean government at the time the mall was built,[10] which was pervaded by assertions of independence from the former colonial power and capability that characterised the early policies of young post-colonial nations. The conflation in the mall of consumption, an expression of aspiration, and symbolism from the culture of the former colonial power creates the impression of an aspiration towards cultural assimilation.

Class and racial divides

The relationship between Zimbabwe and its former colonial power is a complex one.[11] The link between post-colonial consumer culture in Zimbabwe and the global commodity market produced largely through British colonialism in Zimbabwe is more clear, as 'it was with the rise of western industrialism that global commodity markets became a central feature of cultures and economies not only in the west but throughout the world' (Iqani, 2016: 23). Notwithstanding the different attitudes of Zimbabweans towards Britain, spanning from resentment to admiration, the economic advantage Britain has had over Zimbabwe made it a viable subject for the projection of aspirations in the architecture of the Village, which needed to signify wealth and safety, and encourage consumption.

The choice of theme is especially significant because the Village was one of the first malls to be built after independence in the city of Harare, even before the centrally located Eastgate Mall, which opened in 1996. In fact, as with other public infrastructure, most of the malls which sprang up during

9   This is the uniform worn by the first policemen or 'Bobbies' dispatched by Sir Robert Peel in London in 1829.
10   The anti-British stance of Mugabe, the Zimbabwean president at the time, has been well documented (Tendi, 2014). The disassociation went so far as to see Zimbabwe expelled and then withdraw from the Commonwealth in 2002 and 2003.
11   The complexities of Zimbabwean notions of Britishness, and the relationships between the two countries are discussed by Julia Gallagher (2017).

this period, such as Westgate Mall and Arundel Village, were predominantly situated North of Samora. As one of the earliest malls in the very prominent suburb of Borrowdale, the Village reflects particularly strongly the hopes and expectations about where in the city consumption would flourish post-independence. The primary target group was the wealthy people who would inhabit the low-density housing found in these areas. These include the predominantly white-settler communities which were only just becoming mixed with the wealthy black elite.

The Sam Levy administration is at pains to contradict this narrative. In order to preserve the image of Sam Levy as a philanthropist who wanted to make goods available to all, they frequently refer to a nickname, 'cutthroat king', allegedly given to him because his Macy's department stores[12] were notorious for keeping the prices of goods low.[13] Levy was a shrewd businessman and former politician[14] with positive ties with the post-independence ruling party through close friendships with political figures such as husband and wife Samuel and Joice Mujuru (Matambanadzo, 2012) who were heavily involved in the war for independence and aligned with the Zimbabwe African National Union-Patriotic front (ZANU-PF), the ruling political party which strongly denounced British intervention in Zimbabwe (Tendi, 2014; Gallagher, 2017).

The Village administration explains the unlikely decision to build a mall that, through its theme and architecture, promotes a positive image of the culture of the former coloniser of the country, by pointing out that Levy was a visionary who brought many international business concepts to Zimbabwe. This is a popular description of Levy; after his death in 2012, his eulogy read: 'He always said, when I see a good idea, I take it and bring it back to Zimbabwe. His intention was always to let people here get a taste of what was only available overseas. He had so much pride in bringing new things to this country' (Kangondo, 2014). This glowing report of Levy's visionary role was repeated almost verbatim to me in an interview with a security employee at Sam Levy's Village, which was held in an office displaying a framed copy of the newspaper report.[15]

The English theme of the mall is therefore meant to underline its international inspiration and increase the perception of it as prestigious. This has

[12]   These department stores were not connected to the American franchise of that name.
[13]   Informal interview with senior employee in security at the Village in 2019.
[14]   Sam Levy won a seat in the Harare City Council elections in 1975 and sat as Ward 8, Waterfalls councillor.
[15]   Interview held on 2 October 2019.

been reinforced by the way in which the mall has stayed in good business even during the times when many shops with empty shelves were shown in news reports of Zimbabwe around the world (Hanke and Kwok, 2009).[16] A particularly popular anecdote about the Village is that, like many buildings constructed during the first years after independence, it was built without municipal permission.[17] In 2005, many Zimbabweans lost their livelihoods as the Zimbabwean government destroyed structures in urban areas as part of Operation Murambatsvina with the justification that they were illegal (Olaleye and Tungwarara, 2005) as they had been built without permission. About 700,000 Zimbabweans were directly affected by the operation (Sachinkonye, 2006). However, Sam Levy's Village was spared from the demolition, and eventually got its permit retrospectively in 1993.[18] This reinforced the image of the mall as an oasis in a perhaps hostile environment (which I explore in the following section), but also illustrates the dissonance between the realities of different social classes in Harare.

There is a stark contrast between those who benefit from the Village as a vehicle for their 'conspicuous consumption', and the majority who cannot afford the privilege of shopping in the prominent northern suburb and pursuing chargeable activities during their leisure time. In the middle of the decade during which most malls in Harare were built, more than 60 per cent of Zimbabwe's households fell below the national poverty line, and poverty has increased significantly since 1990 (Alwang et al., 2002). In 2008, the period of particularly severe economic crisis marked by hyperinflation, unemployment rose to over 80 per cent (Mhike, 2017). Overall, massive de-industrialisation and job cuts have been on the increase since the 1990s (Mhazo and Thebe, 2020). In practice, there has been no point at which the majority of Harare's society could afford to constantly consume during their leisure time. Indeed, the nature of the luxury goods that are traded in many stores within the Village (including, among others, a Persian carpet store), make a stark contrast with the struggle of most Zimbabweans to access basic commodities. This highlights the economic inequalities in Zimbabwe's society, and the deeply exclusionary nature of this space.

While class and race are conflated in this space because of Harare's post-colonial context, some aspects of the mall are specifically racialised. Viewed in light of the aforementioned contrast between the realities of the

[16]   The impacts of the 2008 crisis in Zimbabwe was widely publicised due to the hyperinflation approaching the world record.
[17]   For a discussion of informal architecture see Kuukuwa Manful's Afterword, this collection.
[18]   See Paidamoyo Muzulu and Zisunko Ndlovu, 2015.

patrons of the interior of the mall and the many who remain outside it, the 'Little England' theme which envelops the patrons harks back to a time when Britishness, through its connection to whiteness, ensured preferential treatment in Rhodesian society. The building reflects the colonial idea of foreignness and particularly Englishness and whiteness as prestigious, or better than the local.

The Village is a place perceived as welcoming by many white Zimbabweans who occupy it in the natural manner in which one occupies a space successfully designed with one's patronage in mind. On a typical afternoon, I observed that among eight or so customers at Pistachio Café in the old part of Sam Levy's Village, only one was black. In the combined outdoors seating area of several cafés in the new mall row of the Village, all twenty occupants are white. The phenomenon is publicly acknowledged and has been referred to for example in newspaper articles about the Village. In an article called 'Sam Levy, the man and his legacy' in the *Saturday Herald*, Fanuel Kangondo correlates it to the English theme of the Village that is still visible in the architecture by asking 'was this designed to attract the white people who initially patronised the village? Even today, there are far more white people at the village than any other mall in the city' (Kangondo, 2014).[19] This comment illustrates how the design of the mall is perceived as not being marketed to black people. The Village occasionally makes headlines for the odd scandal and accusations of racial violence that occur there.[20]

The peculiarity of these dynamics is powerfully contrasted at a neighbouring mall. The Village Walk, by a company called Innscor, is a recent commercial development adjoining Sam Levy's Village. It is therefore a particularly suitable site for comparison, as the malls share a common location in the northern suburbs of Harare. At the two cafés at Village Walk – which go by the names Nush and Freshly Ground – this racial separation dissipates and the continuously changing clientele is made up of a crowd of up to fifty black, Asian and white Zimbabweans.[21] While the demographics here still reflect the situation of the mall in the more well-off 'North of Samora', where more non-black people in Harare live than in southern high-density areas, the stark divide observable at the Village is not as visible.

[19]   A cutting of the original newspaper article from 2012 was framed and hanging in the Village manager's and security offices in October 2019. A similar version of the same article was published online in May 2014.
[20]   *Pindula News*, 14 October 2016.
[21]   Observations made on a Wednesday afternoon, September 2019.

Exclusionary architecture

Tellingly, then, in practice the relaxed, welcoming setting which the architecture at Sam Levy's Village appears to invoke is undermined by its occupation by a set of citizens homogenous in race and class. It keeps out citizens who are not part of this group, thereby limiting contact between those in the interior and those in the exterior. One manifestation of the actually exclusionary nature of the mall's architecture is the introversion of its structure, which is excessive when compared to commercial architecture in the tradition of the American mall from which the Village stems. Venturi et al. (1977) point out that the side elevations of buildings on the Las Vegas strip, which are built to the scale of the highway, are particularly important because they are the primary elevation for oncoming traffic. The shophouses 'turn their ill-kempt backsides toward the local environment' (Venturi et al., 1977: 35)[22] only on the far side from the highway from which they are inaccessible. Sam Levy's Village with its large parking lot is similarly built to be most easily accessed by car. Yet, at the Village, on the longest stretch of the structure along the major road, even the façades towards the outside are completely neglected. The structure completely closes off from the local environment, including the street from which advertising to the general public would be visible. This implies that the mall, from its conception, was notorious enough not to need further advertisement for all the services it offers, and that its interior oasis with its cafés and green islands is intended only for those in the know.

The main advantage of the enclosed structure of Sam Levy's Village, according to a senior employee of the sizeable security team whom I interviewed, is safety.[23] It is easy both to oversee the enclave and to close the mall to prevent anyone from entering after closing hours. The emphasis on safety by the Village administration does give way quickly under scrutiny, however, as the high fence, wide island and deep ditch that run around the parking lot in the safe neighbourhood ought to fulfil adequate safety requirements, as they do for the Village Walk. For comparison, the U-shaped structure of the latter opens towards Borrowdale Road. While it is set well away from the busy road and, like at Sam Levy's Village, the token parking lot typical of commercial vernacular architecture (Venturi et al., 1977) takes up the highly visible space between the road and the mall, yet the structure engages much more with the outside than the Village does. The cafés in the Village Walk are all located on large, open verandahs which face the parking lot and Borrowdale Road. The signage of the shops at Village Walk is clearly visible from the street.

22 The 'local environment' refers to the area away from the main strip, from where the casinos and shops are not approached by the public.
23 Informal interview with senior employee in security at the Village in 2019.

Conversely, at Sam Levy's Village the patrons of the interior are well shielded from passers-by. The omnibus stop in front of the Village is used in particular by people who come to work in Borrowdale in the shops, or as domestic workers for surrounding households. The bare-back façades towards the street prevent their visual participation in the interior of the mall from the outside, while a wide ditch and fence in front of the parking lot, which wraps protectively all the way around the structure, physically separates them from the Village. The primary function of the enclosed structure of the Village is therefore effectively the exclusion of people, rather than protection.

Someway off from the large gate through which cars enter the Village, a small opening in the fence allows pedestrians arriving by bus to enter the Village after they have crossed the car park on foot. This makes access difficult even for the workers who keep the mall running. People who are neither white nor wealthy, even when they enter the mall on the grounds of formal employment, rather than becoming actors in the public space of the Village, take on the role of another design motif. The uniformed security guards stationed at some entrances and occasionally manning the walkway, but otherwise generally ignored by visitors, are an example. The moment they cross the ditch and pass through the fence to enter the Village they become part of the set-up. Their role, like that of an extra in a film, is to contribute to the atmosphere of safety within the Village. They also visually preserve the colonial racial hierarchy within the mall, as during my numerous visits to the mall the security guards were always black men, just as cleaners and other lower-level employees were black and usually women.

By heightening the aforementioned 'quality of being in an oasis in a perhaps hostile context' (Venturi et al., 1977: 53) this fortification evokes colonial imagery in which the British settler enclaves were havens of safety and order that contrasted the wild landscape to be colonised, in this case symbolised by the rest of the city. The enclosed form reminds of the shape of the *laagers*[24] formed by white settlers as they first moved into the area that is present-day Zimbabwe, to protect themselves from both wild animals and people. This architectural form continued to play an important role in the colonial architecture of segregation, for example in the form of forts. Harare, for example, was first established as Fort Salisbury by the British pioneer column. The black workers such as security guards, who only enter the mall to work, have a similar role in the Village as the black bodies exploited for labour in colonial

[24] The Afrikaans word which was used by the British pioneer column is symbolic here of the generic notion of whiteness in Zimbabwe today, which the design of the mall presents through the British term used for a mall known to be marketed to white people in general.

forts and cities. This historical legacy strengthens the idea of Sam Levy's Village as a stronghold of colonial order, from the moment it was designed as a haven of consumption against the backdrop of a young independent government beginning to face the economic challenges that have led to a continuous decline until the present day.

Historically, either unspoken rules or official laws such as the Native Urban Areas Act[25] reinforced the racial segregation of the colonial era. Sam Levy's Village is a powerful example of how architecture reproduces this division even in the absence of such laws today. The racial segregation of the colonial era in the city of Harare has today become conflated with the segregation between different classes, as the growing black population in previously white-only suburbs consists mainly of the wealthy elite. At the Village, the racial exclusion is reinforced by the exclusion of the poor, who cannot afford to spend money in the mall. In the case of the patronage of a café such as Pistachio, it may be both the price and the product sold that precludes people who are neither wealthy nor acquainted with the food served there.[26] The result is a sense of exclusiveness that prevents the mall from functioning as a place of social interaction between different social groups.

Village extension and current developments

Two interviews held with a shop manager and a visitor to the mall, neither of whom work directly with the administration, expressed negative views about the architecture of the Village, in contrast with those who work closely for or with the Levy family. Neither of the two found the architecture of the mall 'modern'. The architecture of the buildings by which the mall has been extended in recent years appears to be increasingly distanced from the original design scheme of the mall as a response to the public sentiment that this is old-fashioned.

---

[25] This law, introduced in 1947, split urban areas into African and European sections. As late as 1976, when several laws enforcing spatial segregation were reviewed, a Rhodesian government commission 'recommended that white residential areas should remain closed to black ownership' (*The New York Times*, 1976: 7) Another rule which ensured the exclusion of black people from leisure facilities was a by-law that forbade people of different races from using the same toilets, which resulted in the legal 'Battle of the Toilets' when a theatre opened its doors to all races in 1966 (Waters, 2006).
[26] The menu in August 2020 at Pistachio was in US dollars, which are not easily available to all Zimbabweans. It included a small box of macarons for US$5 – a luxury food in European tradition. A cappuccino cost US$3 at a time when the monthly minimum wage converted to US$7 officially.

Figure 6.2 Extension to Sam Levy's Village (Tonderai Koschke, October 2019).

This change in architectural direction goes hand in hand with the change in the views of the clientele of the Village since 1990. However, while the newness in Harare of the concept of the mall in 1990 may have linked it to modernity, the brick architecture which was often seen in colonial architecture was no more modern then than it is now, and was as romanticised in Harare's society then as it is today. It is the 'Little England' theme of the original structure that has become outdated. For comparison, both interviewees with whom this aspect was discussed further perceived the more generic architecture of the Village Walk as more modern, despite this type of commercial vernacular architecture predating the entire mall. What has become more modern, however, is the notions of identity of the clientele of the mall. Today, the spending power of the public extends further than a small white minority, and changes in the design approach of the Village extension reflect this. Due to new attractions such as a cinema[27] and gyms, the crowd in the cafés at the Village extension and at the Village Walk are younger compared to the clientele in the original Village itself. The variety in the buildings' styles that

---

[27]   As of 2019, one of the last running cinemas in Harare, it draws movie enthusiasts from all around the city.

make up this new part of the complex produce a less severe order with which this crowd appears more comfortable.

Within the Village, the more recently the structures were built, the more they diverge from the design of the original structure. The first addition after Sam Levy's death in 2012, when the Village was inherited by his children and grand-children, was an expansion of the original Y-shaped structure by an L-shaped row of terraced houses behind the car park on the far side from Borrowdale Road, which also face inward, away from the access streets. The two-storey houses have a similar but less fussy design than the old structure, featuring red brick and front-facing gables but a sleeker façade without decorative arches and windows. On the ground floor is a wide arcade which provides an outdoor seating area for several cafés and restaurants. The arcades are screened from the parking lot by a wide island with several shrubs and palm trees. In keeping with the tradition of the original structure, the cafés in the new part of the Village also provide a strong sense of privacy.

Following this, a large entertainment/lifestyle complex was added, which is similar to the old terraced houses only in the use of exposed brick in the façade. This is built with glass and a hidden reinforced concrete structure which allows for a wide underbridge, shown in figure 6.2, to serve as the entrance of the structure. The façade above the underbridge is divided into three parts by brick-clad pillars, two of which allow a view of a modern gym through ceiling-height fixed glazing. The central pane of this façade is a plain brick wall which serves as a backdrop for a large clock face with roman numerals. This quaint detail, so incongruous with the rest of the building, alludes to the terraced houses in an obvious attempt at visually uniting the different building styles in the new mall into a whole.

The most recent addition to the mall, as seen in figure 6.3, is even more obtrusive in the context of the English-cottage resort theme. It is a roughly cubical, four-storey high spa and office building whose reference appears to be the International Style, with a skin of copper-tinted glazing. Due to its double story ground floor and hidden roof structure, it appears about six-storeys high. A large sign reading 'Sam Levy's Tower' runs along the top of the building in an allusion to monumentality. This new building clearly distances itself from the English theme by choosing a more generic architecture of consumption.

The new cinema complex and restaurants in the Village extension encourage visitors to spend longer periods of leisure time within the mall, and this entertainment complex appears more lively than the original mall structure. The less rigidly planned section of the mall extension leaves some unbuilt space, which allows one area, used as additional parking, to be appropriated by a flea-market on Sundays. This flea-market is one of few opportunities for informal traders to trade at the heart of the suburb in which many tourists

Figure 6.3   Sam Levy's Tower (Olaf Koschke, 11 January 2022).

and visitors to Harare stay. It is one of the main draws for the more racially diverse, if not means-diverse public from the Village Walk which adjoins the Village on the opposite side, with its back to Sam Levy's Village.[28] The market atmosphere in which negotiating is the norm encourages a more familiar communication between traders and visitors than occurs in shops, an illustration of the potential that spaces for consumption provide for social interaction between different parts of society.

Conclusion

Harare is a polarised post-colonial city with a need for public spaces for social interaction to foster understanding between the different parts of Zimbabwean society. Architectures of consumption, as infrastructures used by all, have the potential to fulfil this need. The small-scale open-air mall model, which characterises Sam Levy's Village, creates a small-city or village-centre environment and encourages spending time in public and communication, could fulfil this function. Yet, the mall fails to facilitate the bridging of gaps between the different parts of Harare's society.

Despite serving only a small percentage of Harare's population as a public space, Sam Levy's Village has continued to thrive over the years as a source of international products and luxury goods for those who can afford them, even as Zimbabwe's economy faced several severe financial crises. However, the methods used for the objective of encouraging consumption are incongruous with the objective of fostering a welcoming environment for all members of Harare's society. The very motifs which make the mall suitable for conspicuous consumption and therefore encourage Zimbabweans with the means to spend at the mall, as well as the high prices and luxury goods which make the mall a prestigious place to shop, prevent many Zimbabweans from shopping there. The original structure of the mall in particular is perceived as being an exclusionary place in which division in Harare's society is reinforced.

The social division observable at the mall is not only between classes, but also racialised. Through its theme and architecture, the mall reflects early post-colonial notions of whiteness in Zimbabwe. Its success and steady use by a similar demographic reveals the continuity of the racialisation of public spaces into the present day. The exclusionary nature of the architecture of the

---

28 While the Village and its extension are under the same administration, the Village Walk is distinct from it. In an informal interview with a senior employee at Terrace Africa, the company developing the Village Walk, competitiveness to the point of enmity between the two malls was highlighted. Movement between the two malls is therefore not encouraged by the administrations but nevertheless occurs naturally.

mall in particular facilitates this. The pleasure-zone architecture, which creates the atmosphere of an oasis in a hostile environment, plunges any person who enters the mall into an environment so far from the reality of the actual city and society in which it is situated, that it impedes the functioning of the mall as the kind of public space which would benefit the city's society as a whole.

For comparison, the adjoining Village Walk shows how a different kind of mall architecture can create more inclusive spaces; most evidently, the racialised segregation is reduced within this mall. Indeed, recent developments around the original mall structure of Sam Levy's Village have responded to a shift in the identity of the mall clientele; and the extension of the mall, like other newer malls in the area, is more inclusive than the original structure. The Sunday flea-market in particular allows a more racially and class-diverse crowd to interact.

However, the unchanged main structure still takes up the most space on the prime property on Borrowdale Road, and more comprehensive, conscious changes to the aesthetics and accessibility of the entire mall would be required to change the message sent by the symbolism of the mall and encourage a different perception and use of the architecture. Ultimately, Sam Levy's Village, as an architectural landmark and household name in Harare, is an illustration of the import of commercial architecture particularly in the African post-colonial context. As this chapter has shown, it can be seen as both a symptom and facilitator of the enduring racialised segregation of Zimbabwean society post-colonisation.

7

Public spaces? Public goods?
Reinventing Nairobi's public libraries

MARIE GIBERT

In a fast-growing and changing city such as Nairobi, some public buildings and services have changed remarkably little over the decades. Such is the case with the McMillan Memorial Library, built in 1931 and situated in Nairobi's Central Business District (CBD), but also of the less known public libraries of Kaloleni and Makadara, two poorer areas of Nairobi. Ever since their respective creations all three libraries, which are referred to collectively as the 'McMillan libraries', have continuously delivered a much-needed public service to a population thirsty for education and safe spaces to study, in spite of a lack of investment and increasing state of decay. Book Bunk, a small civil society organisation founded in 2017 by Angela Wachuka and Wanjiru Koinange, two Kenyan book professionals, has resolved to address the matter by setting up a partnership with Nairobi City County Government, assessing needs (from an architectural, inventory and users' perspective), rehabilitating the buildings and exploring new ways in which they and their historical and new contents might be explored, questioned and appropriated by Nairobi's population.

In this chapter, I first show that the libraries, through Book Bunk's work on them, have become the sites of an important reflection on the role libraries can play in better representing and understanding Kenya's colonial past, building a more inclusive culture and offering a different public space and service. In other words, Book Bunk's work on the libraries is placing these three outdated but tranquil refuges at the heart of crucial and heated public debates about history, memory and collective imagination and representation. In the remainder of the chapter, I discuss how Book Bunk is attempting to define a fine line between discarding and preserving history with regard to the libraries' buildings, books and purpose. In doing this, Book Bunk and the libraries are offering their own answers to global debates about decolonising our public spaces, making history and memory accessible to all and offering a platform to Kenya's many, including female, voices.[1]

Tranquil refuges, heated debates

Although Book Bunk rarely, if at all, uses the term 'urban library' in its communications or in interviews,[2] it is clear that this is how it sees the McMillan libraries – that is, as crucial social infrastructure in a fast-growing and changing city that, like many developing world cities, has relatively little public space and infrastructure. A quick drive through Nairobi gives residents an immediate sense of the mixture of aggressive capitalist drive, economic and social dynamism, little regard for urban planning and rules, and the shocking inequality that characterises the booming city. Roads are packed with *matatus*, Kenya's private collective transport vans, but most notably by single-occupancy cars – driven by their owners or one of the now well established hail-and-ride company drivers – and some motorbikes. Above the – so-often jammed – traffic, drivers and passengers can browse the multiple billboards advertising luxury flats for sale throughout the city's most sought-after neighbourhoods, or observe the ongoing works on the ever-greater number of high-rise buildings mushrooming everywhere with little respect for workers' safety or distance requirements from neighbouring constructions and height of buildings. The general disregard for driving courtesy and rules on the road reflects Nairobians' frustration with traffic, a fatalistic approach to risk but also the go-and-get-it culture that dominates much of the city's life.

In the midst of all this, Nairobi's public libraries appear as tranquil refuges, whatever their sorry state. Our three libraries remained popular studying spaces up until their closure both for renovation (for the Kaloleni and Makadara branches) and, from March 2020 to June 2021, because of the Covid-19 pandemic. The central library was full of University of Nairobi students and CBD workers, especially in the afternoons, and the libraries in Kaloleni and Makadara provided a quiet environment for pupils and students who wished to do their homework away from their crowded homes. A survey conducted by Book Bunk in January 2018 showed that the Makadara Library hosted an average of 182 readers a day,

---

[1]   My discussion speaks to many of the same themes Laura Routley addresses on the transformation of a colonial prison site into a public park in Lagos, Chapter 11, this collection. Although Nairobi's libraries have maintained their original raison d'être, contrary to Lagos' Freedom Park, the projects share a common objective of 'overwriting' a colonial past while 're-inscribing' it into debates about the country's identity and future.

[2]   They tend to refer to 'public libraries' instead. See, for example, Book Bunk's statement of purpose on its website, www.bookbunk.org [Accessed 1 November 2019].

Figure 7.1 The McMillan Memorial Library front entrance (Marie Gibert, July 2021).

the McMillan Memorial Library sixty-two and the Kaloleni Library thirty-nine (Book Bunk, 2019: 16). They did not, however, use the library for its books, following in this a universal trend as online contents tend to replace hard-copy elements, albeit for very different reasons. The libraries' books remained mostly unreferenced when they were not totally irrelevant and out of date, and no one knew where to find which book. Book Bunk's survey thus showed that 55 per cent of users came to the libraries to revise for their exams and 41 per cent to read their own books, leaving a mere 3.5 per cent to borrow books and 2.1 per cent to read newspapers (Book Bunk, 2019: 18).

Because of the history of the buildings and their contents, however, these tranquil refuges are also at the centre of debates that reflect current controversies about both the representation of colonisation and that of Kenya's own past, and important reflections over how to deal with these representations. The original McMillan Library (figure 7.1), situated at the heart of Nairobi's CBD, is most clearly linked to Kenya's colonial history. It was inaugurated in 1931, as Kenya's second public library.[3] Built by Lady Lucie McMillan in memory

---

3   Kenya's first public library was the Seif bin Salim Library, opened in 1903 in Mombasa by the then British East Africa Protectorate capital city's Indian community (Mangat, 2010).

of her late husband, American-turned-British explorer William Northrup
McMillan, with a significant participation from the Carnegie family,[4] it was
a segregated library open to white Kenyans only until Kenya's independence
in 1963. Its architecture and contents have not changed since the early 1930s
and bear all the grand signs of the unabashed colonial spirit of the time:

> The building features a neo-classical design with towering granite-clad
> columns dominating the façade and a grand white marble trapezoidal
> stairway leading up to the portico. Twin lion statues stand guard on either
> side of the entrance way … Walls are built of smooth rendered stone
> under a flat roof. Windows are glazed in tall steel casements providing
> ample natural lighting. Doors are made of heavy hardwood panels hung
> in timber frames, pedimented to the lintels. A bust of McMillan finished
> in Makonde black sits atop a mock fireplace overlooking the main reading
> area, as if in watchful vigil. Twin elephant tusks are mounted at a short
> distance in front of the mock fireplace. (Kiereini, 2016a)

More than fifty years after Kenya's independence, white men remain
omnipresent throughout Nairobi's central library. The unmistakably Western
name of the central library, the very central location of McMillan's bust
within it (as described above), the elephant tusks reminding us of white
men's safari/hunting culture, the statues all made by Western male artists,[5]
the many pictures of white men, including that of Andrew Carnegie in the
upstairs reading room and those of the Nairobi City Council – made of
white men only – found in the library's recently rediscovered archives, and
(in all three McMillan libraries) the many books mostly published in the
early twentieth century and authored by mostly white men all attest to a
controversial past.

All this resonates very strongly with debates that have recently shaken
Africa and Europe, Kenya and its British former colonial power. In 2015,
in South Africa's Cape Town, a student-led movement targeted the statue of
British mining magnate, politician and Prime Minister of the Cape Colony at
the end of the nineteenth century, Cecil Rhodes. The statue, situated on the
campus of the University of Cape Town, was first defaced, and later removed
after the university's senate and council decided to follow calls to revisit a
'rose-tinted memory of empire' (Chaudhuri, 2016) and its statuesque symbols.

---

[4]   The McMillan Memorial Library was one among 2,500 libraries around the world
built with Carnegie money. In fact, its external architecture very closely resembles
that of the Carnegie Library in Dallas, Texas (Mars, 2019).
[5]   Among them, an Italian carved alabaster figure, called Passo del Ruscello, made
in 1890 by Cesare Lapini.

The South African 'Rhodes Must Fall' movement prompted parallel calls in the West, most notably in Oxford, where students also called for a statue of Rhodes to be removed from Oriel College. More importantly, however, the movement has prompted calls, worldwide, to decolonise education and academic scholarship and their curricula, and has unleashed a vast debate as to what this could mean and how it should be done (Charles, 2019: 24). Buoyed by the greater visibility of academic and civil society movements calling for gender equality and the explosion of the #MeToo campaign from late 2017, but also by the role played by women in the 'Black Lives Matter' movement, the call to decolonise has also been accompanied by calls to give women of colour a greater voice. A 'feminisation' of both the current political, social and cultural scenes and our understanding of history has been added to calls to decolonise, thus recognising the strong patriarchal nature of colonialism.[6]

Kenya, and here I include both its state and citizens, seems to constantly oscillate between a wish to forget, or at least downplay, colonial and post-colonial violence, and a strong desire to shed light on it and to revisit its most prescient symbols. In a historic move, and with the help of historians who had uncovered archives documenting the repression of their movement,[7] former Mau Mau combatants who fought against the British colonial power, sought reparations in the early 2000s for the ill-treatment and torture they suffered in special detention camps. A first legal battle resulted in the uncovering of 'migrated' archives documenting the repression of the Mau Mau movement, and a settlement between the UK Government and 5,228 Kenyan claimants who were paid a total sum of GBP £19.9 million, as well as support for the construction of a memorial in Nairobi to the victims of torture and ill-treatment during the colonial era.[8] In a second legal battle launched in 2014, more than 40,000 Kenyan claimants sought to bring the UK Government to justice. Following 230 hearing days spread over four years, however, the case was dismissed because the passage of time and absence of corroborative evidence made it impossible for the Crown to mount a meaningful defence. These cases have helped to shed light and put the spotlight on a movement that is now

6   A flurry of articles, children's and adult literature has been published in recent years celebrating Black and African American women and their role in history. See Neema Begum and Rima Saini, 2019: 196–201; Bernadine Evaristo, 2019; and, for an example of a children's book, Vashti Harrison, 2017.

7   Many documents were destroyed before the British withdrawal from Kenya in 1963 (Parry, 2016).

8   The monument, showing a woman handing food to a Mau Mau fighter, was unveiled in 2015 in Nairobi's Uhuru (Freedom) Park.

celebrated in school history textbooks but whose history and handling by both the colonial and post-colonial authorities has been controversial.[9]

Other episodes of Kenya's twentieth-century history and political violence, from the First World War to political repression by the post-independence governments, on the other hand, remain largely unacknowledged and undebated,[10] thus confirming what Kenyan scholar Joyce Nyairo has called a 'deliberate institutionalisation of amnesia'.[11] Yet signs of Kenya's troubled past are omnipresent, starting with those of its colonial history, as underlined above in the case of the central McMillan Library. Much of Kenya's richest land continues to be owned by white Kenyans and foreigners, while the tourist industry, notably the country's many luxury lodges and safari agencies, entertains a nostalgia for the colonial era by offering experiences in tented camps refurbished to resemble the colonial experience as portrayed in the film *Out of Africa*. This way of selling the 'Kenya Colony brand', as William Jackson terms it, to international tourists was instituted during the colonial era but the post-colonial African state has been eager 'to endorse and indeed encourage the marketing of colonial nostalgia through international tourism' (Jackson, 2011: 358). The colonial imagery is thus intensely familiar to Kenyans and this may explain the clarity and lucidity, mixed with a surprising lack of resentment and anger, with which Book Bunk's interns, when guiding visitors around the central library, pointed to its display of male whiteness,[12] as well

---

[9]   Although Kenya's first president, Jomo Kenyatta, was convicted and imprisoned by the British authorities for being part of the Mau Mau, he was not, and his post-independence government included more people who had fought against than with the Mau Mau. Kenyatta's motto was to forget and move on from the past, and his government maintained the ban on the movement introduced by the colonial authorities (it was only lifted in 2002), used 'silent tactics of repression' against it, and ignored its claims over land redistribution (Angelo, 2017).

[10]   David Lammy, British Member of Parliament for Tottenham, visited Kenya and Tanzania in 2019, putting the spotlight on the absence of official graves for the tens of thousands of porters who served Britain in the First World War (Lammy, 2019). Likewise, there is no state museum, or state museum section, devoted to this episode of Kenya's history. (A private hotel situated in the Taita Hills, where the First World War's East African Campaign started, has thus taken it upon itself to create a small museum section dedicated to the issue.) The outpouring of tributes and grand state funeral organised in honour of Kenya's second president, Daniel Arap Moi (in office 1978–2002) in February 2020, further underlined the unwillingness to revisit the myth of Kenya's post-independence pacific and stable politics and to shed light on the country's history of political violence (Adebajo, 2020; Musasia, 2020).

[11]   In Joyce Nyairo, 2015 (cited by Mutonga, 2020).

[12]   Author's visits of the McMillan Memorial Library on 8 December 2018 and 31 October 2019. On both occasions the interns guiding us around quietly acknowledged

as the sense of 'quiet revolution'[13] that emanates from the organisation's plans to reinvent and decolonise the three libraries it has taken on, as I will show in the remainder of this chapter.

Rehabilitating the buildings

While the central McMillan Library bears the most obvious symbols of the colonial era, the two other libraries also reflect important moments in Kenya's history. The much smaller Kaloleni Library (figure 7.2) was built, as part of the Kaloleni Social Hall ensemble, between 1943 and 1948 by Italian prisoners of war, as part of the Kaloleni estate in Nairobi's eastern parts (the then-'African zone').

Kaloleni estate, unlike the estates built previously to house single African men only, was equipped with communal facilities in recognition of the fact that African men and women, and their families, had become permanent residents of the city.[14] The library was part of these facilities, built to cater for the education, development and recreation of Nairobi's African workers and their families. As described in a recent news piece, the Kaloleni Social Hall is constructed in a very different, much simpler (but sturdy) style from the central McMillan Library:

> [It] is constructed in rough dressed stone walls under a Mangalore tiled roof. Doors are made of ledged and braced timber while windows are

different dimensions of the library's white male identity and emphasised Book Bunk's determination to both conserve some aspects of this identity and engage in a decolonising exercise.

13   'Quiet', as shown above and throughout the rest of this chapter, should certainly not be taken to mean 'unquestioning'. One intern guiding a small group of visitors around the McMillan Memorial Library thus explained that he was conducting academic research into the origins of the land on which the library had been built: Who had owned that land? How had it been acquired? These, he felt, were important questions – certainly the issue of land appropriation in colonial times is one that continues to preoccupy many Kenyans who feel their ancestors were brutally deprived of their property and who are seeing land value increase exponentially in many parts of Kenya – that needed to be answered to fully comprehend and appropriate the history of the McMillan Memorial Library. Interview with Book Bunk intern, 31 October 2019.

14   Nairobi was founded in 1899 as a rail depot on the Uganda Railway. It became the capital city of the British East Africa Protectorate in 1907. In the first decades, the colonial authorities were thus able to tightly control who, among the African population (essentially African male domestic servants and labourers), was able to settle in the new city.

Figure 7.2   The main room of the Kaloleni Library, renovated in 2020 (Marie Gibert, July 2021).

glazed in timber casements. The floor is finished in cement screed. The facility comprises a large hall with a stage, offices, two other smaller halls [one of which houses the library] and an external ablution block. (Kiereini, 2016b)

The large hall which adjoins the library served as a meeting place for Kenya's independence leaders and as Kenya's first parliament in the early 1950s, giving the set of buildings historical significance. This was officially acknowledged in 2015 when Kaloleni Social Hall was gazetted as a national monument after a campaign by the Kaloleni Residents Association (Kiereini, 2016b).

The Makadara Library dates back to the 1960s and is thus the only one of the three to have been built in the independence era,[15] at a time when the young Kenyan state was looking to put together its own, new public social infrastructure. Its architecture and materials also bear the signs of the times, however, in that it is, very simply, a big hall built in brick and wood aggregate supported by steel beams (see figure 7.3). This gives it perhaps less character

---

[15]   Kaloleni library was housed in a pre-existing building but set up and inaugurated in the 1960s, alongside libraries in Makadara, Waithaka and Kayole, with UNESCO and British Council Funding. The libraries of Waithaka and Kayole were closed in the 1990s. Online interview with Book Bunk staff member, 28 September 2020.

Figure 7.3 The main room of the Makadara (or Eastlands) Library, renovated 2020–21 (Marie Gibert, July 2021).

but an airy and spacious touch that the two other libraries lack, and its more recent construction also means it is possibly in a better state overall.

As well as those of history, the three libraries bear the marks of age and decay. When I first visited the three McMillan libraries in December 2018, three entire rooms at the central library had been rendered unusable because of the broken chairs and tables, tightly amassed shelves or stacks of newspaper volumes piled into them. One had to tread carefully through Kaloleni Library as buckets had been placed throughout to gather the rainwater trickling down from the unrepaired roof, above the studious school pupils carefully completing their homework. By October 2019, the rooms in the central library had been cleared of much of the clutter and all newspaper archives moved below ground to be inventoried, but the damages caused by decades of lack of maintenance works were still visible within and from the portico.

In spite of the double weight of their complex historical symbolism and material decay, however, Book Bunk was resolved from the start to keep and rehabilitate the buildings and their names. In this, they were partly just being pragmatic. Two of the three library buildings are protected by specific laws[16]

16   The McMillan Memorial Library is the only building protected by a specific Act of Parliament, the McMillan Memorial Library Act Cap 217 of 1938. See Kiereini

and bringing down government buildings is near impossible, as noted by one of Book Bunk's key-staff.[17] In addition, the three libraries' central location – in the midst of the CBD for the central library, at the centre of Kaloleni, and at the heart of an Eastlands compound that hosts other government buildings and services for Makadara – is part of their on-going attractiveness and identity, so there was no question of building more modern libraries elsewhere.[18] Beyond these practicalities, however, the decision to rehabilitate historical buildings, rather than destroy and rebuild, or radically transform, is based on a broad understanding of their history and potential role as keepers of memory. This is most clearly expressed in Book Bunk's statement of purpose: 'We see [public libraries] as sites of heritage, public art and memory.'[19] The buildings are to be preserved and rehabilitated, notably with regards to their external architecture, in order to keep a clear trace of the past, while the internal decoration and library contents are reinvented in order to help the libraries best serve their purpose of hosting users.

This approach was implemented in the case of the Kaloleni Library, the first to be restored because of its smaller size, and whose full renovation was completed in June 2020 in the midst of the Covid-19 crisis (thereby preventing its immediate opening and use by the neighbourhood's residents). The library's façade and roof were restored in exactly the original style, while its internal space was radically transformed to better suit the needs and expectations of young library users: a playful black and white chequered floor, with orange, blue and green furniture in some areas of the library, and more sombre, solid wood shelves in others.[20] One of Book Bunk's key-staff noted that their hope is that the libraries, by retaining some of their historical features, could become conversation starters to revisit and debate Kenya's troublesome past.[21]

This process of using the library buildings to trigger reactions and questions has already started. A clear example is a video clip by Kenyan rapper Muthoni Drummer Queen for the feminist song 'Power', where she both explicitly and implicitly rejects the kind of patriarchal, white-dominated society so clearly

---

(2016a); interview with Book Bunk intern, 8 December 2018.
[17] Online interview with Book Bunk staff member, 28 September 2020.
[18] Ibid.
[19] Book Bunk's website, www.bookbunk.org [Accessed 1 November 2019]. Angela Wachuka, one of Book Bunk's co-founders insisted on the value of the McMillan Memorial Library's history: 'We want to keep that history because it is important – the building wouldn't be here if it was not for McMillan – but also mix it with our history' (AFP, 2018).
[20] Photographs are available on Book Bunk's website: www.bookbunk.org/photos/our-first-restoration-kaloleni-library.
[21] Online interview with Book Bunk staff member, 28 September 2020.

embodied by the McMillan Memorial Library. The video was part-shot in the library itself, complete with its most significant artefacts, thus suggesting that historical buildings can be unapologetically but creatively re-appropriated. The song itself alludes very clearly to Kenya's post-independence, autocratic history:

> You would have us forget how the mother's pressure
> Freed the sons and daughters caught in torture chambers.[22]

Meanwhile, shots of a boxing woman, women counting money made by driving *matatus*, the city's privately owned collective transport vans, and collecting fares (professions usually held by men), dancing and drinking and the rest of the song's lyrics, outline a different world to come, one where women get 'loud and louder', work, 'write [their] own scripts' and do not wait for men to marry them.

Decolonising their contents

If the libraries' walls are to be preserved and their furniture revamped, Book Bunk intends to focus its critical approach on the libraries' primary contents: their books. Book Bunk staff, reporting on their conversations with users, note that what most of them took issue with was not the buildings or their historical artefacts but the degrading image of Africa and Kenya presented in many of the books on offer on the libraries' shelves. Therein lies Book Bunk's chosen challenge and decolonising project: to explore, transform and appropriate a content that was not initially meant for African users (Forster, 2018).

The three libraries' very outdated content has thus been 'weeded': unwanted books have been removed from their shelves to make space for new books. Book Bunk's interns have undertaken an ambitious inventory process, listing on spreadsheets each and every book and archival item contained in the three libraries. While doing this, the interns also identified books of intellectual or historical importance that should be kept on the shelves.[23] The next step

---

22   Muthoni Drummer Queen, 'Power' (official clip), on YouTube: www.youtube.com/watch?v=GQUMbOn7EzI, and lyrics: www.musixmatch.com/fr/paroles/Muthoni-Drummer-Queen-2/Power [Accessed 15 September 2020]. President Moi's regime is known to have jailed, starved and killed its opponents in the torture chambers of Nairobi's Nyayo House (Adebajo, 2020).

23   Cataloguing in the three libraries was completed in early February 2020, with a total of 90,594 items recorded (including Kaloleni Library's 6,007 books and Makadara Library's 19,462 books), see Book Bunk, Update posted on the Global Giving website, www.globalgiving.org/donate/53595/book-bunk-trust/reports [accessed 15 September 2020]; interview with Book Bunk intern, 31 October 2019.

consisted in weeding the libraries' contents, which had not been updated since the 1970s, using the MUSTIE method. This is a common – if not undisputed – library weeding method whose acronym stands for Misleading (factually inaccurate) – Ugly (beyond repair) – Superseded (newer editions are available) – Trivial (no intellectual merit) – Irrelevant (to the needs of the community) – Elsewhere (available from other libraries). Book Bunk made this an inclusive process as much as possible: surveys were conducted to evaluate users' understanding of the currently owned books and users were further called upon to decide on the fate of these books. During the Covid-19 lockdown, Book Bunk's interns undertook the weeding process from home, identifying books they felt might be discarded before the Book Bunk team could meet and make final decisions. A Book Bunk member of staff estimated that as many as 90 per cent of Kaloleni Library's and 70 per cent of Makadara Library's books might eventually be done away with. Like all book lovers, Book Bunk staff shudder at the thought of simply destroying books, however problematic their contents may be, and the organisation is thus looking for recycling ideas. One such idea would be to use them to create art installations.[24]

The final stage is to bring in a host of new books, in English, Ki-Swahili and Kenyan local languages, authored by Africans and notably by women so that the libraries can contribute to, as worded in Book Bunk's statement of purpose, 'the Kenyan collective imagination'.[25] The list Book Bunk has established prioritises authors in the following order: Kenyan authors, east African authors, African authors, authors of colour. The organisation has secured funds from Dubai Cares, the United Arab Emirates-based philanthropic organisation, as well as a partnership with one of Kenya's main bookshop chains, to renew the libraries' contents. There may, however, be limits to this process. While the wish list established by Book Bunk includes books by Africa's great authors, such as Chinua Achebe or Chimamanda Ngozi Adichie, but also a variety of Kenya-published children's novels, some of them are of much lesser quality with regards to contents or editing quality.[26] There is an increasingly rich

[24] Online interview with Book Bunk staff member, 28 September 2020.
[25] Book Bunk presentation video, Book Bunk website, www.bookbunk.org/about-us. html [Accessed 1 November 2019]; interview with Book Bunk staff member, 22 October 2019; Book Bunk's website, www.bookbunk.org [Accessed 1 November 2019]. The feminist agenda will likely be strengthened by Book Bunk's partnership, with British Council funding, with Glasgow's Women's Library see Women's Library, 'Introducing Book Bunk', 19 June 2019, https://womenslibrary.org.uk/2019/06/19/introducing-book-bunk [Accessed 23 October 2019].
[26] Book Bunk Wishlist, Text Book Centre: https://textbookcentre.com/bookbunk/?mc_cid=f65efe30f5&mc_eid=00b90d7a19 [Accessed 14 September 2020].

Black and African literature for children and youths published throughout the world but still, sadly, mainly in the West. Thus a too-great focus on African publishers, which continue to lack the means to attract the continent's best authors, may deprive library users of access to this rich literature.

Book Bunk's founders, who hail from the publishing world, are clearly aware of this caveat. One of their answers, with all its limits, has been to create a publishing sister organisation, Bunk Books, to bring publishing closer to home. While Bunk Books' first publishing endeavour, that of Book Bunk founder Wanjiru Koinange's *The Havoc of Choice*, may have raised eyebrows and suspicions of a conflict of interests, the second book very obviously addresses the issue of bringing Kenya's global authors back to the country. Bunk Books has republished the English version of Lupita Nyong'o's children's book, *Sulwe*, originally published in New York, and published Ki-Swahili and Luo versions in addition.[27]

Having a catalogue of books that is more in line with current debates and users' identity and wishes, however, is not enough as libraries can remain complex mazes for many users, and all too often unwittingly promote racial and gender biases through their classification system.[28] In order to make sure that the new catalogue is fully visible and accessible to all, Book Bunk therefore intends to revisit the libraries' classification systems and create a new system based on the work done by the Akshara women's library in Mumbai, India, the European Women's Thesaurus collective, and the Glasgow Women's Library in the UK (Patrick, 2020), with which Book Bunk has established partnerships. The idea is to have a system that is less Eurocentric and will make for greater space and visibility for African Studies and women.[29]

Book Bunk's outfit itself is an invitation to rethink the identity of Kenya's intellectual scene. It is notable that until 2021 all its core staff, from its two founders to its research, programmes, events and fundraising managers were women.[30] Its interns also include a majority of women, among them working mothers hailing from the libraries' neighbourhoods. Although the organisation does not put this feature forward, let alone claim an outright feminist agenda, its work and choices – including that of the Glasgow Women's Library as a

27   Book Bunk website, 'Presenting *Sulwe* by Lupita Nyong'o', www.bookbunk.org/newsletter/presenting-sulwe-by-lupita-nyongo [Accessed 27 November 202].
28   There have been calls to decolonise the Dewey classification scheme that is used internationally and has its basis in an eighteenth-century view of the world (Charles, 2019).
29   Online interview with Book Bunk staff member, 28 September 2020.
30   Jonathan Bii became the organisation's communications manager, and first man to join the core team in 2021. There are also a minority of men among the support team and interns.

privileged partner, and the female artists and intellectuals featuring in its events – are testament to the search for a different, more inclusive and diverse approach in a male-dominated Kenyan book, and more widely intellectual, world.[31]

Reinventing their purpose

The rehabilitation of the library buildings and in-depth revision of their contents have triggered relatively obvious but complex debates, and forced Book Bunk to define a fine line between keeping and throwing away. As if this was not enough, however, the organisation has also resolved to reinvent the libraries' purpose and has been attempting to draw in a wider public – thus possibly strengthening the sense of public space the libraries can offer – by offering a range of services and events that go beyond those one would traditionally expect in a library.

Book Bunk's co-founders have seized on the fact that the libraries, despite their physical state and their deeply outdated and prejudiced contents, continue to draw in users and have thus not lost their important social purpose. They are aware of the role that libraries, alongside other social infrastructure, can play in cities. Book Bunk staff, in online communication and at events, refer to the libraries as 'palaces for the people', quoting sociologist Eric Klinenberg's work on public libraries in the United States. Klinenberg notes that '*liber*', the Latin root of the word 'library', means both 'book' and 'free' and that libraries are among the public institutions that serve as the bedrock for civil society and can help maintain social links and solidarity in a city (Klinenberg, 2018a, 2018b). Book Bunk has set itself the objective of re-inhabiting the libraries in order to re-establish those crucial social places and links but also to offer a refuge away from the challenges of urban life. One such solution Book Bunk has in mind is what it plans on calling 'Hepajam': introducing longer opening hours on week-days to encourage users to come and spend a while at the library after class or work until the peak hour traffic jams have subsided.[32] This would also mean going against most Nairobians' perception (and, to some extent, its reality) of night-time criminality, something Book Bunk has not yet addressed.

Book Bunk has also been conducting its revival efforts through the organisation and/or hosting of events within the library buildings, thus perpetuating

---

[31]   There are other notable exceptions to this generalisation about the Kenyan book world. Binyavanga Wainaina, who died aged 48 in 2019, was a widely read Kenyan author and founder of the influential African literary magazine *Kwani?*, as well as an LGBTQ rights activist who had openly disclosed his HIV-positive status in a country where homosexual activity remains illegal and HIV/AIDS is still taboo.

[32]   Interview with Book Bunk intern, 31 October 2019.

a long tradition of using libraries to host communal events (Jemo, 2008). Among these are free events that have several objectives. One is to draw the local community, and notably children and young adults, back into the libraries. With this in mind, Book Bunk organised free film screenings, as well as story-telling afternoons and a music holiday camp. It has partnered with, for example, an optician company to run free eye-tests for Kaloleni's inhabitants at the library. The enthusiastic popular response to these events has tended to confirm that there was a demand for them, and for re-appropriating the libraries in this way. This has also enabled Book Bunk's staff to consult with and conduct surveys among users.[33]

Book Bunk has also used all types of events in a more strategic way, to showcase the McMillan Memorial Library as a place that is much more than a random library and to publicise its work, but also to attract a social and political elite audience that had given up on the idea of a public library, and to become part of important debates and networks in Nairobi and the wider Kenya. Events have included a guided tour for some of Nairobi's artists, the screening of 'Operation Legacy', a documentary about uncovering and debating the archives on the repression of the Mau Mau movement, followed by a debate; an evening of presentations and debates about urbanisation led by Kenyan academics and civil society organisations; a day of workshops and debates on archiving data; and annual, fund-raising gala events.[34] The video clip shot by rapper Muthoni Drummer Queen, mentioned above, is another example of cultural collaboration, and a way for the McMillan Memorial Library to be reinvented. Book Bunk has thus already found many ways of 'increasing the circulation of stories' (AFP, 2018), but also to assist people and sister organisations in creating information, a role South African librarian Lara Skelly feels African libraries should take up as libraries cease to be just collection points for information (Skelly, 2015). More prosaically, some of these events have also been about giving Book Bunk greater visibility and raising funds.

This broadening of the libraries' social purpose, well beyond a simple book-centred and meeting place, echoes the project to decolonise their contents. By drawing in Kenyans of all ages, genders and social classes, events of all sorts are repopulating the libraries and symbolically ousting the white male ghosts

[33]   Some of the results of these surveys and interviews can be found in Book Bunk's 2018 Annual Report (Book Bunk, 2018).
[34]   The latter events all took place at the central McMillan Memorial Library, on site or online. At some of the on-site events, Book Bunk interns offered to take guests through the library and explain the organisation's work and plans, see Book Bunk (2019); Book Bunk event e-mail updates; observant-participation by the author on 31 October 2019.

that are so visibly present in some of their artefacts. Their diversity, and the debates they trigger, also extend the conversations launched by the rehabilitation of the buildings and transformation of the catalogues and, alongside these more material processes, point to the fact that the act of decolonising is a long-term and complex process that can take all sorts of forms. In other words, Book Bunk's work on and in the libraries reflects the debates about decolonisation, notably with regards to the desirable boundaries between erasing and preserving traces of a white male past, to the actors and spaces best suited and most legitimate to host a conversation about colonialism's legacy, to the form this conversation might take, and to the extent of the transformation that is needed, in particular when it comes to questioning the global privilege still enjoyed by Western countries and peoples as a result of colonialism. Book Bunk's multi-layered answer to these questions is one that attempts to offer both a serene space for these conversations but also the freedom to take part in them or not, a position no doubt too consensual for the more radical proponents of decolonisation.[35]

In line with this same desire to offer different experiences, and with library developments in other parts of the world, Book Bunk is hoping that the central library's rehabilitation will enable its transformation into a multi-purpose space that will include a café and a museum.[36] An increasing number of libraries throughout the world now house a café and research has shown that the existence of a space where people can meet, talk, and enjoy a cup of coffee or tea, has helped libraries strengthen their role as 'third places', distinct from work and home, where all generations and social classes can meet, and become 'community focal points' (Harris, 2007). Kenya, a tea- and coffee-growing country, has not only fully adopted the global coffee shop trend but also developed its own brand, making the idea of a café in the central library building, right in the middle of the CBD, all the more natural. The association between a museum and library is no doubt more straightforward and, in this case, in line with Book Bunk's resolve to safeguard the libraries' historical legacy – all of it – and to let the libraries act as conversation starters. The museum part of the restored central library could thus house the historical artefacts and archives found in the libraries and described in the first part of this chapter, and could also be an exhibition space for new objects, some of them possibly made from the libraries' discarded books.[37] As Syokau Mutonga, Book Bunk's research and inventory manager, notes, 'as Kenya fights to

[35] On the debates around decolonisation, see Chaudhuri, 2016; Macamo, 2018; Begum and Saini, 2019.
[36] Online interview with Book Bunk staff member, 28 September 2020.
[37] Online interview with Book Bunk staff member, 28 September 2020.

have artefacts both tangible and intangible returned from museums and other collections in the West, making the memories housed at the library accessible to the public is one way that [Book Bunk is] working to reverse a collective amnesia' and to offer a space where people can 'contest, reinvent and reconcile personal and collective memories of Kenya's recent past' (Mutonga, 2020).

This comprehensive process of reinventing the purpose of Nairobi's three public libraries points to the fact that Book Bunk, a small, non-governmental organisation, has taken on a public service delivery role. Like many other sister organisations in Kenya, it is doing this in response to public institutions' inability to fulfil their mandate but with their approval and under their monitoring.[38] This process of devolution from local government to civil society is one that is increasingly familiar in Kenya where a well-educated and professionally trained middle class is resolved to take matters into its own hands and seize for itself public services, public spaces and public debates when it feels local authorities have failed to deliver. In doing this, the middle class is, as Jacob Mati puts it, acting as a 'stabilising and pacifying agent on society, thereby perpetuating and consolidating the status and condition for the hegemony of free market' but also as an agent of social creativity, where a new social order can emerge (Mati, 2015). In Book Bunk's case, as I have shown here, this new social order may encompass a different relationship to public buildings, their history, their contents and their purposes and, more broadly, a different understanding of Kenya's memory and history, as well as a revised sense of what public spaces and services might look like and how citizens can interact with them.

Conclusion

In his 2017 Lugard Lecture at the European Conference on African Studies, Elísio Macamo reflected on the uncomfortable situation of giving an African Studies lecture named after a colonial administrator and offered his own answer

---

38 The agreement signed with the Nairobi City County Government in March 2018, following a three-year-long negotiation process, gave Book Bunk responsibility for fundraising and fund management, architectural restoration, management of the libraries, and the design and delivery of programming for five years. Although Book Bunk staff note that no major decisions, notably with regards to the disposal of the libraries' contents or the use of the buildings, can be made without the approval of the County Government, and Book Bunk's work is closely monitored by County Government staff, they also admit that the agreement leaves Book Bunk with considerable freedom. Book Bunk is already working on the renewal of the agreement for another five-year period. Online interview with Book Bunk staff member, 28 September 2020.

to the decolonisation debate, which he called 'urbane scholarship'. Drawing on his understanding of African cities, he noted that 'taking the other into account becomes the condition of possibility of life in African urban settings' and that this was also a pre-condition for knowledge production (Macamo, 2018: 7–8). In other words, he advocated an acceptance of the historical legacy, with all its 'blunders and sins', that enables us to see things the way we see them today. One could argue that Book Bunk, by rehabilitating Nairobi's library buildings, decolonising their catalogues and reinventing their purpose, is in the process of defining its own 'urbane librarianship' that builds on the libraries' history to construct more inclusive spaces and services and a new collective imagination.[39] I find the concept all the more appealing as it points to the libraries' deep-seated urban identity: situated in the heart of Nairobi's most iconic neighbourhoods, they have offered a tranquil refuge to learners and scholars for decades and have the potential to provide ideal, serene, public spaces to start important conversations. The idea of 'urbane' also conveys the multiple layers with which Book Bunk is working. Decolonising and reinventing the libraries is not, they have decided, working from a clean slate but accepting the historical legacy and working from it to enable important conversations. By keeping and rehabilitating the library buildings but changing their contents and reinventing their purpose, Book Bunk is also, crucially, giving users a choice: they may debate their legacy and Kenya's past as well as more current identity issues, if they so wish, or simply read the newspapers and grab a coffee with a friend while Nairobi's traffic jams clear up. In a city that moves as fast as Nairobi, having this tranquillity of space, choice and thought will no doubt be a precious public good.

[39] This creation of an inclusive public space that seeks to engage colonial history in a thoughtful way stands in stark contrast to the more troubled account of Sam Levy's shopping mall discussed by Tonderai Koschke in Chapter 6, this collection.

8

The role of architecture in South African detention cases during the apartheid era

YUSUF PATEL

In October 1974 Ahmed Timol was arrested at a roadblock, handcuffed and driven to the Newlands Police Station in Johannesburg. The reason for his arrest was that anti-apartheid pamphlets were found in his car. Eventually, the police constructed a report wherein Timol admitted to working with the South African Communist Party in London to overthrow the apartheid regime. Later that month, the police handed Timol's body over to his family (Myburg, 2017: 1). As the family began the painful task of preparing his body for burial they noticed that Timol's nails had been removed, his elbows burnt, his body savagely bruised and his neck broken. The result of a magistrate's inquest into his death a few months later found Ahmed Timol to be responsible for his own death – as he had willingly chosen to commit suicide by jumping from the tenth floor of the John Vorster Police Station (Cajee, 2005: 54). No details of torture were mentioned, leaving the apartheid state absolved of any responsibility for Timol's death (Myburg, 2017).

The Timol case, as are the cases of other death-in-detention inquiries, relies on the space and architecture that housed human rights violations. In particular, police stations – such as John Vorster Square where Timol met his death – were used to facilitate the torture and deaths of anti-apartheid activists. This use by the state of architectural elements in enforcing law has previously gone unexplored. Yet, through the seventy-three recorded death-in-detention cases, numerous mentions were made of doors, windows, corridors and staircases, all typical architectural elements, which were complicit in the torture and deaths of anti-apartheid activists in detention and recruited to assist in absolving the Security Branch officers of blame and ridding the crime scene of evidence. These simple architectural elements were manipulated to become violent forms of torture and abuse. This chapter seeks to understand how such common architectural elements were used in the torture of political activists under the apartheid regime. In particular, it sets out to explore how these otherwise unsuspecting elements assumed agency and became the tools with which the apartheid regime successfully orchestrated control and suppressed political opponents.

Detention in apartheid South Africa was a definitive societal experience. Over three decades, from 1960 to 1990, a reported 80,000 people were detained without trial, thousands became political prisoners and seventy-three people were murdered in South African prisons (Gready, 2003: 1). Notions of detention and imprisonment were intimately intertwined with the government's pursuit of control. As a result, several political activists lost their lives in South African prisons. The apartheid government attributed these deaths to suicide and in some instances to simple misfortune.

The significance of these modes of oppression and the nature of the confrontations and human sufferings left lasting impressions on the families of the victims of apartheid murders (Van der Kolk and Ducey, 1989: 259–74). The 2017 re-opened inquest into Timol's death sparked life into the fight for reconciliation (Specter, 2014: 2), using his case as a departure point to investigate cases of a similar nature. My intention in this chapter is to analyse cases of torture and death to highlight the role architecture played in obstructing justice, to highlight architecture's complicity in death-in-detention cases and expose the manner in which architectural elements were manipulated to absolve the crime scene of evidence. The method used to unpack these cases involves the re-creation of the crime scene through architectural techniques, such as plan drawings, axonometric drawings and sectional perspectives. By unpacking the crime scene through architectural techniques, a catalogue of elements that were used as weapons is created to reveal how Security Branch members used buildings' agency as an alibi.

My suggestion that architecture can be complicit, and therefore anthropomorphised, requires, first, a discussion of theories around agency and its application in architecture. I identify three main arguments concerning agency as applied to architecture, before going on to link each definition to individual case studies. The chapter discusses apartheid architecture, the experience of imprisonment, and in particular the role that John Vorster Square Police Station played in defining the apartheid legacy.

Agency and anthropomorphism in architectural theory

Agency can be described as a state of acting or exerting power onto a person or thing in order to achieve an end (Krupansky, 2017). Architecture on the other hand can be described as both a temporal and spatial feature; it thus does not define the way things work and how people perform but can be reinterpreted. In other words, architecture is usually viewed as passive, illustrating in its uses how things or people can work, rather than acting as an agent on its own (Doucet and Cupers, 2009: 6). An agency approach explores architecture's ability to be critical, and be itself the vehicle for reinterpretation. While the explicit use of architecture and spatial planning has been addressed extensively by apartheid specialists, what has gone unnoticed is the regime's use of the simplest forms of architectural elements in suppressing dissent. However, my reading of witness accounts makes evident how simple architectural elements were manipulated in the torture of political enemies. The use of such everyday elements meant that the scene of death or torture left no evidence of foul play. In effect, architectural elements such as doors, windows, corridors and staircases aided in human rights violations.

While agency has been extensively addressed across multiple disciplines, agency and anthropomorphism in architectural theory has been relatively undefined. As a result, the understanding of agency in architecture has lent largely on the exploration of its application in other disciplines. Theories can be condensed into three main schools of thought. I will suggest ways in which definitions of agency in architecture can borrow from each. The first interpretation of agency prioritises the role of the creator and the intent of humans in their creation of particular objects. Therefore, a person's creation of an object automatically imbues that object with a purpose that its creation aims to fulfil (Hodder, 2003: 23–42). As manufacturers of products, intentionally or unintentionally, creators use the material objects they produce to manipulate their worlds. In turn, Ian Hodder suggests, '[s]ubordinate groups use material culture to counteract dominant forms of discourse' (Hodder, 2003: 32). Human constructs ranging from pens or pencils to walls and windows are created purposefully with the intention of influencing society. In other words, their creators give objects an agenda during the manufacturing process, which in turn imbues the object with an agency of its own (Russo, 2007). This theory prioritises the intention of the manufacturer, with the user playing a lesser role, in mis- or re-using the object in different ways than those intended by the maker. The application of this theory in architecture prioritises the role of the architect. By imbuing the architect with agency to act in service of the client, or guiding society towards a common ideology, the architect is responsible – as is most easily distinguishable in apartheid spatial planning.

The second interpretation states that agency is 'the socio-culturally mediated capacity to act' and is deliberately not restricted to persons, and may include spirits, machines, signs, and collective entities' (Hoskins, 2005: 74). The purpose of the creation of objects is to act upon other objects, on people and upon the world. Therefore, innate agency is possessed by objects, imbued upon them by humans that allow them to affect change (Hoskins, 2005: 75), in ways not necessarily designed or anticipated. Janet Hoskins (2005: 76) theorises that 'things have agency because they produce effects, which can make us feel happy, angry, fearful, or lustful. They have an impact, and we as artists produce them as ways of distributing elements of our own efficacy in the form of things'. Therefore, those objects that possess true agency make some sort of impact on the mental or physical states of human beings (Russo, 2007). The application of this theory in architecture prioritises the architectural object itself. The architectural object, whether it be an element such as a door or window, a whole building, or large-scale urban and regional planning, is imbued with the agency to convince its user about the virtuous lifestyle it hopes to instil (Doucet and Cupers, 2009: 6).

Finally, the third approach avers that the meaning of an object is determined when it is used by a person or group of people, and thus 'meaning is created out of situated, contextualized social action which is in continuous dialectical relationship with generative rule-based structures forming both a medium for and an outcome of action' (Tilley, 2001: 260). In essence, an object gains agency when it is used for a specific means by a human. This theory prioritises the intention of the user over the intention of the manufacturer. Its application to architecture invokes the role of the user who through their intended use of the architectural element imbues agency onto it in the make-up and trans-formation of society.[1]

Although understandings of agency fluctuate in meaning for different authors, what is consistent is that objects and their subsequent actions and legacies are dependent upon human interaction and societal intentions (Martin, 2005: 283–311). The application of agency onto architectural elements in apartheid torture escapes a single definition and, as I shall show, elements are imbued with multiple forms of agency. Importantly, the three understandings on how objects gain agency are not necessarily mutually exclusive, but can be observable at work in different circumstances. A holistic approach is required to recognise the different ways in which architectural elements gain agency, under different circumstances. I will return to differences in the application of agency later in my analysis of the case studies.

Apartheid architecture and the experience of imprisonment

Prison architecture and the experience of imprisonment is central to the political history of apartheid and the legacy of post-apartheid South Africa, as it is in many post-colonial contexts (see Laura Routley on a Nigerian

[1]   This discussion of the agency of an architectural object shares some of the under-standings described by Julia Gallagher and Yah Ariane N'djoré in their argument about the relative roles of creators and viewers of art in Chapter 5, this collection.

example in Chapter 11, this collection). The documentation of that experience has long been a cornerstone of South African literary production in which imprisonment and torture have become synonymous with the apartheid era (Gready, 2003; Jacobs, 1991).

Architectural elements have been used in explicit ways by authoritarian regimes. The use of particular styles can be used to impress viewers of the power and violent potential of the state (Sudjic, 2011). For example, the use of formal elements such as flat roofs, horizontal extension, uniformity, and the lack of decor can be used to create 'an impression of simplicity, uniformity, monumentality, solidity and eternity', elements to which the apartheid regime subscribed (Hartmut, 1981: 33). Statues, symbols and signage have all been used to promote socio-political divisions, dominance and patriotism (Curl, 2006). The influence of apartheid's spatial planning is still visible in modern-day South Africa's built environment. Inscribed in the nature of racial enclaves, this is where the most notable impact of the regime remains. On the one hand are monuments and buildings signifying wealth and symbolising power, and on the other are underdeveloped spaces, described as 'townships' or 'informal settlements' (Murray, 2010: 19). The division of wealth and power were distinguished by the segregation of racial groups and the pooling of resources and infrastructural advancements in areas of dominance. Architecture was used to propagate the apartheid agenda, as it was used in Nazi Germany and by other authoritarian regimes (Hartmut, 1981).

The colonial influence on South African prisons is present in modern South Africa, as it is in much of post-colonial Africa (see Routley, Chapter 11, this collection). Organised punishment and imprisonment were introduced by European settlers in the 1800s and prisons were introduced as a mechanism to protect settlers against populations that might pose threats (Sarkin, 2008), although earlier slave castles built on Africa's West Coast, carried out similar functions (Hernæs, 2005). The first record of an organised, cohesive prison system in South Africa was in the nineteenth century. From the early stages of South African prison development, a culture of racial superiority was pervasive, a trend that succeeded colonial rule into the apartheid era. White European prisoners benefited from acceptable living conditions and were trained for potential release, while black prisoners faced much tougher conditions which resulted in longer sentences (Sarkin, 2008).

One feature that defined the interiors of South African apartheid prisons was that there were no raised beds in prison cells. Prisoners often slept under blankets, on a mat placed on the cement floor. Cell interiors differed from one prison to the next: some prisons and holding cells included a basin, others a toilet and a basin and in many instances, cells had no facilities at all. The exteriors of police stations and prisons were predominantly composed of hard-wearing materials, often a composition of concrete and face brick was used on the façade to give the impression of the building being impenetrable (Raman, 2009). Façade design of police stations and prisons were not prioritised and the only notable design feature was the inclusion of the colour 'blue', which distinguished the South African Police (SAP).

In 1968, Prime Minister Balthazar John Vorster opened John Vorster Square Police Station which was characterised by its square-shaped, blue structure in downtown Johannesburg. The building comprised ten storeys and included holding cells, administration offices and interrogation rooms, and overlooked the busy M1 highway that links Johannesburg South to the City Centre. The portion of the highway passing John Vorster Square included a double-decker carriageway, which meant the top tier of the highway passed the building at its second floor. The high volumes of traffic and resultant noise, as well as the central position of the police station, provided an ideal backdrop for Security Branch members to conduct their work. The police station was heralded as a 'state-of-the-art' modern police station, and as the largest in Africa. It housed all of the major divisions of the police force, including the Special Branch of the police force dedicated to curbing anti-government sentiments. The reputation as a site for torture and brutality soon followed as the building became the primary location for detention, interrogations and imprisonment. Harsh detention regulations were directly attributed to the eight deaths of prisoners there between 1970 and 1990.

John Vorster Square's uppermost, ninth and tenth floors were dedicated to the Security Branch task force. Officers of the Security Branch were given top-secret status and authority denied to other officers. The building aided in the privilege given to the department as the buildings lifts only went up to the ninth floor which gave the Security Branch the ability to restrict access into the notorious tenth floor. The tenth floor was accessed through a dedicated final flight of stairs where numerous detainees were tortured (Cajee, 2005). Evidence by former Security Branch officer Joe Nyampule given during the re-opened inquest into Dr Neil Agget's 1982 death revealed that there were 'strict security measures in place to keep the offices and work of the Security Branch separate from the rest of the police station. These included restricted areas, code systems and bells to ensure that access to the ninth and tenth floor offices was strictly controlled' (Smith, 2020).

The detainees' cells were located on lower floors and were particularly designed for solitary confinement. The cell interiors were painted dark-grey and the floors were black. Depending on the importance of the prisoner, which was determined by their role in the resistance, some detainees were afforded a foam mattress and a toilet while others slept on a mat in a cell without a toilet. Windows facing public roads were boarded with thick fiberglass and security bars, and in the centre of the room was a single light bulb suspended from the ceiling, which was never turned off (Ngwenya, 1981).

The blue of the building's exterior and the grey of the interior remains an integral part of the description of the building from ex-prisoners:

> Visually, I never forgot the blue colour of the building, even when I was in exile. I couldn't forget the blue of this building, the structure, what it looks like ... the shining floors, the metallic, shining, grey floors in the corridor ... the clanging of those gates ... the force and the ringing keys, almost every time there is a ringing key and you would wonder, which cell are they going to open or are they coming to my cell? (Molefe, 1975: 3)

Architecture and the experience of imprisonment were closely related as the spatial arrangement was used to instil a sense of insecurity and paranoia, as is described by an inmate: 'Cells were openly monitored through video and audio systems. The police had three video screens, which they rotated in order to monitor all the cells. One could do nothing in private' (Suttner, 2002: 125). The unwelcoming interiors coupled with limited views of the outside world created a sense of delusion and seclusion. Suttner (ibid.) narrates his recollection further:

> There were two types of cells. The better ones had windows, out of which one could see what was going on outside. I later took advantage of this view, until the police stopped me. The other cells, in which I spent most of my time, had no access to the outside. The bars, windows and door were covered with Perspex, which was perforated with small ventilation holes. When the police brought food, they did not open the door but shoved it through a gap in the Perspex – similar to the feeding of rats in a laboratory experiment. Having a 'view' was an advantage, but these cells were very far from the office where the police sat. That meant it was a complicated process if you needed something and wanted to contact them. Generally, the bells did not work and you had to shout. There was a terrible sense of insecurity and dependence on the police for everything, and you could go for 12 hours without seeing anyone.

The cell interiors consisted of a mat and blankets, there was no pillow and through a small hole in the door drinking water was served in unhygienic plastic containers. Prisoners were seldom taken to the showers on the lower floors and were not allowed to wash or brush their teeth in the fear that prisoners may congregate and conspire. 'There were probably about 60 prisoners at that time. Officers were supposed to let only one prisoner go to the showers at a time. We were not supposed to have contact with other prisoners' (Suttner, 2002: 125).

The experience of being incarcerated in John Vorster Square was clearly an unpleasant one: one comment from a prisoner, written on a cell wall, read: 'This place is hell, I want to get out'. However, those very same walls in some instances bore messages of strength and encouragement, in a response to the despair, one prisoner wrote, 'Look here, comrade, don't despair. Despair leads you to forget your beliefs' (Suttner, 2002: 129). These brief notes reflected the private agonies of people who, faced with hard choices, were trying to keep their courage up.

Agency and architecture's complicity in practice

Some seventy-three deaths in detention were recorded between 1963 and 1990, as well as numerous counts of torture in South African prisons and police stations during the apartheid era. No individual has ever been held accountable for any of these. The twenty-second person to have died in detention was Ahmed Timol, on 27 October 1971, four days after being arrested at a roadblock (Cajee, 2005). In Timol's case, as with previous deaths in detention, inquests confirmed police accounts and absolved the Security Branch of wrongdoing. According to the police officer's version of events, Timol committed suicide by jumping out of the tenth floor of John Vorster Police Station. Other death-in-detention occurrences were ascribed to suicide or accidents, such as slipping in the shower.

At the time, those who knew Timol and knew about the brutality of the apartheid state police, strongly believed the sequence of events detailed by the police officers was untrue, however, there was no avenue to appeal the inquest findings. After many years of pressure on the South African justice system, a re-opening into the inquest was achieved in 2017. After days spent in court hearings listening to testimonies from pathologists, trajectory specialists, fellow detainees and former Security Branch members, Judge Billy Mothle ruled that Ahmed Timol did not commit suicide but 'died as a result of having been pushed to fall, an act which was committed by members of the Security Branch with "dolus eventualis" as a form of intent, and prima facie amounting to murder' (Mothle, 2017).

Evidence given by fellow inmates and Security Branch officers made several references to architectural elements in the description of torture around the events leading up to Timol's death. During the inquest spatial consultants, including architects, were brought in to analyse and assist in the court's decision. The reason for using incidents around Timol's death is that these testimonies were given in court during the inquest and are on public record. The re-opening of the inquest is the first of its kind in South African history and has encouraged families of other death-in-detention inmates to pursue similar legal recourse.

The method used in the analysis of architectural elements firstly involves the identification of any or all references made to it in court documents. The elements' role in torture and death is thereafter analysed to understand which category of complicity it falls into: either it aided in the act or was used as an alibi. Finally, the architectural element and the context it was used in is looked at to identify what definition of agency is applied. The legitimacy of the testimony is determined by its acceptance in court during the inquest, however Case study 5 strays away and explores architecture's complicity outside the Timol case to illustrate the diversity of the application of the theory. Although Case study 5 is not extracted from court documents, it meets the credibility standards, as its events were cited in South African prison literature i.e., inside apartheid's prisons.

An architectural element may be defined in terms of aspects that make structures liveable or usable. A furniture piece may be described as an extension of architecture, creating a direct connection between structure and inhabitants. Furniture in death-in-detention cases and torture during apartheid incarceration was used as a form of fluid architecture. In other words, paired with the more rigid components tables and chairs were used as effective tools in dressing and undressing the architectural crime scene.

These architectural elements played a role in recreating the crime scene during inquests. With the aid of architectural prompts, memories around torture and death were successfully recalled by eyewitnesses during the inquest into Timol's death. The reliance on architecture meant that spatial specialists, such as architects, were introduced into the South African legal sphere to assist in providing empirical data. The forensic recreation of the crime scene unintentionally lent on the theory introduced by Eyal Weizman (2017) called 'Forensic Architecture'. Weizman writes, 'Forensics is a state tool; counter-forensics, as we practise it, is a civil practice that aims to interrogate the built environment to uncover political violence undertaken by states' (ibid.: 64–71). Delving into the highlighted case studies, each incident is forensically and architecturally recreated strictly through eye-witness recounts. Unlike 'Forensic Architecture', the recreation of these case studies is not to prove innocence or guilt but to highlight architecture's role in torture and deaths. Agency is the theoretical framework and forensic architecture is the methodology, and both are, used as a point of intersection to dissect architecture's role in torture and deaths.

Case studies

Case study 1: complicit chair

Ahmed Timol – death

> The Indian asked me to go to the toilet. He was sitting on the chair
> opposite me. We both stood up and I moved to my left (clockwise)
> around the table. There was a chair in the way. When I looked up, I
> saw the Indian rushing around the table in the direction of the window.
> I tried to get around the table but his chair was in the way. Then I tried
> to get around the table (anti-clockwise) and another chair was in the
> way. The Indian already had the window open and was diving through
> it. When I tried to grab him, I fell over the chair. I could not get him.
> (Rodriguez, 1971: 18)

This is the testimony of Joao Rodriguez, an ex-Security Branch officer[2],
regarding the events around Timol's alleged suicide.

Rodriguez claimed to have been the only eye-witness to the alleged suicide
of Ahmed Timol and was the state's star witness during the first inquest in
1972. Rodriguez, a white South African of Portuguese descent, worked as
an administrative clerk at security police headquarters in Pretoria (Cajee,
2005). After ten years of service to the force, Rodriguez had reached the
rank of sergeant.

Nearly fifty years after the incident, Officer Joao Rodriguez's account was
deemed improbable and the decision around Timol's death was overturned
during the 2015 inquest. Through the architectural unpacking of the crime
scene, it was determined that with Timol's height (1.6m) and the height of
the window (1m), it would have been difficult for him to get through the
window, and that the Security Branch officer would have had time to intervene
(Statement – High Court of South Africa, Case number 2361/71: 11). The
Officer's version was deemed highly unlikely by the court as both Rodriguez
and Timol had been sitting at the interrogation table, only a metre apart – yet
Timol had allegedly managed to reach the window; unlatch and open it, and
exit through it without Rodriguez being able to prevent him. Rodriguez argued
that the chair prevented him from getting to Timol in time. The chair was thus
described as complicit in Ahmed Timol's death. The implication of agency of
the chair leans heavily on the role of the user. The careful positioning of the
chair and the manipulation of the spatial make-up of the interrogation room in
relation to the object provided an alibi for the Security Branch officer, which
he used to absolve himself of blame.

---

[2]   Rodriguez died September 2021.

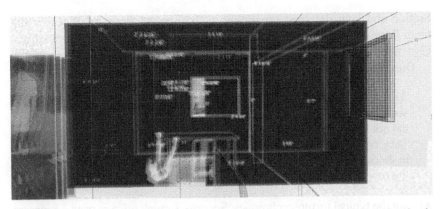

Figure 8.1   Forensic recreation of the architectural layout surrounding the death of Ahmed Timol (Drawing by Yusuf Patel, 2018).

The image in figure 8.1 is an architectural recreation of the scene of Timol's death, created strictly through eye-witness recounts. A forensic analysis of the room dimensions, the height of the window, positioning of chairs and choreography of the events leading up to Timol's death is overlaid to describe the complicit role of architecture.

Case study 2: complicit staircase

Salim Essop – torture

> At one stage I was taken to the stairwell on the 10th floor, close to the room where I was held. Two police officers held me first by my body and then by my legs and put me down. They then threatened to drop me if I was not forthcoming with the information they were looking for. At this stage, after going through so much pain and torture, I felt it was better if they dropped me and relieved me of the pain I was going through. You are literally surviving on fleeting consciousness and trying to make sense of your life. (Cajee, 2005: 132)

These are the words of Salim Essop concerning a time when his mind was drifting as he was looking down. His glasses had been removed which obscured his vision. 'I was thinking of family, friends, dear ones, praying and making peace that this is now the final moment', said Essop years later in reliving his ordeal (Cajee, 2005: 132). Dr Salim Essop was detained together with Timol by the Security Branch in Terms of Section 6 of the Terrorism Act. Before his arrest, Essop was driving Timol when police allegedly found Communist Party propaganda in their car. They were initially taken to Newlands Police

Station and later detained separately in the Special Branch Offices on the
tenth floor of John Vorster Square (Statement – High Court of South Africa,
Case number 2361/71: 11).

During his time in John Vorster Square, Salim was severely tortured:

> Ahmed and I knew the dangers involved in doing underground work.
> We expected to be tortured, but did not know how to prepare for this. I
> did not have knowledge of the different types of torture they were using.
> They would dip your head in a bucket of water. I heard of people dying
> in detention. I had no concept of time. There was a fluorescent light in
> the room where I was detained. (Essop, 2005)

Among the typical torture techniques, Security Branch officers used a staircase
and metal railing from which to dangle Essop. The staircase forms part of the
building's circulation core and would often be left empty. It made for a more
quiet, low-pedestrian area and served as an uninhabited ground for torture.
The staircase is an architectural element traditionally used within buildings
and forms part of a genre called 'circulation spaces'. The term 'circulation'
refers to the movement of people through, in, around and between buildings
and other supporting structures in the built environment (Ching, 2014). Within
buildings, circulation spaces are areas that are predominantly used as linking
routes, such as lobbies, entrances and foyers, and most commonly corridors,
stairs and landings. They are often high-use pedestrian routes as they transition
people from one space to another. However, in the instance of Essop, the
staircase of the Security Branch wing of John Vorster Square formed its own
core. The lift would take passengers from the ground floor up to the ninth
floor where passengers would have to exit the lift and ascend the flight of
stairs to access the tenth floor which was heavily restricted. This not only
assisted in restricting unauthorised people in and out of restricted areas but
also privatised and secluded the staircase. The staircase in the instance of
Essop was used as an agent of torture.

In Essop's case, the staircase gained agency through the architect who, in
an act to service the client, restricted the flow of pedestrian movement through
the space. The spatial planning does not designate areas for torture, but by
isolating the staircase leading to the tenth floor, opportunities were created.
Isolated circulation spaces, in particular the staircase, were weaponised by
Security Branch officers and aided in Essop's torture.

Figure 8.2 is a recreation of the staircase involved in Essop's torture. The
staircase, although only recounted in the torture of Essop, was mentioned by
several other inmates in descriptions of their interaction with John Vorster
Square. The recreation of the staircase strictly through witness recounts details
the circulation core that was complicit in Essop's torture.

1985 INDUSTRIAL STAIRCASE

01. **Dangling by ankles from a stairwell**

02. On one occasion the officers led him out of the vault to a bathroom near the stairwell where they told him to wash himself of all the blood.

03. and took him up to an office with a vault on the tenth floor. to the vault, ascending the flight of stairs

04. The Stormtroopers of the Apartheid State was the hated Security Branch.[1] The SB, acting under the instruction and blessing of their political overlords, targeted those like Timol who questioned the legitimacy of the entire system. They did not hesitate to brutalize, and where necessary, to murder in an attempt to stem the tide of freedom. Some 21 detainees died in security detention before Ahmed Timol died and by the demise of Apartheid that figure would climb to 89. Eight of them perished in John Vorster Square (**JVS**).[2] Thirty three were alleged suicides.[3] Six involved falls from buildings or down stairs.[4]

05. *After Timol's fall Rodrigues ran out of room 1026 screaming that Timol had jumped. Before going to the impact site he did not go to any other floor, he remained on the tenth floor. When he went to the ground floor he did not use the lift because it was too slow. Because of his adrenaline rush, he ran all the way to the* **ground floor using the stairs**.

-EXTRACTS FROM REFERENCES MADE IN COURT

Figure 8.2 Forensic recreation of the complicit staircase in the torture of Saleem Essop (Drawing by Yusuf Patel, 2018).

Case study 3: complicit table

Kantilal Naik – torture

> They weren't satisfied as to how to I was responding and decided to tie
> my hands and knees with a cloth, between my elbow and knees they put
> a broom-stick and they suspended me between tables. They carried on
> hanging me like this and rotating me. From Saturday night to early the
> next morning, Sunday, they tortured me like this. Once they had undone
> the cloth my hands were immobilised and that remained for quite some
> time. It's called the 'Helicopter Treatment'. (Naik, 2017)

This is part of Kantilal Naik's recollections of his time at John Vorster
Police Station. Naik, previously a professor of applied mathematics at the
University of Witwatersrand, was accused of conspiring with his former
colleague, Ahmed Timol, against the apartheid government, and subsequently spent seven months in prison. Leading up to his arrest, Naik was
visited by Security Branch offices at his home, and they demanded the keys
of the Roodepoort School in which he and Timol had previously taught.
He was forced to accompany them to the school and witnessed the officers
confiscate his typewriter and rummage through his belongings. Later that
day he was revisited by Security Branch officers and escorted to John Vorster
Police Station. Naik was taken to an office on the tenth floor and made to
wait for several hours before the torture for information began (High Court
of South Africa, Case number 2361/71: 36–47).

In the accounts of his time in prison Naik explains how Security Branch
members accommodated tables – a simple architectural component – in
his torture. The table, a part of any common interrogation room, was thus
weaponised and aided in the torture process. The use of these unsuspecting
elements meant that the crime scene was completely devoid of any kind of
evidence. In the case of Naik, the table's meaning was recreated through the
situated, contextualised social action through which it was given agency. The
role of the Security Branch members was invoked through the reinterpretation
of the functionality of the table.

Figure 8.3 architecturally unpacks the 'helicopter treatment' as described
by Dr Naik, creating the impression of the viewer undergoing that. The image
describes how tables were carefully orchestrated in the crime scene and how
easily the interrogation room could be returned to its dormant state, and rid
of evidence.

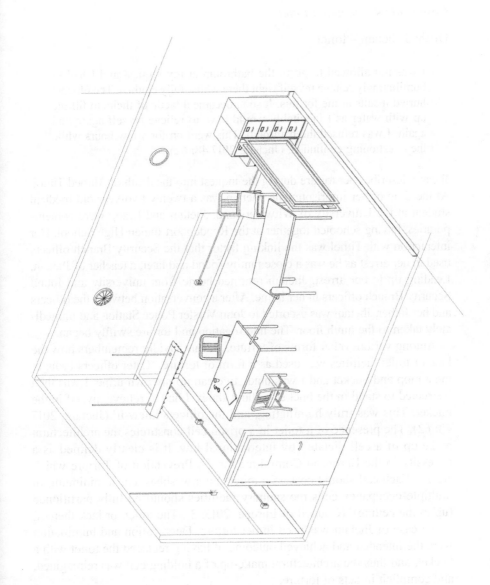

Figure 8.3 Forensic recreation of the architectural layout surrounding the torture of Kantilal Naik (Drawing by Yusuf Patel, 2018).

Case study 4: complicit toilet

Dilshad Jhetam – toilet

> I was not allowed to go to the bathroom at my request and I had to humiliatingly relieve myself right there whilst fully clothed. The officers hurled insults at me for this. It soon became a tactic of theirs to fill me up with water as I inevitably would have to relieve myself again and again. I was refused the bathroom. This went on for a few hours while the questioning continued. (Jhetam, 2017 48: 62)

Jhetam describes her torture during the inquest into the death of Ahmed Timol. At the time of her imprisonment, Jhetam was a twenty-two-year-old medical student at the University of Witwatersrand. Jhetam and Essop were contemporaries, having schooled together at the Roodepoort Indian High School. Her interaction with Timol was the linking factor that the Security Branch officers used in her arrest as he was a close family friend and later, a teacher of Jhetam. Leading up to her arrest, Jhetam returned home from university and found Security Branch officers in her home. After a conversation between the officers and her father, Jhetam was escorted to John Vorster Police Station and immediately taken to the ninth floor. The interrogation and torture swiftly began.

Among various other forms of torture, Jhetam vividly remembers how the lack of toilet facilities was used as a form of torture. 'Later officers brought me a mop and bucket and I was made to clean up my own urine. I was then instructed to stand in the bucket without shoes. I had to relieve myself in the bucket. This was truly humiliating, and the officers knew it' (Jhetam, 2017 48: 62). The presence of a toilet in a prison cell constitutes the architectural make-up of a cell dictated by international law. It is clearly defined as a necessity in the European Committee for the Prevention of Torture which states: 'Each cell should possess a toilet and a washbasin as a minimum. In multiple-occupancy cells the sanitary facilities should be fully partitioned (up to the ceiling)' (Council of Europe, 2015: 3). The toilet, or lack thereof, in the case of Jhetam was used in her torture. Degradation and humiliation were the intended and achieved outcome of having replaced the toilet with a bucket, and thus the architectural make-up of a holding cell was reimagined, and complicit in acts of torture.

Two classifications of agency in architecture can be applied to the Jhetam case, both interpretations using different architectural elements as tools for torture. Firstly, the argument can be made that the architect, in conversation with the client, imbued the holding cells with agency through designed spaces that omitted basic necessities. The toilet was deliberately left out of the holding cells of the tenth floor of John Vorster Square to aid in dehumanising the

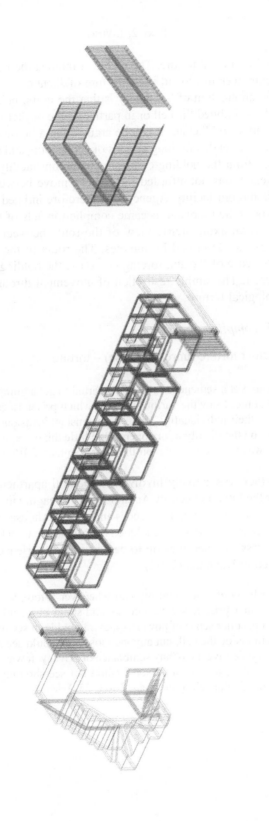

Figure 8.4 Forensic recreation of the architectural layout surrounding the torture of Dr Dilshad Jhetam (Drawing by Yusuf Patel, 2018).

inmate and aid in mental torture. The architect imbued the holding cell with agency and empowered it to aid in the torture of Jhetam.

The second application of the theory is that the users, being the Security Branch members, imbued the cell or in particular the bucket with the agency to aid in the torture of Jhetam. It can be argued that a holding cell, unlike a prison cell, is not intended for long periods of occupation, and usually inmates are transported from the holding cell to the bathroom facility outside of the cell itself. Jhetam was not afforded the right to move between the holding cell and the bathroom facility. Agency was therefore imbued by the Special Branch officers as the users and became complicit in acts of torture.

Figure 8.4 is an axonometric view of the route between the bathroom and holding cell as described by inmates. The route to the bathroom was restricted in the case of Jhetam, forcing her to use the holding cell as a place to relieve herself. The simple restriction of movement through space aided in her psychological torture.

Case study 5: complicit door

Raymond Suttner torture (unrelated case) – torture

> Although not yet a sentenced prisoner, I started to get a glimpse of what lay ahead of me. I saw the various ways in which prison rules try to rob prisoners of their individuality. There were constant invasions of privacy and attacks on the dignity of prisoners. One little thing that immediately struck me was the 'Judas hole' on the door. (Suttner, 2016: 1)

Raymond Suttner was actively involved in the anti-apartheid struggle and charged under the Internal Security Act in 1975 for engaging in illegal political work. Suttner served two prison sentences and a further house arrest, serving a total of eleven years for work that included his role in the then banned African National Congress. Suttner goes on to describe his experience of the 'Judas hole', as quoted in Buntman (2002):

> Any passer-by could look into my cell whenever it took his fancy and sometimes other prisoners would do so, and shout obscenities at me. I felt, then, a peculiar sense of powerlessness. I could not see much of the outside from inside the cell, but anyone looking in could see as much as they liked and deprive me of any semblance of privacy. It was sometimes quite intimidating to have a person I could not see shouting threats at me from outside the cell. (Buntman, 2002: 252)

Suttner, through his stints in prison, experienced the complicit door. The door's prominent feature, a hole in the steel framework, not only robbed Suttner of privacy but also of sleep:

> Sleep was difficult, since the young warders on patrol did not bother to be quiet. When they looked into my cell at night, they would switch on the light long enough to wake me and then go away. Sometimes a young warder would just stand around, apparently aimlessly, but lightly jingling his keys, enough to cause considerable irritation and make me realise how frayed my nerves were. (Ibid.: 254)

The door in this case is both a temporal and spatial feature. The make-up of the door does not define the way the door functions, but the physical construct of the door, whether imbued by the architect, manufacturer or end-user, dictated the performance and manipulation of the guards' use in the torture of inmates.

Conclusion

There has been a tendency in the history of South African architecture to focus on buildings and large-scale spatial planning as methods of apartheid suppression (Manning, 2007: 527–36). Architecture's role has clearly been distinguished by its explicit declaration to the regime through statues and monuments. Boards in front of buildings that read 'Whites only', and mass relocation of races into segregated enclaves, were impossible to overlook and this factor has been extensively addressed by commentators. However, what has previously gone unnoticed is the role simple building constructs played in aiding the apartheid regime. This approach hones in on individual architectural elements' role in apartheid torture and deaths. The utilisation of otherwise unsuspecting individual architectural elements meant that the building as a whole could absorb the atrocities and provide alibis for its conspirators.

By intersecting theories of agency and anthropomorphism with the methodology used in forensic architecture, a new approach to proving architecture's complicity has been outlined. Through analysis of the Timol case I have used eye-witness accounts to argue for the important role architectural elements played in the torture and deaths of inmates. I have used the various interpretations of agency to highlight elements (tables, chairs, staircases, toilets and doors) that were not only weaponised, but gained agency through the architect or user, and thus were complicit in acts of torture and death. The successful manipulation of these commonly found elements meant that during the judicial inquests held, no trace of evidence was left, which ultimately absolved the Security Branch members of blame. The final unrelated case, suggests that these complicit architectural elements transcend John Vorster Police Station and the Timol case, and have application in unrelated apartheid torture and deaths.

The landmark Timol case has set a precedent for others seeking truth and justice post-apartheid. The success in the re-opening and subsequent overturning of the verdict lent heavily on architectural constructs. Architecture proved to be a vital trigger in South Africa's legal system and the unpacking of its role in future inquests could prove pivotal in the success of those cases.[3]

---

[3]   Ahmed Timol's accused murderer, Joao Rodriguez, died on 7 September 2021 officially ending the family's quest for truth and justice. While the re-opening of his case was a historic event, complete justice was not served as Rodriguez was never tried for murder. Surviving Timol and Rodriguez are a number of other cases involving apartheid victims and perpetrators awaiting the indignity of false inquests being overturned and justice served.

PART 3

IMAGINING

9

Pan-African imaginations: The African Union headquarters and its popular imagery in Ethiopia and Nigeria

DANIEL MULUGETA

In the heart of Addis Ababa, the capital city of Ethiopia, stands the African Union Commission (AUC) headquarters, a conference centre and a twenty-storey office complex fully funded, designed, built and furbished by China as a gift to Africa.[1] It was inaugurated in 2012 in grand style, creating, at the time, the tallest building in Addis Ababa. The inauguration was accompanied by quite a fanfare. The surrounding roadways, as usual for international summits, were locked down to all but dignitaries, including 'China's most senior political adviser', Jia Qinglin (BBC, 2012). While the ceremony was dominated by the usual pompous speeches it was filled with literal and metaphorical references to the building as a symbol of hope, change and renewal. It was variously depicted as metonymic for 'Africa's Renaissance', a vision of rejuvenation for the continent rising like a phoenix from the ashes of poverty and conflict (Mathews, 2005). The office complex itself, reaching a height of 99.9 meters, commemorates the founding date of the African Union (AU).[2]

For the African leaders, the building became the public face of the newly founded, self-confident Union of the African states. This dominant narrative was, at the time, splashed across media headlines around the continent. In

[1] The building, costing US$200 million donated by the Chinese government, was designed and constructed by a collaboration of Tongji University, China State Construction Engineering and the China Architecture and Design Research Group. It is just one example of the many prestigious new buildings being constructed on the African continent by the Chinese – see Innocent Batsani-Ncube, Chapter 3 this volume for a discussion of others.

[2] In particular, it refers to the adoption of the Libya declaration of 1999 in which African leaders pronounced the decision to establish the African Union.

Addis Ababa, the building emerged as a symbol of a booming international city and epitomised the process of urban regeneration. Media images often used the silhouette of the building as a backdrop, showcasing the city's rise and its embrace of 'modern' architectural styles. Many other images of the building were produced through aerial photography that depicted the architectural structure from distance, and magnified its presence in the cityscape. On the other side of the continent, in Nigeria, the inauguration of the headquarters was covered in varying degrees across broadcast media and in leading newspapers, giving it transnational publicity to urban middle-class audiences.[3]

The building was presented as a symbolic expression of the growing cooperation between Africa and China based on a new type of strategic partnership, featuring political equality, mutual trust and economic 'win-win cooperation' (Lintao, 2012). In this narrative, Chinese partnership is envisaged as filling Africa's lack by providing the continent with techno-logical support and ushering in the winds of progress. In a symbolic gesture to this partnership, the panoramic view of the conference centre features two hands holding each other.

For many ordinary people, however, the building is regarded as an undesirable foreign import, referred pejoratively as 'the Chinese building'. Shortly after commencing my fieldwork, for example, Ahmed,[4] a City Hall official living in an adjacent neighbourhood, told me: 'You can take a walk around the compound every day, almost everything there is just ordinary buildings. There is nothing that tells you it is in Africa; there is nothing striking in anything about it, all is quite ordinary; there is no effort ... to make a pan-African [statement].'

Another day, while we were sitting at the neighbourhood shop, he gestured towards the compound and questioned, 'what is pan-African about this place?' He continued with revulsion and incredulity: 'Disappointing! This is something else. It is imported. It doesn't smell African. If it is African, it should feel African ... you know what I mean spiritually and physically ... the colour, and everything'. Similarly, Amos, a Nigerian academic who had visited the AU headquarters building in 2016 for a conference, told me that the 'building is remarkable in and of itself but there is nothing African in it'. He continued 'when you are there you expect to feel the pan-African spirit. Unfortunately, the building doesn't inspire it ... a pan-African building should inspire all Africans to feel connected, to feel love for Africa ... to feel admiration for the African Union'.

---

[3]   Most of the middle-class Nigerians I interviewed in Abuja vividly remembered the wide media coverage and debate surrounding the inauguration of the building.
[4]   I have changed the names of all my informants to protect their anonymity.

Ahmed and Amos live in different parts of the continent. While Addis Ababa is located on the eastern edge of Africa, Abuja is located on the west at the other end of the continent. There are few material, cultural or historical ties that link the two cities. Yet Amos expressed similar views to Ahmed's concerning the organisation and the physical structures of the AU built environment. Throughout my interactions with them, in a characteristically acerbic manner, both refused to identify themselves with the AU and they rejected the idea that its Chinese-funded headquarters building represents the concept of pan-Africanism.

The term pan-Africanism[5] to which Ahmed and Amos referred carries different meanings to different people and institutions. In official circles, it denotes formal and often elite-led projects and processes of political and economic integration of African states (Francis, 2006; Murithi, 2020). This understanding is based on the principle of continental unity that once inspired anti-colonial movements across Africa, and which provided the basis for the establishment of the Organisation of African Unity (OAU). The AU is seen as a successor of the OAU and a carrier of the ideals of continental unity, one that promotes the ideology and practice of pan-Africanism (Mathews, 2009; Murithi, 2020). Unlike the official substantialist notion of pan-Africanism, popular conceptions emerge from multiple discourses, extending well beyond the formal, mixing affect and materiality, ethics and politics, and traditional and modern languages of representation. Such understandings of pan-Africanism are immanent, divergent, in constant flux and rather difficult to pin down, but at the same time pervasive and impossible to escape. In this chapter, in dealing with this slippery concept of pan-Africanism, I pay particular attention to the manner in which the divergent expressions of pan-African imaginations emerge and how they can be elucidated through the exploration of popular perceptions of the AU built environment.

My argument, stated briefly, is that architecture is a prominent mediator in the production of transnational forms of belonging and pan-African meaning-making. I posit the AU headquarters as a catalyst enabling citizens in Abuja and Addis Ababa to talk about and imagine pan-Africanism. The focus here is on the arrangement of form, material and space of the AU built environment, to highlight how connections between pan-African imaginary and particular

---

5   Pan-Africanism as a movement and ideology emerged in the diaspora as a reaction against racism and imperialism. It posits a sense of a common history and fate for all people of African descent (Gilroy, 1993). By the 1950s and 1960s it was adopted by African intellectuals and anti-colonial leaders such as Kwame Nkrumah who advocated for political and economic unity of Africa against European colonial rule (Mathews, 2009).

idealised forms of architecture are established in popular imaginations. I particularly juxtapose experiences of people from Abuja and Addis Ababa to show how architecture serves as a 'technology' (Sneath et al., 2009) where pan-African fantasies are embodied in the description of buildings. While there are significant differences in the ways my informants from these two countries engage with and experience the AU built environment, both groups experience similar material sensations. I argue that my Abuja and Addis Ababa informants' common emphasis on specific physical features of the AU building shape their experiences, perception and imagination of pan-Africanism. I also show that multiple cleavages in class and profession, including cleavages within the AU elite such as between high-ranking and low-ranking officials and between the AU elite and the rest of society, are more important than geographic origins in determining my informants' identification with similar imaginations of pan-Africanism. In focusing on different sets of interlocutors from two of the most populous countries of the continent, I thus aim to provide examples of how different conceptions of pan-Africanism manifest in two distinct places.[6]

This chapter draws principally on field research conducted in Addis Ababa in March and August 2019 and February 2020, and in Abuja in October 2019.[7] During ethnographic fieldwork in Addis Ababa, I lived around Mexico Square (the closest urban centre to the AUC) and made frequent visits to the AU and its surrounding residential areas. I focused on how people who work in, live around and pass by the compound made sense of the built environment, and how they talked about pan-Africanism. I 'shared walks' (Lee and Ingold, 2006: 65) and observed how people talked about, moved and peered around the compound and gazed upon the different buildings. I carried out 'object-based interviews' (Woodward, 2019) with AU staff members and visitors to understand their embodied and sensorial engagements with the built environment, and how such experiences help them in meaning-making activity. The AU officials that I interacted with fell into two broad categories: high-ranking officials responsible for overall management of the Commission, and low-ranking officials tasked with the day-to-day running of the AU bureau-cracy. I also travelled around Addis Ababa, interviewing a cross-section of

---

[6]   Besides size of population and geographic location, another reason why I chose Ethiopia and Nigeria concerns history. Ethiopia was one of the driving forces of the pan-African movement, independence and unity, much more so than Nigeria. Ethiopia and Nigeria provide two examples of the different kinds of meaning-making that can found around the continent.

[7]   Some of the material in this chapter previously appeared in Mulugeta (2021).

residents including scholars, civil servants and students who frequently or occasionally come into contact with the AU.

Similarly, my informants in Abuja included academics, students, residents, architects and civil servants. However, unlike my informants in Addis Ababa, most people I interacted with in Abuja, apart from a handful,[8] had no direct experience of visiting the AU headquarters buildings. For the majority, knowledge of the AU came from the media. In Abuja, media coverage of the AU annual leaders' summits is considerable and long established. On television, almost all channels present news programmes on important AU activities. National newspapers have articles on meetings, featuring the image of the building. Thus, my Nigerian informants' perceptions about the AU built space came largely through the media (Meyer, 2010).

The experiences of the actors who occupy differential positions in relation to the AU – officials of the AU and African diplomats based in Addis Ababa,[9] architects, and local residents, academics, and civil servants in Abuja and Addis Ababa – provide the core material for this chapter. This allows me to illuminate how the AU built environment as an affective site refracts contested imaginations of a pan-African sense of belonging.

This chapter consists of five sections. The first presents a discussion of the key analytical foundation of imagination, which includes a consideration of the importance of sensations in human engagements with buildings. Second, I discuss the ways in which the AU building serves as an important catalyst enabling what residents of Abuja and Addis Ababa imagine pan-Africanism to be. Following on from this, third, I examine popular narratives about the building as related to the distinction between the AU and pan-Africanism. In the fourth section, I tease out AU staff members' perceptions about their built space and how it triggers within them contested notions of pan-Africanism. I analyse how negative reactions to the AU built space trigger desires for alternative spaces. In the final empirical section of the chapter, I reflect on how architecture constitutes the complex texture of the articulation of the politics of belonging in post-colonial political discourse, providing points for ongoing public contestation of what pan-Africanism is and should be. I conclude by bringing together the various ways in which the AU building triggers pan-African sensations and imaginations.

---

[8]   Some Nigerian informants had visited the AU headquarters as conference participants or during transiting and layovers in Addis Ababa.

[9]   The diplomats I talked to were not AU staff members but country representatives who regularly liaise with the AU and are stationed at country embassies in the city.

Imagination, senses and architecture

In his pioneering book on imagined communities, Benedict Anderson (1991) demonstrated the elaborate ways by which the spread of the concept of the nation is mediated by practices related to technologies such as the media. Similarly, Arjun Appadurai (1996: 5) wrote that new 'imagined worlds' are being created by global networks and flows, which are able to 'subvert the legitimacy of the territorial boundaries of nation states'. Anderson's and Appadurai's works are part of an important body of literature on the new forms of imagining made possible through media assemblages. Here, though, I focus on architecture to explore how the interactions between objects, actors, institutions and structures enable and constrain the imaginative process of constructing communities.

Indeed, buildings are objects of a fundamentally different sort. They are not like Anderson's print media that transmit ideas of the nation or collective identities through multiply copied and distributed objects. They are immovable objects which generate different sorts of imaginations through people's multiple forms of engagement with them. Architecture, unlike print media, enters the imagination of people through two sets of perceptions. The first set consists of the sensorial (form, shape/visual and verbal) accounts of people who work in and come in contact with the buildings (see Julia Gallagher and Yah Ariane N'djoré, Chapter 5 in this volume). The second set consists of communicative networks that are not necessarily direct or personal in nature but passed on through a person's social engagement with others such as oral transmission of narratives or through television and other media (Meyer, 2010). As 'affec-tively loaded' objects (Navaro-Yashin, 2007: 81), buildings are thus capable of provoking imagination both through direct engagements and through the medium of communicative networks.

This interpretation resonates with recent calls within anthropology of the imagination to 'explore the heterogeneous processes through which concrete imaginings come about' (Sneath et al., 2009: 9). In order to do this, David Sneath, Martin Holbraad and Morten Pedersen advocate a 'focus on the concrete processes by which imaginative effects are engendered, or, what we call "technologies of the imagination"'. Architecture can be seen as such a technology contributing to the imagination of transnational forms of belonging. Rather than merely focusing on their utility, that is, the work that buildings do in hosting political institutions, I argue that buildings, encountered through people's direct and indirect engagements, aid the very imagination of a collective identity. Here it should be noted that while architecture serves as a tool for a particular understanding of pan-Africanism to emerge, the imaginings are not fully determined by the technology of the architecture. As Sneath et al. (2009: 24) argue, 'the imagination is defined by its essential indeterminacy, so that imaginings are distinguished from other human phenomena by the fact that they cannot be fully conditioned'. In the context of this chapter, pan-African imaginations are thus treated as influenced, rather than determined, by the physical architecture of the AU built environment.

By bringing anthropological notions of imagination into dialogue with the study of material culture, I am showing the ways in which architecture is central to the expression of people's collective sense of identity and allegiance to the concept of pan-Africanism. The manner in which people come to engage with the AU built environment provokes intense feelings that constitute the contours and sentiments of pan-African imagination. Anthropological literature on materiality (Ahmed, 2010; Archambault, 2018; Nielsen, 2014; Bennett, 2010; Stoler, 2008) and analytical frameworks that illuminate the sensorial and performative qualities of objects (Ingold, 2007; Kapferer and Hobart, 2005), help establish the AU built environment as an 'affective space' (Navaro-Yashin, 2012: 24) essential to our experience and understanding of an imagined and shared sense of belonging (Meyer 2010). The emphasis here is on human engagements with buildings that are crucial in generating sensual experiences and grounding 'imagined communities' in reality (Meyers, 2015). My analysis also builds on other scholarship that stresses the phantasmatic aspects of imagination. Through her work in north Cyprus Yael Navaro-Yashin (2012) shows us how imagination is part of the 'make-believe' space that people inhabit. The concept of 'make-believe' refers to 'something that exists, but not really; an entity that has been crafted and erected phantasmatically, that has been believed through the making or materialized in the imagining' (ibid., 28). The 'make' denotes to the doing, and the 'believe' to the phantasmatical aspect of constructing spaces. Imagining can thus be thought of as 'forming mental images or concepts of what is not actually yet present to senses' (Bjorkdahl, 2018). This approach opens up space to think of not only pan-Africanism but also materials and architectural styles.

The texture of pan-Africanism in public discourses

The AU headquarters compound is surrounded by high stone walls with four main entrance and exit gates, one on each side. The walls, acting as barriers, distance the AU from the surrounding city and society. Like the compound, the main building, with its expansive setback distance, stands aloof from its environs and is hidden from clear view by the surrounding buildings (figure 9.1). It is visible at an angle, almost out of sight for those who do not have immediate business within it. Although it is distinct and distinctive, because of its size and scale, the building is inconspicuous and not easily visible to Addis Ababa residents. Unlike most landmark buildings in the city, it does

Figure 9.1   View of the AU building from a nearby street (Daniel Mulugeta, March 2019).

not serve as a central identifier for residents of the district. When giving directions, residents refer to the rather smaller local landmarks of the National Tobacco Enterprise or the Genet Hotel on either side of the AU compound.

As I suggested in the introduction, the building has come to be an object of indifference and dismissal. Even my Nigerian informants who only saw the building on TV, the internet or newspapers dismissed it as a trite and banal monument of steel and glass. Fatuma, a Nigerian academic who only saw the building on television, for example, described it to me as 'a copy and paste building'. Such comments provide a glimpse into the widespread popular perception that the building possesses little or no cultural significance.

The simple presence and sheer physicality of the building and its architectural identity however do serve as a catalyst that enables people to talk about pan-Africanism. During the course of my fieldwork in Abuja and Addis Ababa, I found out that people who normally would have little to say about pan-Africanism had no problem talking about it when the building hosting the AU was mentioned. Most of my informants spoke of and imagined pan-Africanism by way of the architectural identity of the building and its design pretentions. For example, when discussing the aesthetics of the building, Hailu, a forty-three-year-old painter from Addis Ababa, said: 'the colour of the building is not agreeable to an African eye ... a dull appearance is not what we want to see in our pan-African building'. He asserted that 'the authentic colour scheme of Africa' is 'primary colours, which are bright and festive'. Similarly, a forty-eight-year-old male primary school teacher remarked that the ideal of pan-Africanism to which the common people are attached is more embodied in 'green, yellow and red ... the colours of the Ethiopian flag' which was central for the nationalist movement in Africa and the diaspora and later incorporated in the national flags of many African countries. Some echoed this sentiment, referring to the dominance of bright colours in West African sartorial traditions. Significantly, my informants' efforts to associate primary colours with tradition and colonial resistance reproduces an image of pan-Africanism steeped in history and heroism.

In the eyes of many of my informants, not only the colour scheme but also the materials of the building lacked the symbolic density of tradition and pan-African authenticity. For example, Michael, a young architect in Addis Ababa, said: 'Building and dwelling in traditional Africa are characteristically developed from organic materials that are sustainable'. He continued, 'organic materials such as wood provide the most immediate form of recognition'. Michael told me that, in addition to its association with nature, organic materials have the function of stimulating all the senses and enhancing the feeling of comfort and rootedness. Notably, almost all the materials considered 'not pan-African' by my informants were manufactured products. Abedela, a Nigerian architect, told me 'what you see in the AU glass-and-steel building is the way modern building materials have suppressed the traditional building materials.' He argued in favour of 'African materials such as stones, thatch, mud and other local materials accessible'. However, he felt cautious about the use of 'traditional materials' in today's Africa:

> we may not necessarily use thatch and mud to build a headquarters to the AU but we should be faithful to traditional African design principles and material [and] use principles ... of sustainable architecture. In Africa freedom flows from harmony with nature. Western architecture undermines our sense of freedom and connection to nature ... it cuts us off from nature.

Such romanticising descriptions of 'organic materials' provided my informants with a consistent cultural repertoire of material signifiers for how pan-Africanism should be represented. This conceptualisation implicitly constructs pan-Africanism as collective identity related to an imagined materiality of an uncorrupted and uncontaminated past.

However, the exterior materials of the headquarters building have neither markers nor cultural frames of reference that resonate with my informants' sense of belonging, affect them deeply or encourage a sustained gaze. The texture of the headquarters building was given as an example. Bethel, a young life-long resident of an adjacent neighbourhood, argued that the building's texture does not 'make you feel good from within … not part of the land, the surrounding … not part of Africa'. Crucially, Bethel like most of my other informants had never been inside the AU compound, so she had no direct tactile experience of the building. Her experience of the texture of the building rather emerged from the ocular sensations that she perceived through her imagination from a distance. Such affective experiences that emerged during visual performances are essential to the imagination of people's senses of belonging and non-belonging in which this experience is part of their reality (Rasmussen, 1964).

It was thus through the experience of negative sensations with the form and materiality of the AU building that 'pan-African' began to resonate in my informants' imaginations. Yet, the criteria of appropriateness, authenticity, and tradition so present in sensations and accounts of the people I interviewed in Abuja and Addis Ababa were construed and drawn upon a clustering of discourses about autochthonous rhetoric of nostalgia and the deleterious effects of colonialism on African societies. Many of my informants traced a rich array of indigenous, pre-colonial architectural traditions in Africa which were supposedly suppressed or destroyed by colonialism. Sarah, a Nigerian graduate student, said: 'Traditional architecture of Hausa that is in heritage sites now in Kano [is a] microcosm of African architecture'. In retrospectively idealising pre-colonial architecture, she celebrated 'African architecture' as 'intricate … fit to African lifestyle and climate conditions' and using sustainable materials. In this formulation, pan-Africanism is understood to be organically linked to African society. This raises the issue of whose architecture in Africa comes to represent pan-Africanism. For example, while my Abuja informants' accounts of pan-Africanism privileged Nigerian architecture, my Addis Ababa informants saw Ethiopian history as the most significant representation of pan-African material civilisation. My informants' idealisation of pan-Africanism was thus itself selective and partial in that it privileged particular traditions of architecture as universal. Nonetheless, the concept of pan-Africanism, retrospectively idealised, served as a discursive resource for my informants in making sense of a collective identity as well as a material representation that they could resist.

The African Union headquarters as a metonymy architecture

More than simply referencing the architectural identity of the building, my informants used analogies that established a metonymic relation between the building and the AU. Petros, a thirty-two-year-old architect from Addis Ababa, for example, used the metaphor of a snail to describe the building and the AU.

He said, 'when you look at it from the main entrance of the compound, it looks like a snail ... the office complex protrudes like a tentacle from the assembly hall. It is actually a befitting symbol to a sluggish organisation ... it is a slow-moving [organisation]'. The building was seen as symptomatic of the fragility and weak capacity of the AU. Michael, when discussing the character of the building chuckled and said, 'it [the building] is an eloquent expression of the problems of the AU. It is cold and distant'. A Nigerian politician, who visited the AU building during a long layover in Addis Ababa, said: 'The building is quite unassuming ... it is pretty average for the African Union. It should have been built in a way that makes visiting the African Union headquarters a crucial part of a trip to Ethiopia ... for all African travellers.' He asked 'why is it not an unmissable cultural sight?' My informant then went on to answer his own question: 'The building tells a story of a weak institution. You know what ... it tells me a story the Commission has difficulty in standing on [its] legs, it is still in the same condition.' Such criticism amounts to the usurpation of the official narrative, dismissing the idea that the building reflects the rejuvenation of the continent.

Another metaphor used when describing the AU and pan-Africanism concerns the African Union Grand Hotel,[10] located inside the compound next to the Chinese-funded headquarters. For example, a West African diplomat said in a faintly mocking tone, 'the big men [African leaders] are "sitting tight" at the heart of the continental organisation'. The allusion here is apparently to the phenomenon of 'sit-tight syndrome', the ambition of African leaders to hold onto power and indulge in spaces of privilege and comfort. The hotel, in my interlocutors' imagination, transformed the AU built environment into somehow a self-contained space where most of the needs of visiting AU leaders are met. In popular discourse, the hotel is recast as a symbol of comfort, the drive for self-preservation and obsession with power displayed by African leaders. It literally embodies African leaders' strong desire to remain insulated, even to people close to the AU. Most of my informants in Addis Ababa mentioned the hotel as evidence that pan-African ideals have been betrayed by the AU. Ironically, their calls for pan-African solidarity were to a large degree promoted by way of contradistinction to the identity of the AU.

In a similar vein, others utilised different analogies of the building to elucidate the characteristics and workings of the organisation. The dome of the conference hall has, for example, been metaphorically described as an 'inverted beggar's bowl' (Poplak, 2012), signifying a 'begging bowl syndrome' (Asante, 2007) or continuation of some of the ways African leaders wilfully

---

10   According to my AU informants, the hotel was designed to accommodate presidential and diplomatic visitors to the AU Commission.

Figure 9.2 The dome of the AU Conference Centre (Daniel Mulugeta, March 2019).

exploit the resources of dependence to finance their programmes (figure 9.2). Here, what attracted such gazes is the metaphoric potential of the building. More specifically, what interested people was what the metaphor itself embodies – that is dependency – not the cultural or political significance of the object itself. The metaphors reinforce the sense of the repetition of the material and temporal continuities of African political practice and offer people leeway to reimagine their perception of the AU more forcefully.

One of the most important functions of the building in popular discourse has therefore been enabling my informants to disentangle the AU and pan-Africanism, stressing the view that the AU only pays lip service to the ideology of pan-Africanism. In drawing this distinction, they often referred to the AU as an impotent organisation and they defined pan-Africanism in terms of the imagined glorious past of Africa. Embedded in this imagination was popular anxiety that wholesale absorption of foreign material artefacts and ideas would destroy what Edward Blyden (1908) called the 'distinctive personality of Africans'. This 'ontological anxiety' (Giddens, 1984) comes from an imagined ill of foreign cultures. However, despite its own claim to the contrary, pan-Africanism, like other forms of nationalism, is a fairly recent 'invented tradition' (Hobsbawm and Ranger, 1983).

African Union employees and pan-African sensations

The AU staff members I interviewed expressed a variety of imagined pan-Africanisms as they shared their experiences with their built environment. Most low-ranking AU staff members were largely evasive about their feelings of their work environment during our interviews, but they did admit a strong sense of shame and uneasiness. In a moment of frankness, a junior AU official told me, 'I am acutely embarrassed by [the sight of] the building ... because we received it as gift.' Such sentiments were heightened by the lukewarm and antipathic public reactions. 'People think we're not serious or a tool of foreign powers', another AU official from Ethiopia said of how the public evaluate the AU's decision to accept Chinese architectural gifts. When I asked him what the public reaction made him feel, he replied 'disappointed [a rush] of shame all over me'. My informants situated pan-Africanism vis-à-vis the building in a very complex way. They often made distinctions between the idea of Pan-Africanism and its representation in the African Union, identifying the former with the realm of an idealised optimism that has not been given adequate material expression. In so doing, they discursively place pan-Africanism in a position superior to the current material representations, but are simultaneously frustrated as they are unable to experience the power of its material aesthetics. These acute recognitions of negative emotions go beyond an experience of disappointment. Significantly, they disturb the consistency of narratives and meaning. For most of my interlocutors, the building represents the absentminded mismatch between the pan-African vision and practice, that is, between the idealised image of Africa's past as told by former South African President Thabo Mbeki[11] and the future vision that is found in the African Renaissance rhetoric and the AU constitutive act.[12] In a sense, the building seems to accord with what Roland Barthes (1972) calls a 'photographic punctum', a prick, which punctures the viewers' engagement with it in a way that makes the experience momentarily but singularly arresting to them, and in this case, cringeworthy. The punctum powerfully pinpoints the building's real meaning that it represents a weak and disappointing institution.

By contrast, to high-ranking officials pan-Africanism is lived in the texture of diversity of staff members and is materially evident in the arts that decorate the buildings. One senior AU official told me that 'this is a pan-African compound tip to toe. You can find people of different nationality and religion; we have

---

11   Mbeki had been a leading proponent of the notion of an African Renaissance which denotes the belief that Africa is capable of re-making itself.

12   The AU Constitutive Act is the founding document of the AU which defines the visions and aspirations of the organisation.

African food; we have African art ... we represent the larger continent of Africa in several ways'. My informant said that the art exhibits showcased regional variations of pan-African cultural themes and represented all AU member states.[13] In speaking with me about the art exhibits that filled the lobby of the main building, another senior AU official told me: 'We recreated the space with African art. We have put our mark on the building. This makes it look and feel African. It is made creatively African. It occupies you absolutely.' In these informants' imaginations, the building is just a blank canvas which provides a tabula rasa onto which material objects from different parts of Africa could be displayed to enculturate and transform the space. The building's perceived negative connotations are put into a frame and 'tamed' idiosyncratically. The building hence is no longer be identified with China or the West but accommodated as African in a sophisticated way.

It is here worth noting, by way of contrast, that this is not the sentiment of the large number of architects I interacted with, who believed that African aesthetics should have been an integral part of the architectural design of the building from the very beginning. John, an experienced Nigerian architect who had worked in the public and private sectors, told me that cultural buildings should give the viewer a comprehensive aesthetic sense in form and content:

> Aesthetics that is applied lacks depth. If the essence, the beauty and the flavour of a product doesn't come from within, the core of itself, then it is an application and that application is ephemeral. It is poor aesthesis ... the art is not an integral part of the building ... [we need] African materials, African responses to the built environment, an African narrative.

However, for my high-ranking AU interlocutors, the art exhibits were not superfluous but a source of cultural identification and were often counterposed against the idea of 'westernisation'. During a tea break in one meeting a senior AU official distinguished between 'modern' and 'Western' forms of art and said that he was 'anti-Westernisation' and that 'Westernisation is another form of colonisation'. He described the exhibits as 'African modern art' and hence 'pan-African'. Clearly, the 'taming' or appropriating of the building enabled AU officials to differentiate themselves from what they called the phenomenon of 'Westernisation' in a way that evoked a sense of being 'cultured' and sophisticated. By becoming modern and cultured Africans as opposed to being 'Westernised', they created a sense of distinction, *esprit de corps* among themselves, and of attachment to what they considered to

---

[13]   This is despite the fact that, according to one informant, the paintings were produced and donated by China as part of the furnishing work.

be the real, but idyllic, Africa. Thus, the building decorated with African art creates an opportunity for elites to capitalise on traditional cultural markers.

Materialising pan-Africanism: a search for a holistic model

The AU built space thus, when seen, touched and felt, provoked in my informants feelings and desires to see 'accurate' architectural representations of Africa. However, my informants were not particularly articulate about what their desired pan-African architecture should look like. Their expectations of a pan-African building bore very little resemblance to either historical or contemporary models of architecture. According to several of my informants, 'authentic African architecture' should be rooted in the 'glorious, pure' but lost past. Bethel, for example, told me that 'our tradition is dying. We need to return to our pure cultural roots'. When I asked what she meant by 'pure cultural roots', she said 'a return to cultural traditions … our past uncontaminated by colonialism'. The building rekindled the fear of sustained colonial domination in some of my interlocutors. Railing against the Chinese construction of African political buildings, Nathan, a thirty-six-year-old who worked at a construction firm, like many other informants, lamented African leaders' 'reckless [thrill] to foreign culture … rather than [reviving] local building traditions'. For several other informants, pan-African architecture had come to simply mean non-Western and non-foreign. Ahmed told me, laughingly, that 'African buildings are not Chinese. They speak to you. They immediately strike you'. Similarly, Hailu told me, that 'when you walk down the streets, you get that feeling [which] would make you say "oh, that is the one" … you just know it'. Africanness was experienced viscerally to my informants. Hailu and many others claimed to feel African material forms in their daily interactions, in a way that enabled them to construe a sense of identification in relation to the threatening presence of material schemes defined as 'foreign'. Here, undoubtedly, in addition to the desire to revive pre-colonial traditions, such popular perceptions stemmed from contrasts with the immediate surrounding environment.

In contrast to these enthusiastic idealisations, any of the architects I interacted with believed that there are no common architectural typologies understood by all Africans to represent a pan-African tradition. For example, Petros told me: 'There is no single African architectural typology [that is] distinct from other typologies. But Africa has architecture with thousands of years of history. Our architecture is historic; not contemporary. This is because of colonial [domination].' He admitted that this presents architects with a difficult job as 'we have never done this sort of cultural project before'. But he continued with firm conviction 'we could extrapolate one from the past and design a novel ... appropriate building for the AU'. Similarly, Michael told me that a pan-African 'hybrid [typology of] architectural fusion is possible'. This conviction that an alternative model of architecture for the AU is possible was recognised and echoed by most Nigerian architects with whom I interacted. John, for example, told me:

> when you want to build a building of that nature, you ask what is it to be African today? What identifies you as an African? Is it the cloth you wear, is it the skin pigmentation, is it the way you speak, is it the name you have ... you are able to understand that argument from different sources ... you look at that and you amalgamate it and from there you are able to extract elements, commonalities which start to form building blocks ... that is the solution.

My informants, both in Abuja and Addis Ababa, generally saw the AU headquarters as a 'great missed opportunity' to revive the 'authentic' African architecture, aimed at both creating a pan-African monument and a workplace for the AU staffers.

The AU built space thus functioned as a powerful affective site around which history, identity and, indeed, pan-African belonging can be imagined and defined. In construing what is pan-African and what it ought to be, my informants oscillated back and forth between their sensorial experiences and pre-existing knowledge about pan-Africanism. Undoubtedly, the notion of pan-Africanism is always contested and contingent. Yet, the affective intensities arising from encounters with the AU built spaces allowed for divergent expressions of pan-Africanism. In particular it permitted people to enter the realm of imagination and construe pan-Africanism in terms of its ideal material wholeness.

Pan-African ideology is clearly highly utopian. However, its utopian dimension is built based on a fundamental 'misrecognition' (Gallagher, 2018)[14] of the diversity of vernacular building forms, construction techniques, building materials, and sociocultural traditions of African history. This misrecognition reflects the core of the idealisation of Africa promoted by 'creole pioneers' (Anderson, 1991) of pan-Africanism. Early pan-African intellectuals have substituted the lived diversity of Africa for an imagined idea of a common history and fate. It is not therefore too far-fetched to argue that popular imaginations of pan-Africanism clearly mirror the sort of elite manipulation that has pushed a certain conceptualisation of Africa from above.

---

[14] Gallagher (2018) discusses the significance of 'misrecognition', the tendency to shape one's own world and imagination through the process of 'splitting and projecting', in the making of identity.

Conclusion

In this chapter, I have explored how the dynamics of direct and indirect engagements with the built space of the AU produce different sentiments of pan-African identification. I began by viewing imagination as a prism through which people in Abuja and Addis Ababa refract different ideals of pan-Africanism. The case of the AU built space shows that reading architecture through the lens of imagination makes visible the ways in which people creatively use imaginaries in the construction of collective identities. Not only are buildings the means by which the reality of national identity comes to be represented (Vale, 1992), transnational political buildings in particular can reveal how people imagine their transnational collective identity – how they aspire to be as well as how they wish to be seen by others.

Clearly, buildings that host political institutions do not emerge in a social, aesthetic and historical vacuum. Rather, they are inflected by symbolic, social and political utterances. As we have seen in this chapter, the different spatial and architectural features of the AU headquarters were not observed by my informants as ordinary functional objects. Instead, for the people I spoke to, all picked up meanings within the realm of history and collective aspirations (Anderson, 1991). We have seen that the architectural identity of the building allowed residents of Abuja and Addis Ababa, architects, diplomats and academics to debate and develop different visions of what pan-Africanism is and should be. Those who work for and have links with the AU largely expressed mixed emotions of comfort at feeling 'being-at-home', indifference and shame at receiving architecture as a gift from a foreign country. For many low-level officials, the AU building in its totality was foreign and not informed by African aesthetic ideals. Of course, for high-level AU officials, such symbols were invisible, but to low-level officials they were not only visible but also potent triggers of imaginations and sentiments of ambiguity, dismay and distance.

By contrast, those with no or few links to the AU predominantly expressed negative feelings of distance, and a longing for the lost past. Despite their different places of residence, culture and degree of engagement with the AU built environment, what the Abuja and Addis Ababa residents shared was a belief of being unrepresented and the desire to be represented. Their engagements with the building open up feelings and imaginations that are otherwise not accessible, giving them a sense of common pan-African value, although many of them do not engage in face-to-face relationships with each other. However, the imagination of collective subjectivity, produced through people's multiple forms of engagement with the AU building, does not necessarily produce cohesive pan-African identity, but it can transform the reality of

African diversity and difference into an imagined appearance of similarity. In this sense, the AU built environment serves as what Anthony Cohen (1985) calls an 'aggregating device' rather than an 'integrating mechanism'.

Moreover, the feel of the AU buildings on the eyes particularly served to materialise the AU as an ineffective entity; and as such the AU was performed and thought of as weak, and thus de-legitimised. The performativity of the AU built space is all the more apparent in the 'make-believe' (Navaro-Yashin, 2012) nature of imagined space it inspires. This imagined space, which is generated by intense emotions like pride in pan-Africanism, is indeed chimeric and elusive, yet it is germane in creating feelings of longing for togetherness.

Overall, the different sets of actors with whom I interacted in Abuja and Addis Ababa occupy different positions in their relations to the AU and its built environment. Their reactions and experiences with the building thus slip and vary according to their social location and the range of cultural references available to them, but their deployment brings out the multifarious nature of the notion of pan-Africanism. In this sense, architecture proves to be a vital trigger of sensations and imaginations.

10

Asantean noumena: The politics and imaginary reconstruction of the Asante Palace, Kumase[1]

TONY YEBOAH

In 1874, the British colonial forces attacked and ransacked the capital of Asante, Kumase, during the war of Toto.[2] One outcome of the war was the relocation of the palace, the seat of government of the Asante Kingdom, from a strategic location in Kumase to what was, at the time, a peripheral neighbourhood of the city in today's Manhyia. In their attempt to establish legitimate authority through conquest, the British replaced the old palace site with a fort, architecturally establishing their presence and demonstrating the transfer of power from the indigenous Asante dynasty to the British colonial administration. Then they set about reinventing the architectural landscapes of the city, beginning with the construction of a European self-contained house to serve as the palace of the Asante Kingdom.

1   I am incredibly grateful to the late Nana Opoku Frefre III, Asantehene Gyaasehene, whose excellent knowledge of Asante culture benefited this chapter. I dedicate this chapter to his memory. It is also dedicated to the memory of my beloved grandmother, Akosua Nkrumah (1919–2020), and to the painful loss of my uncle, Kwadwo Kaabi (1962–2021). May the souls of these departed loved ones find rest in the bosom of Nyankopon. The ideas for this chapter were conceived in three cities: New Haven, Berkeley and Johannesburg. In New Haven, where the paper began as a term paper, I am very grateful to Dan Magaziner for his comments and advice. The paper assumed a new life in Berkeley following extensive conversations with Trevor Getz. It was here that my fundamental idea gelled, thanks to the generosity of Trevor. In 2019, I met Julia Gallagher in Johannesburg; she posed complex questions, meticulously read several drafts and offered incisive comments and advice. I am equally grateful for the comments of Mary Owusu, Marius Kothor, Cajetan Iheka and George Bob-Milliar. Finally, this chapter has profoundly benefited from conversations with Kwasi Ampene and Richard Ansah.
2   This is popularly known as the Sargrenti War, named after the Anglo-Irish general Sir Garnet Wolseley who commanded the British military forces.

Today, if you walk around the streets of Kumase asking the question 'does the Asante Kingdom have a palace?' you would find that people answer in the affirmative. Yet, I am a Kumaseano, born and bred in this region, and for many years I lived in ignorance that the Asante Kingdom had a palace. The palace occupies a liminal space – it is there and not there. Following research into Asante traditional architecture beginning in 2015, I have encountered contradictions within the concept of an Asante traditional palace as I juxtapose the palace at the 'national' level, Manhyia, with those under the paramountcies, subordinate to the palace of the Asantehene. The paramount-level palaces are uncompromisingly patterned on the concept of a traditional Asante palace, while what should be the most important national palace remains half-built, and largely represented by a colonial-era, British-engineered house. In this chapter, I problematise this situation and allied contradictions by focusing on the national palace of Asante in Manhyia. The efforts to rebuild the Asante palace after it was demolished in 1874 have produced several results antithetical to Asante folk architecture. The consequence is discontent and the corresponding pursuit of that architectural past.

I argue that attempts by the Asante Kingdom to rebuild its national palace have proven unsuccessful. The current palace complex is made up of interim structures built to meet the needs of governance, especially satisfying the court needs of the Asantehene's judicial mandate, but it fails to fulfil the ideal of a proper Asante palace. This should be duly acknowledged. However, I suggest that this material shortfall offers instead a powerful mental construct through which the traditional Asante palace could be revived. This involves the idealisation of the 'authentic' palace in an interventionist phenomenon. The attempt to reinvent an Asante architectural landscape by the British and the contestation between local cultural practices and the unsuccessful efforts to fulfil old obligations and needs have necessitated this mentally constituted approach. In a similar vein, Daniel Mulugeta (see Chapter 9, this volume), has demonstrated the mediating role of architecture in the question about belonging and people's capacity to imagine that which ought to represent an idealised worldview, customs, institutions, and symbols of a people. Thus, architecture provides meaningful interventions in the absence of idealised forms of practice.

Even though I give a background from the nineteenth century, my starting point can be found in the twentieth century with the ambitious plan by Opoku Ware II (the fifteenth Asantehene who reigned from 1970 to 1999), to reconstruct a new palace for 'the proper housing' of the Asantehene, the Asantehemaa, and the sacred regalia, including the Sika Dwa Kofi, also known as the Golden Stool.[3] Ordinarily, one would have thought that the growing

---

[3]   The Sika Dwa Kofi is the symbol of Asante unity, inaugurated when several groups agreed to form a confederation of state with the Asantehene as their leader. It symbolises

needs of local governance necessitated this decision. Nonetheless, I argue that the decision-making was motivated by a desire to preserve vernacular architecture and local cultural heritage, albeit with a touch of useful syncretic innovation. My principal evidence is architectural, for the proposed structure deviated from the already existing structure (built with European design for the occupation of the thirteenth Asantehene, Nana Agyeman Prempeh I, who ruled from 1888 to 1931) and instead followed Asante traditional patterns of house construction and, in particular, palace building.

In making these arguments, I wish to highlight a broader proposition. I use the palace-building project to highlight what this effort tells us about the position of Kumase within the imagined and real geopolitical landscape of contemporary Ghana and within the context of the global history of resistance to the legacies of Empire. From pre-colonial travelogues by Europeans to post-colonial media reportage, this city has been hailed, first, as an embodiment of culture and tradition, and second, as a site of resistance against Empire. Evidence of this assertion was displayed in 2017 at the funerary rites of the late thirteenth Asantehemaa, Nana Afia Kobi Ampem I (1977–2016), where there was a massive display of Asante culture, which reinforced strong attachment to ancient beliefs and traditions.[4] It was after this same event that Kumase was heralded as 'a region where culture and tradition' have 'shrugged off the influence of westernization' (*MyJoyOnline*, 2017).

The research underlying this chapter employed diverse methodological approaches including oral history and tradition, archival research and documentary accounts of Europeans. Using oral history, I interviewed high-ranking chiefs of the Asantehene and officials of the Manhyia Palace including Justice Brobbey – curator of the Manhyia Palace Museum. I also conducted interviews with ordinary residents of Kumase. Beyond oral history, I carried out extensive research at the national and regional archives of the Public Records and Archive Administration Department in Accra and Kumase as well as at the Manhyia archive, perusing the documents of Asantehenes and matters relating to the palace. I also examined the building plans of palaces under the paramountcy including the Edweso Palace. As already observed, the chapter begins with my reflections of Kumase and the Asante traditional palace. I proceed to theorise the attempt to mentally reconstruct the Asante

---

the essence and unity of the Asante Kingdom. The Asantehene is the political head whereas the Asantehemaa is the female traditional leader of the Asante state.

4   Kwasi Ampene has produced a captivating documentary entitled 'Gone to the Village' that tells the story of the funerary rites of the Asantehemaa. At the time of writing, the documentary has not been made public and interested researchers and individuals may have to request it from Kwasi Ampene, University of Michigan.

palace, using it as a framework to explain the historical processes involved in the rebuilding of the 'authentic' palace.

The mental recuperation of the Asante national palace

I propose to describe and explain the politics surrounding attempts to recreate the 'authentic' Asante ancient palace. Although the temporary structures built by Opoku Ware II incorporated some aspects of that palace, the result cannot be characterised as a replica. There is little material evidence of the ancient palace and no complete photograph of it.[5] For this reason, what we have of it are fragments of a few sections and artists' impressions. However, this does not mean that we cannot reconstruct, either mentally or physically, a replica of that palace today, as palace plans of the paramount states have had a similar, if less magnificent, architectural layout.

In a broad philosophical framework, the physical appreciation of a related palace could be categorised under the empirical theory of knowledge, which is the object as it appears to the observer. Beyond the material world, the transcendental idealist doctrine of the German philosopher, Immanuel Kant, can further explain the pre-1874 palace as against what is presented in contemporary Kumase.[6] Kant defines transcendental idealism as the doctrine that 'all objects of an experience possible for us, are nothing but appearances, i.e., mere representations, *which as they are represented* as extended beings, or series of alterations, have outside our thoughts no existence grounded in itself' (Allison, 2004: 36, emphasis added). The obvious equation of appearances with mere representation might suggest that these objects have no existence outside the human mind. However, the italicised phrase in the above statement shows how the 'representations' are reflected back to the object rather than to the 'appearance'. This makes it possible for humans to perceive objects in themselves, in the transcendental world, without employing empirical sense. We observe, therefore, that there is a clear distinction between objects that exist in themselves and mere representations. The concept of the Asante palace is of course independent of its own terms but could be categorised

5   Even though photography had been introduced to the Gold Coast from the middle of the nineteenth century, the Asante authorities seemed to have banned its practice for security considerations until after 1896 when it was opened up for a gradual colonial imposition (Jenkins, 2005).
6   I do not have the space to review debates about theories of knowledge (Allison, 2004; Kant, 1998; Abela, 2002; Guyer, 1983: 92, 329–83) but will borrow from Kant's treatment of transcendental idealism where it is applicable to my argument of the Asante palace.

Figure 10.1   The British-built 'palace' for Asante, now a museum (Julia Gallagher, 2019).

into similar realms of the mundane and transcendental worlds for the purpose of illustration.

Without any material evidence of the pre-1874 palace, stories I have collected from the people of Asante fit well within a Kantian approach to knowledge of the palace, which remains unbuilt, and thus intangible but mentally recognised. I am calling this phenomenon the 'Asantean noumena' which, following the Kantian theory of knowledge, represents the Asante palace as independent of our sense-experience and any phenomenal attributes. The Asantean noumena speaks to two contemporary, yet steady attitudes within which people of Asante descent approach their national palace: the first is that the palace exists in people's minds and corresponds with the past glory of the pre-1874 palace. The mental process gives people, especially those disappointed at Asante's failure to rebuild its palace, the power to imagine and mentally construct an appropriate structure that excites the self (see Julia Gallagher and Yah Ariane N'djoré in Chapter 5, this volume). This excitement is at the individual level and thus subjective, but the concept of the mental construct is objective because it appeals to a unified architectural past. Thus, people are able to conceptualise a traditional palace that befits the status of the Kingdom's wealth and accordingly describe the current palace complex as an imperfect shadow of the absolute reality that exists in the external world of *Asamando*, where the ancestors and supernatural forces reside.

The second is the group of structures that currently serve as the palace and seat of government of the Asante Kingdom. These structures, excluding the guesthouse, which serves as the residence of the Asantehene, were built for temporary use but after nearly five decades of existence it is difficult to tell whether their purpose has not been refashioned into permanency. People prefer to be silent about them than to express criticism.[7] The mystery surrounding chieftaincy in Asante and the aura at the Manhyia Palace that regulates behaviours and attitudes could partly explain this culture of silence. In addition, even though the might and wealth of the Asante Kingdom drastically reduced at the turn of the twentieth century, its glorious past, existing in an external world, continues to affect *our* admiration and veneration for it in contemporary Ghana.[8] Thus, even in the absence of a national palace, the few who know this fact are not critical of the contemporary leaders for their unsuccessful attempts to reconstruct a 'befitting palace' for the Kingdom.

The return of Asantehene Prempeh I and its aftermath

In 1925, the year after Prempeh I's return from exile in Seychelles, the British colonial government, in collaboration with the people of Asante, raised £3,000 to build a two-storey house on a three-acre plot of land to accommodate him (figure 10.1).[9] The need for this house followed the government's reluctant decision to return the Asantehene to his land of birth. The process by which this decision was reached can help us to understand two conflicting concerns of the British administration: its anxiety about Asante resurgence and nationalism, and the ever-present need to maintain law and order to ensure the continuous supply of raw materials to the metropole.

One motivation for the return of the Asantehene can be found in a secret letter from the Chief Commissioner in Kumase, Francis Fuller, warning of an absolute state of pandemonium if the Asantehene remained in exile. Fuller feared that the continuing exile would create 'a general feeling of discontent and uneasiness amongst the people at the continued sequestration of their hereditary Lord'.[10] We do not know on what evidence the Commissioner reached this conclusion. However, it was corroborated by a letter from one Wilson K. Otibo, sent in 1925, which warned the colonial government that the chiefs of Asante had procured arms and ammunition and were prepared to

---

[7]   I learned this during my interview with the Council of Opoku Frefre III in 2015.
[8]   See Daniel Mulugeta for a similar discussion about the power of the imagination in relation to the African Union building, Chapter 9 in this volume.
[9]   Public Records and Archives Administration Department (hereafter PRAAD), Accra, ADM 54/5/5.
[10]   PRAAD, Accra, ADM 11/1/1901: Ex-King Prempeh.

oppose the government by force if their petition for the return of Prempeh I did not receive assent. This threat among other potential disruptions of peace in the city added to the decision by the colonial regime to free the Asantehene and repatriate him and other members of the royal family and aristocrats in November 1924.

Although this second letter was signed, the police after several investigations could not trace its author. This was not the first time the identity of a writer could not be traced, especially in correspondence directed to the colonial government. Although there is no evidence, I suspect that the letter might have been written by a chief, since as both leaders and advocates of the people, chiefs were at the forefront in the push against the separation of their Asantehene.[11]

In his letter, the Commissioner opined that the lack of a head for Asante constituted a serious drawback to the colonial administration, as it led to endless quarrels and time-wasting. Thus, a decision was reached to allow Prempeh I to return. The question of a suitable palace for him immediately became an issue of discussion. Ahead of Prempeh I's arrival, the Council of Chiefs in Kumase met to discuss his welcoming reception and resettlement in the city. After careful deliberations, the chiefs agreed to welcome him at the palace of the Asafohene, the second in command of the Asantehene's army, and later to relocate to his permanent residence built through a joint Asante-British funding at Manhyia. So began a process of reinvention of the traditional Asante palace, the unsuccessful attempts to rebuild it by successive Asantehenes and the ultimate imagining in contemporary Kumase.

The new Manhyia Palace was built through a collaborative effort between the colonial government and local people. The British contribution was meant to compensate Asante for the demolition of the national palace, which was located in Adum.[12] The new house cost an estimated £3,000, nowhere close to the value of the magnificent palace that had been demolished. This disparity was a key reason why the Asante Council of Chiefs and the people initially rejected Prempeh I's occupation of the house.[13] However, two other explanations are commonly given to account for their reluctance. The first hesitation

---

11   Stephanie Newell (2013: 172) has demonstrated how elites in British West Africa issued articles through pseudonyms in the print media to register their discontent about inequalities and systemic racism in the region from the 1880s to the 1940s. The British colonial administration, worried by the provocative and anticolonial publications by pseudonymous writers, 'used rudimentary and questionable biographical techniques for establishing the intentions of authors'.

12   Justice Brobbey (Curator, Manhyia Palace Museum), interviewed 3 June 2016, Manhyia, Kumase.

13   Ibid.

is a refusal to allow the British the honour of contributing financially to the housing of the Asantehene. As a result of this objection, the chiefs and people repaid the British colonial government's contribution before their 'long-lost hero' was allowed to occupy the facility.[14] The second stated reason for the rejection was that the new house did not conform to the pattern of Asante palace architecture.[15]

This second objection is important because it shows contestation to the British claim that Prempeh I was returning as a private citizen. Their initial rejection of a house that did not support Asante socio-political institutions of governance suggests that many of the Asante people saw him returning as the Asantehene. To be effective, an Asantehene needed an architectural space that facilitated his quotidian kingly obligations and the performance of local governance.[16]

Despite the controversies surrounding his return and housing, Prempeh I did occupy the joint-funded house on the premises of what is today the seat of government of the Asante Kingdom. As a leader who embodied Asante customs and traditions, Prempeh I agreed to rule from this house despite its poor fit to the Asante political system. This was partly due to his reliance on the colonial government for the upkeep of his family and servants. In an emotional letter to the District Commissioner, Major W. R. Gosling, Prempeh I showed his reliance on the colonial regime for his livelihood. Requesting an increase in his annual allowance, he stated that his current allowance 'was too small to enable' him 'to look after the large family I have brought over with me from Seychelles and those I have come to meet at Kumasi and I shall rely on H. Honour's kind reconsideration of the matter in the light of my present state'.[17] Considering his dependency, it is understandable that Prempeh I seemed to prioritise accommodating the colonial regime in Kumase.

Justice Brobbey, current curator of the Manhyia Palace Museum, puts forward an additional and quite convincing explanation for Prempeh I's decision to settle in the house. He postulates that his acceptance of the house could be attributed to an identity shift.[18] During his twenty-eight-year exile, Prempeh I lived in a European-designed house. His return, as Brobbey advances, was made possible after the British had succeeded in transforming him mentally, religiously and physically to suit British and European ideas (this

---

[14]   Ibid.

[15]   Ibid.

[16]   Admittedly, there was some division and contradiction among the chiefs, especially those outside Kumase, about Prempeh's status. For example, some chiefs opposed Kwami Kyem's (a sub-chief of Bantama) offer for the Asantehene to live with him in his palace on the basis that Prempeh I was returning as a private citizen.

[17]   PRAAD, Accra, ADM 11/1/1901: Ex-King Prempeh.

[18]   Justice Brobbey, interviewed on 3 June 2016, Manhyia, Kumase.

idea is supported by Emmanuel Akyeampong, 1999 and Mary Owusu, 2009). Although he continued to observe and preserve aspects of Asante culture while in Seychelles, Prempeh I might have felt that this house aligned with his own sense of identity, changed by his years in exile. Yet this acceptance came at a cost, suggesting that the Asantehene seemed to have brushed aside the ancient practice of subjecting any new idea to scrutiny in the light of Asante tradition and culture (Akyeampong, 1999).[19] Ultimately, the decision demonstrates the power and capacity of the colonial administration at that time.

Prempeh I occupied the new house for the rest of his life. Immediately following his demise, his successor, Prempeh II, with support from the Asanteman Council, initiated moves to abandon the joint-funded palace and commissioned a 'suitable accommodation for the office of the Asantehemaa and Asantehene, and which will make adequate provision for housing' the 'sacred and important regalia'.[20] The proposed project, described below, was an ambitious but unsuccessful attempt to reconstruct the Asante national palace. Rather it complicated the concept and our understanding of the traditional Asante palace as well as disrupting ancient cultural practices. Concisely, by the reign of Opoku Ware II, these initiatives reached an inflection point. In the sections that follow, I will describe three palaces – Opoku Ware II's 1970 proposed palace, the Asante-British funded palace and the Asante national palace. By comparing these three designs, I will demonstrate broader themes of Asante architectural and political history.

Opoku Ware II's proposed palace

Not long after he took over as the Asantehene in 1970, Opoku Ware II inaugurated an interim committee to 'advise him on the technical issues relating to the proper housing of the Asantehene, Asantehemaa and the sacred regalia'.[21] The committee consisted of 'architects, structural engineers, town planners, quantity and geodetic surveyors, and men from other walks of life'.[22]

Within less than a year, the interim committee presented its report to the Asantehene. The report and recommendations culminated in the creation of the National Committee, which had Osei Bonsu (now Osei Bonsu II, the occupant of the Silver Stool)[23] as the interim chairperson. Other members of

19   Also, see T. C. McCaskie, 1995.
20   PRAAD, Accra, ADM 11/1/1901: Ex-King Prempeh.
21   Manhyia Archives, Ghana (hereafter MAG), MAG 1/3/34: Asantehene: Palace Building Committee.
22   Ibid.
23   The Silver Stool is the symbol of authority for the state and chief of Mampon. It is next to the Golden Stool in the political structure of the Asante Kingdom.

the Committee included distinguished personalities including J. A. Kufuor, the Kumase city engineer, and later President of Ghana. Beyond these, the Committee was made up of a sweeping representation from the major constituencies of the Kingdom including delegates from the states of Bekwai, Nsuta, Essumeja, Kokofu, Mampon, Dwaben and Edweso. Nevertheless, several interests, including the non-office holding *nkwankwaa* (Kumase 'young men'), and other ordinary citizens were missing from the Committee. Notably, despite Opoku Ware II's conservative outlook, the interests of the ancestors and deities were ignored in this procees, as his committee included no priest-prophet to represent them.

The Asantehene Opoku Ware II gave the committee the mandate to oversee the planning, financing and building of a new palace for the Asante Kingdom. In an important speech he explained the need for a new palace: 'The present palace [referring to the one built in 1925], planned and built nearly fifty years ago, has become too small and does not possess sufficient facilities to cater for the expanding needs of the Asantehene.'[24] This statement seems diplomatic, as it does not foreground the principal concerns raised by the Asanteman Council – the fact that the structure failed to incorporate traditional Asante building components that facilitated the indigenous art of governance. However, as he continued the speech, it became explicit that the people had an issue with the structure and hence awaited a moment that Asante could abandon its use as the palace of a Kingdom whose hegemony and territorial control once extended beyond the shores of modern Ghana. 'Plans to build a new palace', according to Opoku Ware II, 'were made and nearly got off the ground some twenty years ago'.[25] He excused the delay, stating that, '[i]ll-health and other difficulties prevented my illustrious predecessor from putting the plans into effect'. Thus, Opoku Ware II was to be the leader who executed this project. In other words, he, like his predecessor, was a conservative committed to the restoration of custom and tradition.

The National Committee was given the responsibility for the execution of the entire palace building project, which comprised a guesthouse, the main palace or *Fie Kese*, to house the Golden Stool and other regalia as well as providing all the spaces required for the various customary and traditional functions and ceremonies, the Asantehemaa complex, the permanent residence of the Asantehene and the Dwaberem (Durbar grounds).

It had been planned that the architects would present the plan to the public before beginning construction. That did not happen.[26] Instead, several

24   MAG 1/3/34: Asantehene: Palace Building Committee.
25   Ibid.
26   Ibid.

additional buildings were built over time, in a somewhat haphazard way. The Committee accepted responsibility, admitting that the Accommodation Sub-Committee had delayed the architect and consultants. Even in the absence of a public plan for the proposed palace, however, it was clear that the British structure did not meet the standard for a traditional Asante palace. It is these shortcomings to which I now turn.

The limitations of the Asante-British-funded palace

The Asante-British-funded palace was a two-storey, European-style, self-contained structure consisting of living rooms, dining rooms, bedrooms, a kitchen and a toilet and bathroom.[27] The ground floor was made up of five rooms, two of which were living rooms. The first of the rooms was the administrative office where the Asantehene transacted official duties.[28] Next to the administrative office was the first living room, which was used to receive ordinary and non-official visitors, while the second living room was used to receive special local, national and international dignitaries and diplomats.[29] Next to the second living room was the dining room. The other room on the ground floor was quite disconnected from these four rooms and was later converted into a bedroom for the children of the Asantehene.[30]

The Asante-British-funded palace had two big verandahs, one at the back and the other at the west elevation-end of the palace. It had two flat rooftops situated at the west elevation-end, over the verandah and the other at the east elevation-end. The upper floor had four rooms: two halls, two bedrooms and a washroom. It was on this floor that the Asantehene's bedroom was located. Because of the private nature of this space, it was restricted to meetings involving people who had familial ties to him.

Although it functioned as a replacement for the pre-1874 palace, the joint-funded palace lacked the components necessary to be the national palace, having been designed without recourse to vernacular architectural designs and imperatives. Just like other colonial projects, the construction of the joint-sponsored palace was part of a colonial design aimed at breaking down communal organisation and weakening the effective process of local political administration. This conclusion is corroborated by an observation of Matthew Nathan, Governor of the Gold Coast, as he reflected on the colonial administrator's failure to appreciate that the

27   Brobbey, interviewed on 3 June 2016, Kumase.
28   Ibid.
29   Ibid.
30   Ibid.

complicated system of administration, hallowed by antiquity and historic precedents, which our ignorance and policy have alike tended to break down, and a deep-rooted superstition which we are unable to understand and from which our presence in the country has detached a portion of the people. (Quoted in Kimble, 1963: 132)

Whether by intention or confoundment, the joint-sponsored palace could not provide the space for the local art of governance. To answer why, it is necessary to examine the Asante conceptualisation of a palace. Such an explanation will highlight the retention and changes that Opoku Ware II's project proposed, and indeed, introduced.

The concept of a traditional Asante palace

In Asante, a palace is supposed to be an immense structure primarily built to provide accommodation to an *ohene* (pl. *ahenfo*, traditional political leader) and an *ohemaa* (pl. *ahemaa*, traditional female leader). It is also to house the preserved stools of past leaders and contain other valuable treasures of the state.[31] The precise design of palaces in Asante is uniform but their adornment differs from one place to the other depending on the status and wealth of a particular stool.[32] It is expected that the palace of the Asantehene be more graceful and magnificent than other palaces within the Kingdom and able to assert dominance and authority over the nation's architectural landscape. European travelogues about the pre-Toto War palace of Asante give illuminating descriptions about its aesthetic, and how it markedly differed from others. For instance, Ramseyer and Kuhne (1874: 85) – both European missionaries held captives by Asante – during their captivity in Kumase, were impressed with the palace of the Asantehene because of the 'ostentation and gaudy show' of gold and jewels. T. Edward Bowdich, a member of the first British commercial/peace negotiating envoy to Kumase (1966 [1819]: 308) made a similar observation concerning the adornment of the palace in the following description: 'the piazza is 20 yards long, and inhabited by captains… above is a small gallery… The upper end of the piazza … is more ornamented, and appropriated to the superior captains' (ibid.). We observe from Bowdich's description that the need for the Asante palace to be distinguished is partly informed by its scale and luxuriousness.

---

[31]   Baffour Asabre Kogyawoasu Ababio III (Asantehene Nsumankwahene), interviewed 29 November 2015, at his palace, Ash-Town, Kumase.

[32]   Opoku Frefre III (Asantehene Gyasehene), interviewed 10December 2015, Ash-Town, Kumase.

However, on a close observation, the existing palaces of Dwaben and Offinso paramountcies seem more elegant than the palace of the Asantehene. Nonetheless, the status of Manhyia as the seat of government of Asante could be highlighted as the most important reason for justifying its position within the architectural landscape. Here, we observe a composition of several buildings on a large compound whereas palaces at the paramountcy levels are made up of a few buildings on a relatively small territory. In terms of the political hierarchy and power dynamic of Asante, paramount chiefs come next after the Asantehene and, thus, it is possible that the palaces of Offinso and Dwaben could 'rival' the Manhyia Palace.

At both the national level and the paramountcies, palaces have historically been built with two sections – one each for the *ohene* and *ohemaa*. Fundamentally, this created gendered use of space within a palace.[33] Nonetheless, at the paramountcy level, *ahemaa* usually sit in courts with their male counterparts and cannot pass judgement without approval of the *ahenfo*, even in their absence. This explains the absence of courtrooms in the female section of palaces at the paramountcy level.

At the national level in Manhyia, the situation is somewhat different, because the office of the Asantehemaa is independent of the Asantehene due to the numerous defined roles and areas of jurisdiction under her authority. In addition, all *ahemaa* in Asante are under the authority of the Asantehemaa. Finally, the Asantehemaa has several sub-chiefs who serve and constitute her court. It is for these reasons that, at the level of the Asante national palace, the Asantehemaa has a separate court and independently decides cases with the assistance of her sub-chiefs in a democratic fashion typical of the Asante political system.

Another reason for the gendered division of space in the palace is the monthly process of menstruation, which is regarded in Asante lore as a taboo against the gods and ancestors.[34] Historically, menstruating women were regarded as inactive, a state which is commonly but inadequately interpreted as unclean, and hence unfit to be in the same section where an *ohene*, the gods and ancestors reside.[35] Thus, women who found themselves in a state between puberty and menopause were mostly not permitted to stay in the male section where the stool room – serving as the abode of the gods and ancestors – is situated.[36]

---

[33] For a discussion of a colonial gendering of space, see Marie Gibert's discussion of library spaces in Nairobi, Chapter 7, this collection.

[34] Comfort Asante (Lecturer, University of Cape Coast), informal conversation 3 November 2015, Cape Coast.

[35] Baffour Asabre Kogyawoasu III, interviewed 29 November 2015, Ash-Town, Kumase.

[36] Ibid.

Assessment of Opoku Ware II's intervention

By the end of his administration in 1999, Opoku Ware II had completed the planning of a contested palace complex for the Asante Kingdom. Yet as the description of the proposed complex shows, Opoku Ware II's intervention did not simply restore the 'authentic' Asante national palace. Rather, it introduced novel styles to the architectural landscape of Manhyia. Key among these was detaching the male and female sections by a few metres rather than the tradition of having them as neighbours separated by a courtyard but under one roof.

In addition, the proposed structure created a spatial division between the Asantehene and the gods/deities/ancestors. In Asante cosmology the Asantehene, who is semi-divine, and the ancestors/deities/gods are supposed to be in constant communication within the traditional palace. Given that it is still believed today that the Asantehene has a close relationship with the ancestors/deities/gods, one might wonder whether the separation affects the bond and frequency of communication between them? This question has proven difficult to answer since the Asantehene does not grant interviews to scholars working on oral history and those responsible – state orators – are not expected to answer every question, particularly, an intimate question like this.[37]

Finally, the new construction introduced a guesthouse. In the past, there was no separate house for visitors but rather some of the rooms in the palace were reserved for this purpose. This was true, for example, of the period when an independent Asante engaged in intramural diplomatic relations within the West African sub-region and with traders across the sub-region. Asante in the late-twentieth century again extended diplomatic relations with dynasties and nations across the globe, so building a guesthouse to cater to

---

[37] I have already noted (footnote 1) that between 2015 and 2016, I was privileged to have oral history interviews with Nana Opoku Frefre III, Asantehene Gyaasehene and state orator. The interviews were conducted in his court at Asante New Town with the presence of his council. This is where I was told that state orators and chiefs are not supposed to answer every question after I had asked a question about what goes on in the Stool Room of Asante. When I first asked the question, one of his council members responded by saying, '*Nana ntumi mmua asem yi ano*', translated as 'Nana cannot answer this question'. I switched and asked other questions only to return to it after a few minutes but for the second time, I was given the same answer and by the same council member. I was burning with intense curiosity and my youthful exuberance made me ask for the third time, smart as I thought, paraphrased in a new sentence. At this point, you can imagine how I had aroused the displeasure of the council and I was yelled at by a different council member. I never returned to this question for the rest of the time I spent with Nana Opoku Frefre III and his council. I am grateful for their patience and for tolerating my nuisance.

their needs conforms to the changing dynamics of international relations. With the increasing change in lifestyles, attitudes, and respect for individual privacy, old allies in the sub-region prefer separate accommodation. In an interview, the curator of the Manhyia Palace Museum, Justice Brobbey, made a similar observation by taking us beyond the borders of Kumase and the changing pattern of diplomatic relations to examine the socio-political situation in the country. According to Brobbey, the rationale for building a separate house for the guests of the Asantehene and Asantehemaa was partly due to the unstable political situation in Ghana in the 1970s and 1980s, which affected the tourism industry, making it difficult to get a suitable hotel for international dignitaries and guests. The decision to build a guesthouse as part of the palace building project was therefore appropriate.

Overall, the proposed structure seemed better suited to the needs of the state than the joint-funded palace that preceded it as the Asantehene's residence. However, the key question is, did the proposed building address the funda-mental inadequacies of the joint-sponsored structure? Opoku Ware II might have promised the reconstruction of a 'befitting palace' for the office of Asantehene and Asantehemaa, but he might have failed to factor in all the constituents associated with the art and science of building a palace that corre-sponds to the needs and expectations of Asante socio-political institutions. This has necessitated the need for a creative approach to reconstructing the palace through the principle of 'Asantean noumena', which is the thing that is unknown to the physical. The attempt has therefore received a wider and more radical attention among members of Asante society, and the capacity to reimagine is widespread and gaining prominence over Manhyia's materialist vision of constructing a palace.

Finance and the palace

In his inaugural address, the chairperson of the Palace Building Committee had stated that the Asantehene would only 'live in the Guest house... until his permanent residence is built'.[38] Until his demise in 1999, however, Opoku Ware II ruled from the guesthouse. Even though committed to the construction of the palace, he realised that Ghana's unstable political conditions jeopardised his vision.[39] Traditionally, finances to erect the palace should have been generated communally from members of Asante society and fraternity. Yet Opoku Ware II's reign coincided with the highest number of national coups d'état in Ghana experienced by any Asantehene. With the exception of the

38   MAG 1/3/34: Asantehene: Palace Building Committee.
39   See Mike Oquaye, 1980; A. M. H. Kirk-Greene, 1981; A. Adu Boahen, 2000.

1966 coup, which ousted the Nkrumah-led administration, the remaining three occurred during his administration. This situation led to the collapse of many businesses and other economic activities, which in turn limited people's ability to donate to the construction of the palace.

Public funding of the construction of the palace is not a peripheral topic, but rather central to the theme of this chapter. As already noted, palace construction in Asante is a communal project and it is an honour for every adult member and group to identify and contribute financially, materially or by providing labour. This must have been the reason why Opoku Ware II invited the public with the conviction that 'fund[s] will come from all over the country; from individuals and organisations who cherish our cultural heritage, and who wish to see the Golden Stool properly housed'.[40] The Committee opened three bank accounts, at Ghana Commercial Bank, Barclays Bank and the Standard Bank of Ghana, where contributions to the fund could be deposited. The call received immediate attention from individuals, entrepreneurs and the corporate world. The financial secretary of the Committee acknowledged receipts of several donations. For example, the Member of Parliament for Adansi constituency in the Asante Region, S. N. Mensah, donated NC100.[41] On May 1971, Gaisie (West Africa) Limited, representing the corporate world, presented a cheque of NC100 to the financial secretary. Two months afterwards, The World Key of Christ, a spiritual movement, unlike earlier donations, wrote to seek permission to present NC200 to the Asantehene 'as part of their contribution towards the proposed Palace Building fund'.[42] But it was not enough and so instead of the planned palace, Opoku Ware II decided to build temporary structures to meet the needs of local governance while anticipating a stabilised country and improved economy for the realisation of the ambitious palace project.

This economic resurgence did not begin until 1992 when the Fourth Republic Constitution of Ghana was created, aimed at preventing future coups and dictatorial regimes. Yet just as the country stabilised, the health of the wife of the Asantehene started deteriorating until her death in 1995.[43] Soon after the death of his wife, the health of Opoku Ware II also started degenerating until 1999 when he also 'went to the Village'.[44]

[40] MAG 1/3/34: Asantehene: Palace Building Committee.
[41] NC100 in 1971 was equivalent to about US$26,000. However, this was equivalent in purchasing power to about $135,870 in contemporary values (GBP £103,912).
[42] Ibid.
[43] Phone interview with Justice Brobbey, 18 October 2019.
[44] In Asante, when the Asantehene or Asantehemaa dies we say he or she has 'gone to the Village'. Village is used as a metaphor to represent the spiritual realm or the land of the ancestors.

Although I believe the Asantehene and the royal family could have raised the estimated NC3,000,000 for the project, Opoku Ware II, his family, and the Asanteman Council wanted to ensure the observation of Asante mores regarding the financing of the palace. Because of this communal funding, the palace's magnificence would reflect on the whole community.

Questions of tradition

As earlier stated, a cursory observation of the inaugural speech of Opoku Ware II shows that the Committee did not include a priest-prophet. However, by Asante custom and tradition, libation and certain rituals of spiritual signifi-cance should be performed before a house is constructed (Ramseyer and Kuhne, 1878: 226). In the case of a palace, a priest-prophet in the presence of an *ohene* and *ohemaa* (the Asantehene in the case of Manhyia) performed libation. For instance, when Kofi Karikari, the tenth Asantehene, charged Ramseyer and Kuhne to build him a European house during their four years' stay in Kumase between 1869 and 1872, he had to 'perform a ceremony', 'libation', before the foundation was laid (ibid.). This was done to charge the Asante deities for the successful completion of the house and to ward off any evil attack that could result in the collapse of the building.[45] Thus, a priest-prophet should have been on the Committee to communicate the thoughts of the ancestors and deities regarding any decision taken by the members. As it turned out, Opoku Ware II seemed to have brushed aside this requirement.

Why would an Asantehene committed to the status quo do this? Is it because at this time Asante had architects, engineers, contractors and other skilled workers in the building sector who could be trusted to construct robust houses without the help of the deities and ancestors? Could it be the outcome of Christianity, which by this time had succeeded in undermining certain traditional practices including the institution of Asante priesthood? This last suggestion seems unlikely because even though, at this time, Christianity had taken root in Asante, the priest-prophets were still relevant especially to traditional leaders like the Asantehene. It therefore gives reason to speculate that the advancement in building technology and scientific knowledge might have accounted for this lacuna. Indeed, before encounters with the Europeans, Asante had no professional architects and guilds, in today's scientific/professional sense.[46] The architecture at this time could be described as Asante folk architecture, and information on building designs and methods was passed down from generation

45   Baffour Asabre Kogyawoasu Ababio III, interviewed 29 November 2015, Ash-Town, Kumase. Steve Feierman (1990) calls this 'power against power'.
46   Opoku Frefre III, interviewed on 10 December 2015, Ash-Town, Kumase.

to generation by word of mouth and through the follow-observe-practise form of education. Thus, the younger generation learned the art of building whenever building projects presented themselves within the community.

Conclusion

With the demise of Opoku Ware II, Barima Kwaku Dua took over as the sixteenth Asantehene with the stool name, Otumfuo Osei Tutu II. In an article that eulogises the twenty years of his reign, Baffour Ankomah, editor at large of the *New African Magazine*, reflects on an insightful interview he had with the reigning Asantehene ten years after his enstoolment in 1999. The Asantehene eloquently shared his thoughts about the African personality and worldview, which taken together, could give an idea about his conception of the palace in Asante: 'To me, [African personality] means all aspect[s] of the African. It doesn't matter if other people say we are primitive, but if that is what makes us unique and comfortable, why not?' (quoted in Ankomah, 2019). It seems obvious that Osei Tutu II's worldview converged with that of his immediate predecessor.

Osei Tutu II renewed interest in the palace building project under his flagship development programme for Kumase. The Sub-Committee for the palace building project retained most members from the earlier committee including the architect, F. A. Kufour and the structural engineer, Asafo Boakye. At the time of writing, the architect has presented the ambitious building plan of the palace to the Asantehene but it is awaiting the next stage of action. Osei Tutu II continues to live in the guesthouse and adjudicates cases in the temporary structure built by Opoku Ware II. Many may find it difficult to comprehend, but the wealthy and powerful Asante Kingdom of the eighteenth and nineteenth centuries has not been able to build the palace that was planned over a century ago. In light of this inadequacy and through the application of the Asantean noumena, natives of Asante have creatively, powerfully and mentally rebuilt the ancient palace independent of any material intervention from the Asantehene and members of the ruling class.

Throughout this chapter, I have demonstrated how the British attempt to reinvent the Asante national palace re-opened old wounds about colonialism vis-à-vis tradition and modernity[47] among members of the Asante ruling class and society. In a region where tradition mostly triumphed – even under colonial rule – because of the respect for the state's 'ideological structurations

---

[47]   In this context, I employ Akyeampong's concept of modernity, which he explains as 'the rapid social change introduced by colonialism with its empowering, alienating and subjugating qualities' (Akyeampong, 2001: 76).

and hermeneutical intent' (McCaskie, 1995: 139), the British attempt to reinvent the palace's built space was contested and repudiated. As a response, the Asante state proposed a restoration of the National Palace and allied cultural practices. Even though committed to preserving ancient tradition and practice, Opoku Ware II could not deliver, in entirety, as promised. Whereas he succeeded in restoring certain norms associated with Asante palace building including raising funds, the proposed structure itself was compromised as it incorporated aspects of modern building designs and disrupted tradition. The process has illuminated how tortuous and difficult it has been for the Asante state to restore its traditional palace in a rapidly modernising world. In other words, the process shows the increasingly onerous task involved in the attempt to recuperate the wonderful ancient palace that has taken off in people's minds. The unsuccessful attempts to rebuild the palace emphasise that my fellow Kumaseanos and I were indeed wrong to think that the Asante Kingdom had a palace. However, and most significantly, the physical absence of the magnificent palace is proudly preserved by its non-appearance, the Asantean noumena.

11

From prison to freedom: Overwriting the past, imagining Nigeria

LAURA ROUTLEY

Freedom Park, previously known as Broad Street Prison or more formally, Her (or His) Majesty's Prison (HMP) Lagos, sits on Lagos Island at the centre of Nigeria's behemoth mega-city, Lagos. It was from this stronghold on the coast that Britain established its colonial control over what is now Nigeria. This paper explores how the Park overwrites the colonial brutality that Broad Street Prison represents while re-inscribing rather than obliterating its brutal carceral past. It interrogates how the Park's narrative overwrites the colonial past and opens up an imagined prosperous Nigerian future, while, simultaneously struggling with some of the *difficult heritage* (Macdonald, 2008) of the post-independence era and failing to engage with the current brutality of the Nigerian legal system that troubles this imagined Nigeria.

Broad Street Prison was mainly demolished in the 1970s,[1] and by the 1990s the site was wasteland used for dumping rubbish, despite being prime real estate in the centre of Lagos. Explanations given for this are either that the site was cursed by Chief Awolowo, a prominent political prisoner,[2] or that Nigeria's turbulent history of coup and counter-coup meant that contracts to develop the site were often rescinded on power change and that investors became shy of the site.[3] At one point there was a plan to build a facility on the site to extend the nearby maternity hospital, which did not take place – after all who would want their baby born on site with such a history?[4] That it was neglected, left in a state of ruin, allowed to decay into a rubbish ground emerges from and illuminates the enduring trauma of colonial brutality that

[1]   I have seen different dates given for the closure and demolition of the prison but all are in the early 1970s.
[2]   Awolowo's significance as a figure in relation to Freedom Park is discussed below.
[3]   Interview with Theo Lawson, 16 May 2019, Freedom Park, Lagos.
[4]   Ibid.

produces great tensions around what is to be done with such sites (Stoler, 2008: 197). This chapter explores these tensions through an examination of the site subsequent to its relatively recent – 2010 – repurposing as a park/ arts venue. It is based on autoethnographic engagement with Freedom Park which included both written fieldnotes and photographic recording of the site, conversations with other visitors, and a semi-structured interview with the architect of the Park, Theo Lawson.

The ways in which memory practices shape the debris (Stoler, 2013) of colonialism constitute an important question.[5] These practices are entwined with the contemporary politics of communities and states, and indeed internationally. The material culture, architecture and cityscape of most African cities is littered with buildings and sites whose colonial legacies are, forgotten, rewritten and remembered. These remnants can be used by those in power to project their own significance by occupying the throne built by the colonial power or operate as mnemonic intrusions of colonial pasts into contemporary cityscapes.[6] Where these sites feature in the memory-scape of contemporary African states is an emerging area of research, to which this chapter speaks. How this architecture both shapes and is shaped by politics within Africa is a broader question to which this volume makes a singular contribution.

Building on an initial millennial project idea for a park in Lagos, a green space like London's Hyde Park or New York's Central Park,[7] Theo Lawson, the architect and instigator of the Park project, was able to pitch the establishment of Freedom Park to the Governor of Lagos as a marker for the fiftieth anniversary of Nigeria's independence in 2010. Freedom Park was realised not just as a green space but also as a key Lagos arts venue which houses a museum and an art gallery onsite. It also has food stalls and shops. The billed 'transformation' of this waste ground into Freedom Park does not resolve the tensions of its history but is instead a response to colonialism: both in terms of how the site 'overwrites' these spaces (as I discuss at length below) and how the Park is envisioned to substantiate the position of Lagos as a global city and make claims about Nigeria's place in the world. The architecture of Freedom Park, thus, represents a direct engagement with the memory of colonial brutality, a kind of memory practice which has received surprisingly scant attention in academic literature (Rothberg, 2013: 365–66). The

5   This challenge arises in a huge variety of ways. For two others, see Tonderai Koschke, Chapter 6 and Marie Gibert, Chapter 7 in this collection.
6   For an exploration of the relationship between political authority and architecture see Julia Gallagher and Yah Ariane Bernadette N'djoré's discussion in Chapter 5 of this collection.
7   Interview with Theo Lawson, 16 May 2019, Freedom Park, Lagos.

overwriting which is undertaken presents a fascinating response to this colonial debris that focuses on a prosperous imagined Nigeria of the present and future. While heritage practices are always in some sense about an imagined future (Rowlands and de Jong, 2008) the heart of Freedom Park is its practice of overwriting the past with this imagined future. It initiates a narrative arc about a departure from this past and the renewed vitality of the present and future that is both confirmed and extended by the use of the site as an arts venue. Freedom Park therefore manifests an unusual if not unique approach to engaging with difficult memories of colonial penal brutality, and presents a hopeful narrative arc reinforced by the prosperity and creativity it displays.

This narrative is undercut in two ways. First, Freedom Park avoids confronting some of the more *difficult heritage* of the site that speaks the internal struggles that followed independence, and which remain prominent in Nigeria's contemporary political landscape. Second, the Park's engagement with contemporary incarceration within Nigeria is generally dismissive, an approach which responds to the desire to bring into focus the vibrancy of Nigeria but one which overlooks the injustices that were the focus of the #EndSARS demonstrations in 2020. Thus, while the architectural shaping of the site of Broad Street Prison into Freedom Park is an important example of how it is possible to engage with colonial debris, and how Nigeria's great artistic contribution to the world overwrites the alienation and dismissal of colonial rule, the freedom being celebrated is haunted by spectres of colonial rule that continue to shape Nigeria's politics and carceral practices.

A note on colonial incarceration

The (ex-)prison site at Broad Street, Lagos, is a significant location for the colonial history of Nigeria due to the centrality of incarceration to the European colonial endeavour (Anderson et al., 2015; Alexander and Anderson, 2008). As David Killingray (2003: 100) and Florence Bernault (2003: 2) have highlighted, prisons were often among the first buildings erected by colonial powers in Africa. Broad Street Prison was erected in 1872 and rebuilt as a more permanent brick structure at the significant cost of £16,000 (at that point the education budget for the entire colony was £700) (Freedom Park n.d. c), the financial outlay indicating the significance attributed to the prison. The 'development' of Lagos and the establishment of the prison occurred concurrently with increased British interest in this region and further annexation of other coastal parts of what is now Nigeria (Falola and Heaton, 2008: 95).

Incarceration, certainly in the form embodied by these prisons, was a departure from pre-colonial modes of punishment and social control in Nigeria, and as such was a clear marker of colonial forms of rule (Saleh-Hanna,

Figure 11.1 Main stage, Freedom Park, Lagos (Laura Routley, May 2019).

2008: 57–58). The prison in colonial Africa was a key method of control with prison populations that were per capita three to six times higher than in Britain (Bernault, 2007: 63; see also Jefferson and Martin, 2016). Not only was a higher proportion of the population incarcerated but the sentences given were often considerably longer (Killingray, 2003: 101). Prison heritage sites in Africa are underexplored with the notable exception of apartheid-era sites such as Robben Island (Deacon, 2004; Strange and Kempa, 2003). This absence within the academic literature is accompanied by a broader neglect of many ex-colonial heritage sites including carceral ones in Nigeria (Oyigbenu, 2015). Thus, while incarceration practices and prison buildings were a significant element of colonial control, as well as locales of resistance to colonialism, in the main they remain somewhat marginal in contemporary accounts, marking Freedom Park as a notable site for examination.[8]

Overwriting

While both Lawson and the literature produced by Freedom Park discuss the Park as a heritage site, Freedom Park neither seeks to recreate or preserve; rather the space tries to evoke. By the time Lawson was able to develop the site all of the buildings within the prison compound had been demolished. He used a plan of the prison, located at the National Museum, not to rebuild

---

[8]   For another exploration of architecture and carceral practices see Yusuf Patel's exploration of detention in apartheid South Africa, Chapter 8 in this collection.

it but to put things together so that they resonated in certain ways: 'where the gallows were, we put a stage' (figure 11.1).[9] I understand this process as form of overwriting, where the 'new' is given particular resonance precisely because it is placed over what went previously. This layering on top is marked on the site by information boards located adjacent to features and outlining how these echo what stood there previously. The framing is not simply about equivalence but is in some senses also about overturning. The information board by the main stage (figure 11.1) reads: 'The Gallows was a structure used for execution of condemned prisoners by hanging ... Today, it is interpreted as a stage where people should feel free to express themselves socially or politically without fear of retribution.'

This evocation rather than preservation or re-creation produces something that is much more future-oriented than many other heritage practices. All heritage sites and museums, and indeed histories, are inevitably shaped by and implicated in the concerns and assumptions of their curators and creators as well as their visitors, and as such are situated within their contemporary context. Moreover, as others have explored, the production of events into a sequence itself produces a future – 'for the practice of narration distends each "point" [each present] into the past and future' (Crang, 1994: 31). I am not contending therefore that future effects are unusual within heritage sites, rather that the mode of rendering Freedom Park as a heritage site diverges from many heritage sights discussed in the literature, as does the absence of an attempt to create authenticity. Efforts to create something which presents 'the past' realistically (Turner and Peters, 2015: 74) as what it was 'really like' (Walby and Piché, 2015) are seen in many heritage contexts including prison museums. But Freedom Park does something much less focused on *authenticity* and 'bringing back to life'. While these strategies are not entirely absent from the Park (there is a mock-up of a cell in the museum for example) they are marginal and often authenticity is not the main driver. There is not an attempt at re-creation or a move to ask visitors to 'place yourselves in their shoes'. Even in the case of the cell, the flooring is a continuation of the floor in the museum. It is not on the site of the actual cells, which is particularly significant as the layering over on the location of previous structures governs much of the design of the site. This is not a site where its previous uses are un-mentioned or glossed over, but neither is it one in which there is some act of fidelity to a previous moment and an attempt at recreation. The site is less about the past than the future. The importance of other museums as ways to imagine the future are important. However, in the case of Freedom Park, it

9   Interview with Theo Lawson, 16 May 2019, Freedom Park, Lagos.

is not a subplot but the main narrative arc of the site that points towards a particular future.

Overwriting, while still echoing previous forms, dominates the shape of the site. What is noticeable here is that what is layered on top is about relaxation, art and expression, a clear inversion of what was represented by Broad Street Prison. This inversion is obviously central as the site has been renamed 'Freedom Park'. The pergola cells give another clear illustration of this transposition while evoking previous forms. They sit on the site of one of the cell blocks and map their size. They are called the pergola cells because they are half-height walls with a floating corrugated steel roof, creating a semi-open walkway. These cells have electricity points within them and visitors can hire plastic tables and chairs to use in them. Lawson explained that originally the idea had been to mark out the cells on the grass as has been done for the 'impression cells' but that the structures were added to make more useful spaces so people could stay longer. When I visited, a handful of people – mainly young men – were working (setting up computers, tables and chairs) in them. I spoke to a group of musicians and dancers. They told me that they come to work and practise. One was giving vocal coaching to another. The pergola cells (figure 11.2) are also used for commercial events: a sign next to them reads 'Prison's Cell Block A, Freedom Park's Virtual Commercial Space ... Now an open space used for commercial and retail purposes especially during events or fairs'; this usage is also mentioned in Freedom Park's literature. Thus, while serving as a practice space, for many the cells are also used in other ways. A young man in his early twenties who was with the musicians, told me that he runs an Instagram account and online clothing shop: he was working on that from the 'cells'. The access to electricity in the pergola cells is significant in a city with an unreliable supply and during another visit I came across someone who was there charging their phone and 'relaxing'. These structures have therefore enabled the dwelling envisaged for them. That they are frequently used by musicians and dancers as practice spaces is not incidental. One of those I met told me that there was an agreement between Freedom Park and the company he worked for to waive the entrance fee to the Park. This fits with the Park's role as a key arts venue.

An association made by Freedom Park in its literature is between freedom and culture, the Park being described as: '[a]n existential space where freedom is synonymous with culture and culture is synonymous with freedom' (Freedom Park n.d. c). Artists are seen as central to the Park both in terms of the realisation of its overwriting of Broad Street Prison through expression and culture but also because these artistic endeavours are central to how it is financially viable as a theatre and music venue in the evenings for charged events. Indeed, a few years ago the site was at risk of being turned into an events venue, a

Figure 11.2   Pergola cells, Freedom Park, Lagos (Laura Routley, May 2019).

move championed by the Commissioner for Tourism. Freedom Park was saved by both Wole Soyinka's intervention and because, when the Governor visited the site he liked the trees and the green space and the alternative project did not move forward.[10] Lawson sees the artists as what is keeping Freedom Park afloat, saying that they are people who 'make something from nothing'. That the Park operates both as a prisons/colonial heritage site entwined with an arts venue/park devised for people to be comfortable to dwell may at first seem somewhat contradictory. But I suggest it is in fact central to its overwriting. By engaging with artists of various kinds, this process of overwriting is sustained not only because of the financial viability it gives to the Park but because it means that the Park is not a singular moment of re-inscription but a perpetual one. On visiting, it is not clear which parts of the Park are 'permanent' and which are current time-limited exhibitions.

When discussing the history of the site with the group of musicians, they all said that they were aware of its history; indeed one basically responded – 'we are Nigerians so we know'. When I asked if they thought about this history as they were using the space another said that they knew but that you 'have to move on'. Moving on was, however, not inevitable for the site as the abortive building projects and decades of neglect as wasteland show – for example, as already mentioned, the site was seen to retain ghosts of the horrors of incarceration which made the site unfit for a maternity hospital. Rather, the project of Freedom Park itself is about productively transforming and overturning the macabre associations, not by obscuring them but by transmuting them into markers of freedom. 'This is a symbolic re-enactment of this journey, as the old Broad Street Prison – a colonial fortress of control – is literally dismantled to usher in the dawn of Freedom Park' (Freedom Park n.d. a). The forms of the Park and their marking out while subverting and replacing are then part of this story which has a teleology of movement towards 'freedom' and the site is used to mark the departure from a particular history rather than to preserve it.

A bright Nigerian future, stalked by ghosts

The politics of the Park and its architectural overwriting imagine a prosperous, creative Nigeria, and the activities of the Park as an arts venue work towards the production of this, alongside the imagination of a Nigeria of global consequence. As mentioned above, Lawson envisaged Freedom Park as a marker of Lagos' status as a global city – alongside Hyde Park or Central Park.[11] The overwriting

10   Ibid.
11   The way in which buildings and architecture are utilised to make claims about states' international relations and standing is discussed by Joanne Tomkinson and Dawit Yekoyesew, Chapter 1 this collection.

of colonial spaces of control and brutality within the site is, therefore, also an attempt to overwrite Nigeria's position not as a colony but as an equal on the international stage. While Lawson did not mention the heritage elements of the endeavour as emulation of Western capitals, heritage sites too can be seen to bring African cities in line with the architectural landscape of international cities (Marschall, 2008: 360). Freedom Park is therefore productive of a particular global positioning of Lagos and Nigeria, the arts events that occur within this space being further evidence of international standing. Summoning Nigeria's place in the world also evokes Nigeria itself, which is, however, not an un-contested entity, its post-independence history being marked by: the Nigerian Civil War or the Biafran War, 1967–70 (even the name is a source of tension), a conflict precipitated by the attempted secession of the east of the country; political unrest and a complex insurgency in the Niger Delta from the early 1990s onwards; and the Boko Haram insurgency in the north-east of the country, which intensified from the late 2000s. The unity of Nigeria as a large federal state that binds regions with significant separate pre-colonial histories together has thus been under strain throughout its existence.

The museum is somewhat peripheral within the Park; it exists in the opposite corner to the food court area and on the other side of the site to the main 'gallows' stage. The art gallery sits on this side too and is decorated with portraits on the outside which draw the eye. The museum on the other hand somehow feels more hidden: you enter it through a side door which is obscured from view by a children's play area. On my first visit I was unsure if the building was open, as the lower floor of the museum was deserted with nothing except a couple of items of plastic furniture, rather lost in the midst of the room. I felt compelled to check with a woman who was cleaning that I was permitted to go in. This space is used for temporary exhibitions. The whole of the museum, with the permanent displays housed on the mezzanine floor above the temporary exhibition space, was also empty of other visitors. During my visits to the Park, I did not come across anyone in the museum, unlike other parts of the Park which, while far from crowded, were often occupied.

Climbing the stairs at the far end of the Museum's lower floor leads to a mezzanine which houses the museum's permanent collection. You encounter the first boards discussing the history of Lagos at the top of the stairwell. The museum offers a more expected framing of the site, around artefacts and historical narratives. Once on the mezzanine proper, the first alcove predominantly exhibits items that are understood to be from the era of Broad Street Prison, found when the site was being cleared, but these do not have explanatory card labels. They are accompanied by old photographs and a picture of the plan of the prison used in the designing of Freedom Park. The narrative of the exhibition is mainly presented through the large explanation boards that detail the arrival of colonialism to Lagos, the building of the prison and so forth. The story is framed around the political prisoners that were held here and especially their resistance to colonial rule. One of the first boards, entitled 'From the curator's desk', outlines the colonial history and announces that: 'This exhibition depicts the transition of "Her Majesty's Prison" to Freedom Park while celebrating our heroes past.' The story of Broad Street Prison is rendered as the story of the arrival and ultimately the vanquishing of colonial rule. The exhibition itself shifts from images of Broad Street Prison – photos, plans, and the artefacts the in the first alcove – to detailing the heroes in the second. Large portraits of anti-colonial activists such as Herbert Macaulay and Pa Michael Imodu are displayed with brief biographies on cards below. The third alcove highlights the transformation of the site into Freedom Park with large photographs of the site at different stages in its redevelopment. The exhibition is thus framed teleologically with freedom as the inevitable destination, echoing the statement on the 'From the curator's desk' board at the start of the exhibition that: 'The prison could only hold these prisoners captive but it could not hold back the freedom that was to come.'

The most significant potential disruption to the museum exhibition's narrative arc – from Prison to Freedom – comes from the presentation of 'The Trial of Chief Obafemi Awolowo'. Awolowo, Chief Lateef Jakande and other members of the Action Group political party, were arrested, tried and jailed in the immediate post-independence era (1962) for treason. The information about the trial is given notably on an information board of a different design and type (was it added later?) and there is a set of photos of the key protagonists with their names and sentences. However, how Broad Street Prison is implicated in the turmoil of the early independence period, and how this intersects with the overarching narrative of Freedom Park as a victory over colonial oppression, is not directly addressed.[12] Neither is how these post-independence struggles play into the closure of the prison in the early 1970s. However, the next information board 'The Transformation', which outlines the development of the site into Freedom Park, does hint at these complexities stating:

> Freedom Park holds the key to significant history of the nation with its symbolic testament. It is a representation of a journey to Freedom and a triumph over all that sought to confine people (Colonial or Tyranny). Freedom Park is a prove [*sic.*] that they broke free.

---

12 Will Ross (2014) in a BBC news article says that: 'Some of the last prisoners to be detained here were separatists during Nigeria's post-independence civil war.' If this is the case, it is passed over in silence in the museum – the Civil War is a particularly contentious topic in Nigeria.

'Colonial or Tyranny' thus acknowledges these different historical struggles but simultaneously rolls them together, obfuscating the tensions that the post-independence struggles within Nigeria bring to an implied happily ever after of 'Freedom'. The attention paid to 'The Trial of Chief Obafemi Awolowo' needs to be intellectually situated within Freedom Park's location within Lagos and indeed its connections to the Lagos State Government. Freedom Park is an organisation connected to the Theo Lawson Architectural Practice which runs the Park and is the driving force behind its transformation. However, it sits between a private initiative and the state, the land it occupies being owned by Lagos State to which Freedom Park pays rent, but also from which the Park receives support.[13] The quote above highlights the site's national significance but the same paragraph concludes that: 'The Museum ... depicts the culture, history and heritage of the site and of the Lagos people.' Lagos is often celebrated within the Park with the gallery hosting exhibitions for the Lagos Black Heritage Festival and the Lagos@50 festival. Intriguingly, Lawson originally envisaged the Park's skeletal cells (figure 11.3) as 'flowing from the ramp out of the museum block with some kind of projections of current and future Lagos; a museum of Lagos flowing out into the future of Lagos'.[14]

Chief Awolowo's trial was part of the history of the then-Western Region of Nigeria's struggle with the Federal Government. In this context, Awolowo can be seen to be struggling on behalf of the people of Lagos (which is situated within the Western Region) against tyranny. But the national story is more complex. Indeed, these political struggles of the early independence era in Nigeria were struggles between federal and regional levels, and between regions, for power and influence at the federal level. Awolowo was pursuing theses struggles for the Western Region of Nigeria as a long-term proponent of Yoruba interests (Falola and Heaton 2008: 150, 167). The implied positioning of Awolowo as a hero struggling against tyranny as previous leaders had struggled against colonialism thus roots the narrative in a particular regional and ethnic perspective.

The oblique way in which Nigeria's post-independence internal struggles and the fight against colonialism are elided are, I contend, part of how this site engages with, or perhaps more accurately skirts around, what is its *difficult heritage* in the sense used by Sharon Macdonald (2008: 4) that it: 'threatens to trouble collective identities and open up social differences'. Chief Awolowo appears not only in the museum but outside in what was the prison yard, in prime position at one end of the 'Hall of Fame', a formally laid-out paved

---

[13]   Interview with Theo Lawson, 16 May 2019, Freedom Park, Lagos.
[14]   Ibid.

garden area. Here stands a statue comprised of three larger-than-life figures of Chief Obafemi Awolowo, Sir Ahmadu Bello and Dr Nnamdi Azikiwe, with a board that describes them as the Founding Fathers of Nigeria's independence'. I also found reliefs of the three of them leaning against the railings at the edge of the mezzanine in the museum.[15] The presentation of these three leaders as the founders of Nigeria is frequently used across Nigeria to foster a sense of Nigeria as bonded across what have been contentious differences and senses of marginalisation – with each leader being associated with a region of Nigeria: Awolowo – Western Region, Bello – Northern Region and Azikiwe – Eastern Region. This occurs in a context where the national unit of Nigeria is frequently and currently under strain, including from current Boko Haram activity in the north (Olaniyan and Asuelime, 2014), ongoing agitation for secession in the east (Ugwueze, 2019) and, despite an amnesty programme, continuing conflict in the Niger Delta (Dudu and Odalonu, 2016). In this context, Awolowo's imprisonment for treason and more broadly the role that Broad Street Prison plays post-independence, raises the spectre of struggles around Nigeria's nationhood which are far from resolved and continue to shape its politics. The 'national question', key for Nigeria for many years (Osaghae and Onwudiwe, 2001; Momoh and Adejumobi, 2002), is currently manifest in discussions around 'restructuring' Nigeria's federal system (Ibrahim, 2020). At the same time, however, Awolowo as one of the Founding Fathers of Nigeria represents Nigeria's national identity. Freedom Park places Awolowo centrally in this role – both literally in terms of the 'Founding Fathers' sculpture being positioned near the centre of the Park, but also in terms of avoiding the difficult heritage to which Awolowo's imprisonment speaks.

The centrality of the 'Founding Fathers' sculpture works alongside other sculptures in the Park to centre it as a Nigerian site. Spread around the Park are sculptures that portray the diversity of Nigerian cultures through representations of figures undertaking activities of cultural significance. Most of these figures are marked as donated by the Omooba Yemsi Adedoyin Shyllon Art Foundation.[16] While it is not clear whether they were created for Freedom Park, the information boards imply their long-term residence. They include a figure playing a Kakaki (a long wind instrument made from various materials), which the information board tells us is played when 'leaving the palace of an Emir, Sultan or Shehu'; a chorus leader from Benin; a drummer from Calabar; and the festival of Eyo from Lagos. These statues situate Freedom Park not only as a heritage site of national importance but highlight its significance

---

15   It was unclear whether the reliefs were being stored there or were part of the exhibition.
16   This is an art foundation in Nigeria set up by Omooba Yemsi Adedoyin Shyllon.

Figure 11.3   Skeletal cells, Freedom Park, Lagos (Laura Routley, May 2019).

as a national monument and its representation of Nigeria as a nation, in its diversity but ultimately in its unity. This is fitting as Freedom Park was opened to mark the fifty-year anniversary of independence for Nigeria: the framing of the site speaks both to an overturning of colonial oppression and to the establishment of Nigeria as an independent state. Freedom Park deals more comfortably with Nigeria's colonial history which it beautifully overwrites without erasure, than with the messy post-independence turmoil.

The presence of prisoners?

One of these sculpted figures is different to those portraying cultural practices from across Nigeria. It sits, not in the more open spaces between the depicted cell blocks and other defined areas such as the food court as most do, but within the skeletal cells block. This figure is not of a cultural practice but is entitled 'Contemplation' and is one of the few nods within the Park to contemporary criminality and imprisonment (see figure 11.4).

The skeletal cells (figure 11.3) were the format of recreating the cells that I found the most affective. They stand on the site of cell-block C, a two-storey structure with a ramp which leads you up to a second-storey level. The walkway continues between cells which are marked out by a skeletal-metal framework. This form works to reproduce the cells while still rendering them see-through and somewhat ephemeral. The affective power of this part of the site, for me, is however not solely about the imaginative way in which the cells are brought back without any pretence at an authentic recreation, but

Art in the Park
OMOOBA
YEMISI ADEDOYIN SHYLLON
ART FOUNDATION
Contemplation
It is a general knowledge that the economic down turn is biting hard on the masses. Despite the fact that the majority of the people still look for legitimate source of income, some chose to remain idle and thus turn to crime or become miscreants.
Medium: Resin glass fibre.
Size: 40" x 24" x 44"

Figure 11.4 Contemplation, Freedom Park, Lagos (Laura Routley, May 2019).

that these are the only cells on the site which are 'occupied' by prisoners. Within the cells are sculptures of figures made out of metal and covered in barbed wire – which comes from the top of the prison walls.[17] They sit or stand suspended within the cells and are themselves also semi-transparent. The situation of the skeletal cells means that the retail units (none of which were open any of the times I visited) are visible through them, the cells appearing superimposed over the other activities of the Park. The vantage also gives, as the information board puts it, 'views over the Park'. This vantage also acts to slightly separate you from the rest of the Park, placing you as a more detached observer. This cell-block produces something slightly different to the overwriting of the pagoda cells and other parts of the Park, or the more narrative elements of the museum exhibition; rather it attempts to create a sense of presence, not focused on authenticity but rather relying on modes of abstraction and encounter which are reminiscent of an art installation – fitting given Freedom Park's focus on the relationship between art and freedom.

The presence of prisoners in the skeletal cells thus does something different to the rest of the Park as it engages more directly with the affects of confinement rather than focusing on the overwriting of this confinement. However, the abstract nature of this does not invite connection or sympathies with the imprisoned per se. In carceral geography's engagement with prison museums there is often a discussion of how they enable or hinder visitors to make connections between the historical prison and the situation for prisoners in contemporary institutions (see, for example, Turner and Peters 2015). The narrative of the Park does not attempt to make these connections and indeed the 'ordinary' prisoners of the historical prison are somewhat marginal. Information about some of them are presented in the museum exhibition but they are not woven into the narrative of freedom. Their stories are limited to their name, age, conviction, sentence and time served and the individuals remain just shadowy silhouettes, both literally on the information cards where they are represented by outlined head and shoulder, but also in terms of their experiences of Broad Street Prison which remain unilluminated. The marginal position of these inmates does not invite identification with prisoners historically and therefore short-circuits possible connections of the site to the situation of contemporary inmates.

While the Park does not make these links to current penal practices, some of the visitors do. One member of the group of university students I met 'said that she thought this prison established in 1875 [in most of the literature I have seen it says 1872] was better than contemporary prisons. I asked in what ways and they highlighted feeding[18] and access to family'.[19] Indeed, the expectation of prison conditions is extremely low. Later I re-explored the site with another two of these students:

> They discussed the pagoda cells [and] looking at the size of them Precious[20] declared that they probably housed six people in each (there wouldn't have been room for them to lie down in that case) … Again, when looking at the mock-up of a cell [in the museum] they were wondering if it was for more than one person. I said I thought that it would have just been for one. Rita said 'so this was something like a big man's cell'. I said I thought that it was just for one person because they thought solitude would help them reform … (didn't get much response to this comment).[21]

While Freedom Park works to overwrite or to overlay rather than to reproduce authentically inmates' experience of Broad Street Prison, some visitors use their own referents to undertake this imaginative work themselves. They also make connections to contemporary penal practices.

Over much of the Freedom Park site there is little focus on the non-political prisoners of Broad Street Prison and almost no mention of contemporary prisoners. The exception is the sculpture entitled 'Contemplation' at the end of the walkway to the skeletal cells (figure 11.4). The figure is dressed in a vest and rolled-up trousers – the uniform of poor young men in Nigeria. The text which accompanies the figure states:

> It is a general knowledge that the economic down turn is biting hard on the masses. Despite the fact that the majority of the people still look for legitimate source income, some chose to remain idle and thus turn to crime or become miscreants.

This momentary engagement with contemporary criminality is not particularly sympathetic, which undercuts the affective engagement with imprisonment that the figures within the skeletal cells produce. It also underscores the focus of the narrative of the site as one of political imprisonment and overcoming colonial (and other forms) of tyranny. The absence of engagement with the conditions of current inmates in Nigerian prisons and the censure of those who contemporarily fall foul of law enforcement contained within the text

---

18   Whilst prisons in Nigeria nominally have some funds for feeding prisoners, inmates rely on food brought in by relatives and friends.
19   Fieldnotes, May 2019.
20   These are pseudonyms.
21   Fieldnotes, May 2019.

companying the 'contemplation' statue struck me when I visited in 2019, especially as a scholar interested in Nigerian prisons and prisoners' experience of them. It also chimed with critiques of other prison heritage sights (Turner and Peters, 2015). It seemed to be part of the production of a particular temporality within the Park in which the injustices of incarceration were relegated to the past. This absence feels even more glaring in the light of the nationwide #EndSARS protests in 2020.

These protests focused on the disbanding of the police Special Anti-Robbery Squad known for its brutality (Amnesty International, 2020) and they received international attention especially after the shooting of unarmed peaceful protesters that killed at least twelve at Lekki Toll Gate – approximately four miles from Freedom Park. About halfway between these two sits Ikoyi Prison which, two days later, was subject of an attempted prison break (Olufemi, 2020). Elsewhere in the country – Benin, Oko and Ondo – in the same week prison attacks associated with the protests resulted in over 2,000 prisoners escaping (ibid.). The press reports framed these attacks on prisons as conducted by thugs under the guise of #EndSARS protesters, and rumours of all kinds are circulating, including that the government released prisoners in order to counter the #EndSARS protests. However, #EndSARS is about resistance to Nigerian police brutality and highlights the illegitimacy of the force used by those who are supposed to be enforcing the law. Freeing of prisoners and the destruction of prison property seem in line with this questioning of the legitimacy of the coercive arms of the legal system. In 2020, 74.3 per cent of prisoners in Nigeria were pre-trial detainees or on remand (World Prison Brief, 2020). According to one Deputy Controller of Prisons, many within the prison he ran should not be there, they had been in the wrong place at the wrong time,and that the overcrowding problem was caused by 'over-zealous' police arresting people, asking too much for bail, and the courts being too slow to resolve these cases.[22] Given the delays in the judicial system, prisons are not separate from police brutality – indeed they are another aspect of it. While the motives behind the prison attacks and escapes in late October 2020 remain unclear, the legitimacy of contemporary practices of imprisonment in Nigeria is far from obvious.

Freedom Park celebrates Nigeria's transition to freedom, overturning, overwriting, colonial incarceration and exhibiting the fruits of freedom through arts and performance. The contemporary prison population of Nigeria does not fit neatly within this vision of the future. For Freedom Park, imprisonment is Nigeria's past, not its present or its future. The Park also, through its role in the Lagos' art scene, produces this future, through exhibits and performances,

---

[22]   Interview, Deputy Controller of Prisons, 26 September 2012, Nigeria.

and with the space being used by musicians and dancers for rehearsals. The arts community, the public that Freedom Park imagines, is also generally a middle-class and elite community. The Park is not open to all as it has an entry fee of 200 Naira – not a huge sum but certainly one that the women selling fruit and street food on the corner outside it might hesitate to pay. This does not undermine its achievements; many world-leading arts venues could be seen to be predominantly for the middle class and the elite. But it does hinder it in engaging with continuing forms of marginalisation, many of which have their roots in colonial practices, of those who cannot afford to dwell within the Park and those who continue to be imprisoned within Nigeria.

The incarcerated past and the freedom of the future

Michael Rowlands and Ferdinand de Jong locate the drive for heritage practices as part of 'modern moods of nostalgia and longing for authenticity' (2007) but Freedom Park is not driven by nostalgia or authenticity. Freedom Park, to a degree, also troubles the distinction often made in the literature between states as monumentalising and private memories (Rothberg, 2013; Rowlands and de Jong, 2007; Werbner, 1998). The broad-brush contention is that heritage as monumentalisation is part of spectacles of state formation that are often disconnected from public memory because they focus on triumphs and erase trauma (Strange and Kempa, 2003). Freedom Park's form of heritage does not simply monumentalise and yet neither does it foreground trauma, despite the site's history. Rather, as explored, it overwrites the space in ways that that foreground the palimpsest nature of the site. This provides a powerful mode of engagement with colonial debris, and yet retains a unified 'triumphant' story of Nigeria in which current traumas and the difficult heritage of the site are marginalised.

The site cannot simply be seen as a state monument. The state's presence and engagement with the Park is somewhat contradictory as it supported and ultimately funded it but has also been the source of a threat to the project – when the Commissioner for Tourism desired to repurpose it as an events venue. When I asked Lawson about his concerns about changes in administration impacting the future of Freedom Park he said – 'I am an architect not for the state but for the people'.[23] This claim highlights I think an idea of Nigeria beyond its governmental bodies; a community imagined by Lawson that Freedom Park serves. This community is, however, implicitly if not consciously imagined as middle-class Lagosians and other such discerning people who can afford the entrance fee. It is not those currently residing in Nigeria's prisons.

23   Interview with Theo Lawson, 16 May 2019, Freedom Park, Lagos.

The inscription of the past onto the city emerges in European nation-building wherein establishing a long history through the visible material culture of cities works to both cement identities and to convey a sense of the endurance and legitimacy of the nation (Macdonald, 2008: 2). In a broad-brush way Freedom Park conforms to this celebration of the triumphs over colonialism as a Nigerian endeavour which both highlights the endurance and the legitimacy of the nation. The inflections here are, however, divergent from the practices in Europe in important ways, because the endurance for European states often is about persistence over the longue durée, whereas to endure for (post?)colonial nations often references endurance as 'the capacity to "hold out" … a countermand to "duress"' (Stoler, 2016: 7). Freedom Park represents the overturning of the colonial restrictions on the Nigerian soul. The legitimacy of Nigeria is also conveyed by this overcoming. The trans-formation of this space announces the joy of freedom post-imprisonment, freedom post-colonisation and the establishment of a confident, sophisticated Nigeria. The Park speaks to a prosperity entangled with its emergence from an ambition to be like London's Hyde Park or New York's Central Park, a desire to claim Lagos' place as a global city and, in so doing, to overturn colonial practices of marginalisation. By this means, the divisions and injustices that continue outside the Park's boundaries are rendered out of focus, yet creep back in round the edges.

Maybe I am wrong; maybe it does not edge back in; maybe these elements are always present. The largest building on the Freedom Park site is Kongi's Harvest Arts Centre. This is obviously a tribute to Wole Soyinka a long-term supporter of the Park. But of all his great works the building is named after a play which engages head on with the struggles, division, trauma and brutality of post-independence African leadership.

Afterword: Theorising the politics of unformal(ised) architectures

KUUKUWA MANFUL

The introduction to this book began with a discussion of the much-celebrated opening of the Unity Park in Addis Ababa in October 2019. With its architectural centrepiece, the magnificent former palace of Emperor Menelik II (constructed 1886), the Park complex represents what Daniel Mulugeta, Joanne Tomkinson, and Julia Gallagher describe as 'significant centres of political power in recent Ethiopian history' (Introduction, this volume). About eight months before the opening of Unity Park, the government of Ethiopia started a mass demolition of about 12,000 homes in the Legetafo and Legedadi neighbourhoods on the outskirts of Addis Ababa. Calling the buildings 'illegal' and referring to a master plan that did not include those homes, the government rendered thousands homeless in the space of a few days. A week before the Legetafo and Legedadi demolitions, the 29 Billion Birr (US$900 m), Chinese-aided 'Beautifying Sheger Project' was launched to clean up and develop rivers and riversides in Addis Ababa. Here too, there were demolitions of homes to make space for the government master plan. A former resident expressed the view that the state was 'treating [the residents] like enemies' as she narrated how the police were 'sent' to carry out the demolition 'during holidays which led [them] to live on the streets for 4 months' (Terefe, 2020).

These homes are called 'Moon Houses' as they are 'built illegally overnight in the moonlight' (Meseret, 2019). Among the reasons people built them in the first place is that the Ethiopian government has been unable to provide adequate housing for its citizens. Biruk Terefe (2020: 377) has argued that the government[1] has 'shift(ed) away from pro-poor schemes towards a new

---

[1] The Ethiopian People's Revolutionary Democratic Front (EPRDF) Government governed the country from 1988 to 2019. The EPRDF emerged out of the resistance to the brutal Derg Regime of Mengistu Haile Mariam. The last EPRDF chairman who is also the Prime Minister Abiy Ahmed, dissolved the EPRDF and created a new

emulated urban form that focuses on luxury real-estate projects and a vibrant urban tourism sector targeting domestic elites, the Ethiopian diaspora and international tourists'. This shift in the government's urban development focus contributes to ever-growing inequality, precarity and housing deficits for residents of Addis Ababa. So, people take matters into their own hands and build when they can, how they can, and where they can. In interviews with the press, some of the former residents of Legetafo and Legedadi said they paid rents on the land, ostensibly to some government officials.

State demolition of buildings rendered illegal or informal is a recurring theme across much of Africa. In some cases, as in Ethiopia, homes built by citizens in response to the inability of governments to provide adequate housing to accommodate massive urban migrations (see Irene Appeaning Addo's analysis in Chapter 4, this volume) are destroyed to make way for elite visions of grand, modern cities. In other cases, it is not just homes but places of work, rest and worship that are destroyed in service to government master plans or development schemes, as seen in Ashaiman, Ghana, on 5 July 2021 when buildings in the Nii Annang Adjor Market were demolished without warning (Nyabor and Washington, 2021). Traders were left to salvage items from the rubble that used to be their shops as they wondered where they would go or how they would survive in the post-Covid 19 pandemic economic slump. On a much larger scale and earlier in 2005, the Zimbabwean government destroyed thousands of homes, industries, and businesses in 'Operation Murambatsvina'. This targeted destruction of 'illegal, informal' buildings had an additional political dimension in that it was it was in part the ZANU-PF government's response to opposition (Vambe, 2008). It was also an 'an attempt by the government to punish the urban poor for having turned their backs on the ruling party' (Mlambo, 2008: 21). In Lagos, parts of the Makoko waterfront settlement, which dates back to the nineteenth century, were demolished to make way for a much snazzier waterfront 'regeneration development'. The residents, primarily low-income fisherfolk, were given only seventy-two hours' notice to make alternative arrangements. The police killed one person, and thousands of people lost their homes in the Lagos State Government demolition of Makoko in July 2012 (*Al Jazeera*, 2012; Morka, 2012). It is important to note that some of the people who lived and worked in these places rendered illegal and informal by governments had actually paid rents or taxes to state officials, showing that they were known to the state and regulated in some formal ways when convenient or profitable.

---

political party, the Prosperity Party, in November 2019. The Prosperity Party is now the governing party.

In these state demolitions of informal settlements, there are common threads of governments maltreating their citizens and viewing their buildings as untidy challenges to elite visions of formal order. Buildings long established and known to the state are removed often without sufficient warning to make way for projects of affluence and exclusivity, which sometimes remain unfinished and incomplete. These demolitions are driven by African governments' 'fetish(es) about formality' (Kamete, 2013: 17) which play out in attempts to rid their countries of what is considered unsightly, dirty or out of place in modern cities and nations. In Operation Murambatsvina, which translates to 'clear the filth or dirt' in Shona (Human Rights Watch, 2005: 1), the 'illegal' structures and their occupants, by extension, were literally characterised as 'dirt' or 'filth' to be removed (Vambe, 2008). In Kigali, Rwanda, which has undergone rapid and extensive transformation, a city official quoted in an interview spoke of a 'new identity' for Kigali, stating: 'We have to be orderly, we have to be clean, we have to be modern' (Goodfellow, 2013: 83). For these governments, modernity is achieved through formal planning (Adama, 2020), and 'informal' buildings, especially those built by the poor, threaten that. Thus, even when governments provide no formal alternatives, the attempts by ordinary citizens to make do for themselves are always at risk of destruction.

In this Afterword, to a book that has brought together scholars thinking through the politics of architecture in Africa, I explore ideas of what is considered informal, illegal, and out of place in African built environments – in a bid to redefine 'architecture'. Although the contributions by the authors in this volume have been elite-decentred and people-centred in their approaches, I seek to challenge and push the boundaries of our thinking around the politics of architecture even further by questioning the designation of 'architecture' in the first place. This is a move towards the inclusion of the everyday and the ordinary in the built environment; buildings that are not constructed by or for the wealthy, elite and powerful; and those constructions typified as 'informal' or 'illegal'. Fundamentally, I want to trouble what it means for something to count as architecture, worthy of study in its own right and not just as aberration occurring outside of the boundaries of formality.

Much – if not the majority – of the built environment in Africa falls into this realm of informal or illegal because many Africans build their own houses, places of work and worship outside of formal planning regulations and without the services of an architect or state-sanctioned professionals. Yet, there is a tendency to exclude these types of construction – sometimes manifesting as slum dwellings and shacks as one might see in Khayelitsha (South Africa), Makoko (Nigeria), Cazenga (Angola) and Old Fadama (Ghana) but also including expensively constructed homes, capital-intensive multi-storey buildings and extensive industrial facilities as one might see in Muyenga (Uganda) and Adum (Ghana) – from the label of Architecture. I use the terms 'unformal' and 'unformalised' architectures to refer to these built forms as I theorise the politics of these state- and architecturally othered constructions and explore how studying unformal architectures could provide an essential lens for examining the politics of architecture in Africa.

In addition to an approach to studying the politics of architecture that centres the poor and non-elite, I discuss how, by studying unformal architectures in their own right, we could open up new lines of inquiry about society and politics in Africa. The chapters in this volume, even where they centre the perspectives of ordinary people, examine these perspectives in response and relation to buildings created for or by elites. In this Afterword, I suggest approaches that centre the knowledge and perspectives of ordinary people about their own architectures. Through this, we can begin to look beyond the 'illegal' and 'informal' as the mere absence of formality, but as distinct types of architectural form and expression worth examining in their own right. Many of the studies of the 'informal' and 'illegal' aspects of the African built environment focus on the poor or 'underprivileged classes' in Nnamdi Elleh's (2014) terminology. But while these kinds of construction form a core category of unformal architectures, there are many other constructions that are not designed and constructed out of poverty or lack of access to state-sanctioned professionals. Therefore, unformal architectures in Africa include all the buildings and structures that occur outside of state purview and formalised design and construction industries.

Using archival material and historical texts, I demonstrate how power refracts through taste, aesthetics and style to suggest that, by reframing what we consider architecture, we can open up new avenues for our studies of the (Politics of) Architecture in Africa. The archival sources I use include newly digitised images from my 'building Early Accra' Project which has digitised 'a collection of building permit applications submitted to the Accra Metropolitan Assembly from its earlier manifestation as the Accra Town Council in the early 1900s'(Accra Archive, 2019).[2] The historical texts I consult include books from travel writers and British commercial and colonial officials who visited what was then the Gold Coast in the nineteenth and twentieth centuries.

---

[2]   The 'building Early Accra' Project (EAP 1161, available at www.accraarchive. com) was funded by a grant from the Endangered Archives Programme, supported by Arcadia and administered by the British Library.

Designation and regulation of architecture in Africa

Many of the current issues around the designation and regulation of archi-tecture in Africa can be traced directly back to European conquest and coloni-sation. Architecture, including the control of architecture and space, was one of the many tools and techniques of conquest and eventual colonial domination. Colonial architectural domination was realised in a number of ways, four of which I discuss in detail below. These are (1) the diminishing, erasure and demolition of existing African architectures; (2) the erection of imposing and intimidating European architectures; (3) the juridical and bureaucratic control of the built environment through planning, permits and licenses and; (4) the influence and imposition of European hegemonies of aesthetic taste. These were complex, often interwoven processes that resulted in the erosion of existing African architectural aesthetics and construction techniques, some of which have been lost forever.

First, historically, the labelling of what counts as architecture in Africa has been deeply political. In European explorer accounts of much of Africa, we often find the built environment referred to in terms meant to denote that they are 'less than'. Words such as 'hovels', 'huts', 'dwellings' and 'shanties', some of which, although not necessarily disparaging, were used in derogatory ways to refer to many of the buildings made and inhabited by Black People in Africa. Even when there was incontrovertible proof of African architectural advancement by European standards, such as in the pyramids in Egypt and the ruins of Great Zimbabwe,[3] there were attempts to attribute them to non-Black, non-African creators. Edith A. Browne, a prolific English travel writer who wrote about early Christian, Norman, Greek and Byzantine architecture as part of a series 'Great Buildings and How to Enjoy Them', presents this account of Accra in her 1920 book titled *Cocoa*:

> On that plain, close behind where we landed, stand the business quarter and native town of Accra, a mixed assembly of up-to-date facilities, pioneer makeshifts, and primitive squalor. Fine premises built in European style, of durable concrete or concrete blocks, are scattered about among weather-beaten, ant-eaten wooden shanties resembling old barns surmounted by a loft, and wedged in among these civilised and

---

3   Some of the most ludicrous theories concerning the origins of the city of Great Zimbabwe and the great pyramids of Egypt were that they were constructed either by or with the help of extra-terrestrial beings or aliens. Some other theories posit that those structures may have been built by long-lost European civilisations who since left the continent. Belief or evidence of alien activity aside, what underlay these theories was the racist disbelief that Africans – Black Africans especially – could have built by themselves anything that met European standards of grandeur.

semi-civilised buildings are mud huts and warrens of mud hovels. The mud quarters are the homes of swarms of black people – men, women, and children. (Browne, 1920)

In this brief extract, Browne's admiring perception of buildings assumed to be built by Europeans reads in sharp contrast to her descriptions of those she attributes to 'natives'. On the one hand, there are 'fine premises' and 'up-to-date facilities', and on the other hand there are 'mud quarters' and 'warrens of mud hovels'.[4] In between these lie the 'weather-beaten, ant-eaten wooden shanties', which she attributes to 'white pioneers … fellow-countrymen' who arrived in Accra before her. Yet, from archival photographs and contemporaneous literature, it is known that there were 'native' buildings that would fall into the categories of 'fine premises' and 'up-to-date facilities', including some built in mud. Buildings such as the Adorso House Hotel[5] and the original palaces of the various Mantsemei,[6] for instance, were in Accra at the time.

Browne's account of Kumase makes it even more clear how, through her writing, she aims to place European architecture above African architecture. She notes: 'In 1875, when the Black Watch made their famous entry into Coomassie, the place was a primitive native village. The first European building of any importance to be erected there was the British Fort, which was begun in 1896' (Browne, 1920). In Kumase, like Accra, even by Western standards, this account of the physical environment is a false one that attempts to diminish and erase. (For an account of pre-colonial monumental architecture in Ghana, see Tony Yeboah, Chapter 10, this collection). Thomas Edward Bowdich's 1819 account, which was intended as a 'most accurate' report for the African Company of Merchants and contributed to the eventual British annexation of the Asante Kingdom, gives an entirely different impression of Kumase. He writes:

The construction of the ornamental architecture of Coomassie reminded me forcibly of the ingenious essay of Sir James Hall (in the Edinburgh Philosophical Transactions), tracing the Gothic order to an architectural imitation of wicker work. The drawings will serve to shew the various and uncommon character of their architectural ornaments, adopted from those of interior countries, and, confessedly, in no degree originating with themselves.

---

[4] The use of the word 'warren' here is enlightening as it refers to habitations of non-human animals, either occurring naturally or artificially created for the purpose of breeding game for hunting.

[5] The Adorso, or Adawso House Hotel was designed by C. Annan Vanderpuye for his brother and was mentioned in Charles Francis Hutchison's *The pen-pictures of modern Africans and African celebrities* by Doortmont (ed.) (2004 [c.1929]).

[6] Mantsemei are kings, or royals of the Ga State.

Figure 12.1 Drawing of Kumase in the 19th century based on historical accounts and images (Drawing by Kuukuwa Manful, 2022).

From Bowdich's account, sketches from his book and other contemporaneous images of Asante architecture as reimagined in figure 12.1, it is even more clear that later descriptions of 'native' Kumase architecture departed from the initial almost positive and admiring tones of the first official reports.

Under conquest and colonial rule, architecture was one of the many sectors in which European authorities exerted their power and attempted to control. This control was expressed overtly and brutally through the demolition of African built space, such as the levelling of entire coastal African towns to make way for European forts and castles. Browne notes with approval the demolition activities of the colonial government and 'private enterprise' towards transforming the town of Accra: 'mud huts are being removed to afford sites for more such premises; the location of destructive and constructive operations suggests that the business quarter will eventually rise clear of the native town' (Browne, 1920).

A second way in which architectural control was expressed was through the erection of buildings symbolic of the government, such as police stations and post offices, as well as grand and intimidating edifices such as courts and palatial official residences in African cities. Maurice Amutabi discusses this as it occurred in Nairobi, Kenya, where 'the power that colonial buildings exhibited was unmistakable' (2012: 326) and Africans both admired and

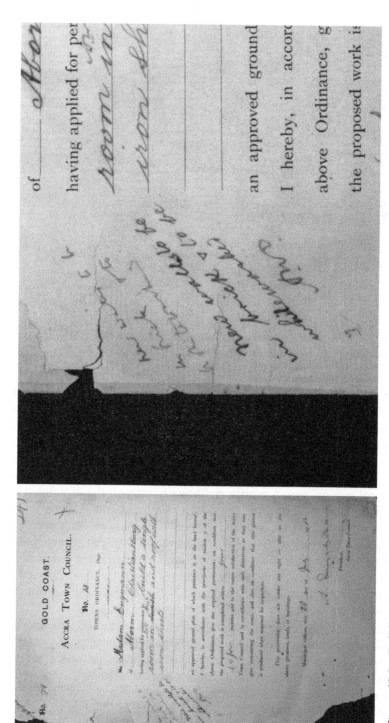

Figure 12.2 Building Permit Application number 13 (The building Early Accra Project, 2021; reproduced with permission of the Project).

were intimidated by European colonial buildings. Italy's occupation of Libya was channelled, among others, through architectural domination, such as in the twenty-six 'villages' that were constructed to house 20,000 (*ventimila*) Italian settler colonisers in distinctly Italian styles without any reference to existing Libyan architectural and spatial contexts (Samuels, 2011; Segre, 1972). In 1930s Ethiopia under Italian control, as Mia Fuller notes, 'a building's function was to confront the local population ... with Italian power', and '[urban] planning was expected to facilitate the precise art of distinguishing and dividing within the living space of the colonial context the metropolitan Self from the colonised Other' (1988: 456).

A third form of architectural domination, less overt and brutal in many cases, proved no less destructive. Channelled through town planning ordinances and building construction bureaucracies, such as the Town Councils of Accra and Nairobi, which regulated architecture and space in colonial Gold Coast and Kenya, respectively, indigenous architectural aesthetics and technologies were eradicated. Colonial Nairobi was designed for racial segregation spatially and through architectural form with Europeans living in 'private houses on the spacious lots in the higher, cooler, north-western sections of the city', 'Asians ... in large extended family houses near the city centre', and 'Africans [in] cramped rental quarters in the lower lying' regions (Gatabaki-Kamau and Karirah-Gitau, 2004).

In Accra, colonial urban authorities outlawed building in earth and other natural materials, prescribing that new constructions in the city had to be made in mostly imported and expensive materials such as cement. Some of the regulations speak specifically to what kind of building materials are permissible. For instance, it is stated that:

> For walls, concrete or concrete blocks is the most satisfactory material ... Swish [earthen] walls will only be allowed for single-storey buildings, and then not within two feet of the ground. Wooden buildings will not be permitted; but verandahs may be of timber ... All materials used should be of the best quality obtainable.[7]

Figure 12.2 shows a note from an Accra Town Council official that approves an application from an African resident with an amendment that strikes out their intention to build with earth and replaces it with 'new walls to be in brick and whitewashed'.[8]

Through these regulations, people who either could not afford to build with expensive, imported materials such as concrete, or were unwilling to,

7   Building Regulations for Accra Under Section 11 of The Towns Ordinance, 1920.
8   Building Permit number 13 Town Council, 28 July 1902.

were essentially barred from building on their own land. Eventually, most of the earthen buildings that were indigenous to Accra disappeared from the cityscape. Thus, architectural control through laws and bureaucracies was a subtle yet insidious process that resulted in the loss of architectural heritage around the continent. To this day, many zones of exclusion of the poor and otherwise marginalised in African cities echo the exclusions of colonial urban planning and architectural control.

Finally, even more subtle sociocultural influences of Western ideas of aesthetics and taste in colonial Africa have helped to undermine African architecture. Under this dispensation, what was considered more prestigious, tasteful architecture was primarily associated with European power and status. Increasingly adopted by African elites, Western aesthetics and architectural styles began to supersede African ones. Even with the eighteenth-century Gone Fantee[9] movement in the Gold Coast that advocated a return to some traditional customs and a careful blending of things European and African, African architectures did not make the comeback that African names and languages did. European architects and builders were valued over African ones, and their clients included both private businesses and the colonial state. They professionalised the industry and formed exclusive organisations on the basis of race, keeping out African architects and builders as they designed and constructed much of the formalised architectural landscape and cemented aesthetic taste in the upper echelons of colonial society.

In post-colonial Africa, control and domination through architecture continues despite independence and the transfers of power from colonisers. African states and individual leaders have often erected monumental buildings to project their power and ideals. Examples include presidential palaces in Entebbe, Yaoundé, Accra and, more infamously, Mobutu Sese Seko's palace in Gbadolite. The bureaucratic control of architecture and space in towns and cities has not changed much either, and the professionalisation of architecture has only expanded from colonial to post-colonial eras. Although there are different actors, agents and aims, the hierarchies of architecture and what is deemed 'architecture with a capital A' remain firmly entrenched. Where there was the Gold Coast Association of Architects, an exclusive group of mostly European and a few mixed-race architects that was the dominant architecture society, there is now the Ghana Institute of Architects (Manful, 2015). Accra

[9]   The 'Gone Fantee' movement or 'The Doctrine of Return to Things Native' was a cultural renaissance movement among the Fante nations in eighteenth-century Gold Coast. They promoted the use of African names, African musical instruments, the wearing of 'native dress', and the speaking of the Fante language (*The Gold Coast Aborigines*, 12 February 1898).

Town Council, run by British officers, is now the Accra Metropolitan Assembly run by Ghanaian civil servants. Fundamentally, what remains the same is that influence, control and regulation of architecture – through bureaucracy or sociocultural norms – remains dominated by a socio-political elite in many African countries. Just as occurred with indigenous African architectures in centuries past, unformal architectures which fall outside the influence, control, and regulation of the state and state-sanctioned professional organisations are viewed as undesirable in built landscapes, especially in urban areas. In the worst cases, those unformal buildings that belong to the poor and relatively powerless are often targets for demolition. Those that wealthier people build are often harder to demolish. Even so, because there are often no professionals from the formal industries involved in their construction, they are not considered as architecture worthy of acknowledgement, respect, or indeed academic study.

A fresh outlook: Challenging the boundaries of designations

Scholarly engagement with architecture in Africa has often been constrained by the boundaries of designation, professionalisation and taste. In his article titled 'Architecture, history, and the debate on identity in Ethiopia, Ghana, Nigeria, and South Africa', Ikem Okoye writes about what he characterises as the 'perceived threat' that instigated the 'African academy's engagement with architectural history'. He argues that:

> Given that the modern state in Africa is relatively weak in that it has few resources to enforce its own laws, the idea that the architect is the only creator whose design proposals had first to be approved by building inspectors and planning authorities before construction could proceed is in reality non-existent ... Anyone can, where enforcement is nominal, design and erect a building. This is the threat to Architecture. (Okoye, 2002: 381)

The threat persists, perhaps at a greater rate, in contemporary times with population explosions in several African cities, the failure of governments to provide adequate housing and infrastructure for citizens and the abundance of people creating architecture outside the control and influence of the state, professional associations and elite tastemakers. Perhaps it is time to expand the boundaries of what the academy studies under the label of architecture in Africa.

The examples of architecture that have been analysed and theorised under the politics of architecture in this book have almost all comfortably fit into formal architectural designations in the African countries where they are located. Some do so because they are grand and monumental, such as the Manhyia Palace studied by Yeboah (Chapter 10) and the proposed national cathedral in Ghana written about by Emmanuel Ofori-Sarpong (Chapter 2). Others, such as Julia Gallagher and Yah Ariane N'doré's state buildings in Côte d'Ivoire (Chapter 5), Irene Addo's public housing in Ghana (Chapter 4), Innocent Batsani-Ncube's parliament building in Malawi (Chapter 3), Marie Gibert's public libraries in Kenya (Chapter 7) and Yusuf Patel's account of the notorious John Vorster Square Police Station in South Africa (Chapter 8), count as 'big-A' architecture because they are important buildings symbolic of the state. At the same time, Joanne Tomkinson and Dawit Yekoyesew's Bole Airport (Chapter 1) and Daniel Mulugeta's African Union headquarters (Chapter 9), both in Ethiopia, count as 'Architecture' because they are state-approved, international-facing structures. Tonderai Koschke's Sam Levy Shopping Centre in Zimbabwe (Chapter 6) and Laura Routley's Freedom Park in Nigeria (Chapter 11) were elite-led projects. This despite the fact that, as Koschke points out, the shopping centre was technically an illegal structure because 'like many buildings constructed during the first years after independence, it was built without municipal permission'. Yet, while Operation Murambatsvina destroyed buildings belonging to the poor and relatively powerless, the wealthy, well-connected owner of the shopping centre was able to regularise it by obtaining permission retrospectively, establishing it as a prestigious commercial site patronised by the upper-class. In the case of Freedom Park and the Ghana national cathedral, the architects are renowned architects or 'starchitects'. Having such famous architects involved brings extra legitimacy and formal recognition to building projects because they are then positioned as big-A architecture by big-A architects.

The authors of the chapters in this book have not just focused on the intentions of the architects and elites where the architecture is concerned. Most have approached the studies from the point of view of challenging and questioning elite-driven discourses of architecture. In Ghana, through their studies of the national cathedral, Manhyia Palace and the state housing schemes, Sarpong, Yeboah, and Addo respectively looked beyond what is presented at face value. Batsani-Ncube, Koshke and Routley have questioned the premises, processes and consequences of the elite-driven 'vanity' projects of the parliament, shopping centre and memorial park. Patel has conducted a forensic analysis of built space to 'highlight architecture's complicity in death-in-detention cases'. In several of these chapters, the authors have sought to foreground considerations such as those of the non-elite which are usually decentred or peripheralised in discourses about big-A architecture. Through this, we begin to understand the politics of architecture beyond elite intentions and processes.

Other authors have explicitly included the opinions and perceptions of ordinary people who view and use the buildings and spaces. In Tomkinson and Yekoyesew's study, these include Addis Ababa residents' conflicting views of the Bole Airport in their analysis as 'an icon of national pride' and 'an alien, strange', and 'un-Ethiopian building', as evidence of a nuanced and 'complex relationship between the global and the local' in Ethiopian state building. Had they relied on the opinions of elite actors, this analysis would not have been possible. Similar threads can be seen in Mulugeta's study of the African Union building and in Gallagher and N'djoré's chapter on architecture and authority in Côte d'Ivoire, which focus on the views of the principal constituency to which political power is projected through architecture.

Although the instances of architecture within this book are mostly formal, the people-centred and elite-decentred approaches the authors have taken to studying the politics of architecture have shown how we can begin to move our studies in different directions, even towards challenging the designation of 'architecture' in the first place. We could build on this start, and look for an even more fundamental challenge to the politics of architecture, one that included studies of the informal and unformal, not solely as a lens through which to talk about struggles between states, governments, elites and the common person, but as architectures in their own right, on their own terms, worth studying, worth theorising about. I end with two vignettes, beginning to explore a few possible points of departure towards such an outlook for the future.

Two vignettes: An uncompleted building and a golden edifice

Duku has always dreamed of living in her own house.[10] That is, a house that she will build on land she owns. But she is only a teacher, and with having to support herself, her children and her extended family on her meagre salary, this is not the most achievable dream. Nonetheless, she intends to persevere and realise her dream, so she has bought a plot of land and started building. Technically the plot of land is not hers yet as she has not finished paying for it, but she purchased it through the Teachers' Credit Union she belongs to, and they will deduct a sum from her salary every month until the cost is covered. She started constructing her house in 2010, and as of March 2020 it stands with most walls at lintel level. She did not use an architect, engineer or any of the other professionals required to get a building construction permit as it was both unaffordable and unnecessary in her opinion. She hired a 'contractor' to build everything, and he 'gave [her] a plan [architectural drawings]' 'for free'.[11]

10   I have used a pseudonym.
11   Interview with Duku, Accra, November 2020.

She progressed the project by building materials piecemeal whenever she had saved up a bit of money – one bag of cement here, 100 sandcrete blocks there – storing them until there was enough to build a part of one element. For instance, her building foundation had been complete for over a year before she had gathered enough sandcrete blocks and money to lay the first few courses of walling. She is literally building her house 'brick by brick' when and where she can find money to spare. Building and land encroachments are common, and people who cannot afford to pay the police or people in the legal system to protect or recover their assets have to be extra vigilant. Already there has been one claim by a wealthy real-estate businessperson on her plot of land, but luckily the Teachers' Credit Union stepped in to protect all the land on behalf of their members. Still, to keep her investment safe, she has allowed a family of strangers to live in it. The family has nailed a few roofing sheets over one of the rooms and boarded off the window openings to shelter from bad weather as they live there. The parents work whatever odd jobs they can find, and their two children are in primary school. Duku's house is one of hundreds of thousands of what are typically called 'uncompleted buildings' in Ghana and Nigeria.

Uncompleted or unfinished buildings are a common element in cityscapes across West Africa. A headline of an article on *The Economist* website, which states that 'half-made buildings are everywhere in African cities', asks 'Why are there so many unfinished buildings in Africa?' (2021). There are many such headlines and questions in the news media and social media. In Nigeria and Ghana, these kinds of buildings often exist in public imaginations, expressed through film and popular culture, as unfortunate, shady, unsafe or even dangerous places. In these public imaginations, the people who occupy them either do so out of poverty because they have no choice, because they are unsavoury characters who have something to hide, or both. The plot of 'Blessing', one of the thousands of low-budget Ghallywood and Nollywood movies released straight to YouTube and other free-to-access video streaming services, revolves around a poor girl who is saved from living in an uncompleted building by a wealthy man who eventually marries her. As in countless other movies, in 'Blessing', urban poverty is portrayed by situating characters in shacks and uncompleted buildings.

Uncompleted buildings are also viewed as hideouts for criminals and social miscreants such as armed robbers, kidnappers, rapists and cultists. In Part One of *The Armed Robbers' Prayers*, featuring a star-studded cast of Jim Iyke, Sylvester Madu and Emma Ehumadu as armed robbers, a police officer tails them into the uncompleted building which they use as a hideout. A news story from November 2021 has the headline 'Lagos residents decry use of abandoned, uncompleted buildings as hideout for miscreants' (Nwannekanma,

Figure 12.3   Menzgold Accra Premises (Kuukuwa Manful, 2021).

2021). Despite the overall negative tone of the story, interviews with people who lived in uncompleted buildings revealed that some were hawkers who only went there to 'sleep when there [was] no traffic' (ibid.). Another had moved there as a last resort after being 'ejected by her landlord' (ibid.). Tellingly, the state government's response was to 'pledge to demolish abandoned and uncompleted buildings across the state' (ibid.).

But these uncompleted buildings do not appear out of thin air, and their owners do not sink their life savings into building intending to leave them partially finished. Many uncompleted buildings represent the ongoing aspirations, imagined futures and desires of their owners. For the average salaried worker in Africa, someone in that vague category of not wealthy and not poor who cannot access mortgages or other means of financing a home, building a house slowly and incrementally over years – decades even – is the only way to own a house. Duku's uncompleted building is likely to remain uncompleted even longer. The global pandemic hit the economy hard, and prices of already expensive building materials have gone up. Nonetheless, she intends to persevere and realise her dream of living in her own house, on land she owns.

My second story takes us along the George Walker Bush Highway in Accra, where sits a golden building that glints and glitters in the bright hot Ghanaian afternoons. The golden building is, or was, the premises of a gold dealership and investment firm known as Menzgold Ghana Limited. Now deemed as fraudulent, Menzgold promised investors anything from 10 to 30 per cent monthly returns. It appears to have operated as a pyramid scheme, using deposits from later investors to pay off the principal investors who had the good fortune to cash out early. All landed properties belonging to Menzgold have since been seized by Ghana's Economic and Organised Crime Office, including the golden building itself. The founder and chief executive officer of Menzgold, Nana Appiah Mensah, was a major celebrity in Ghana when the firm was operating. He was pictured with several religious leaders, national leaders and celebrities, including the Chief Imam and the President of Ghana (*MyJoyOnline*, 2019; Zurek, 2019). He lived lavishly, regularly flying to exotic locations on a private jet and splurging on luxurious cars and extravagant parties.

The design of the Menzgold headquarters (figure 12.3) has not been publicly claimed by any architect. The consensus among the architecture community is that it was not designed by a trained or registered architect in the country. The golden Alucobond cladding and the golden reflective fenestration is also considered quite gauche by many in the community. It is in a style of architecture that I have named 'Despite Architecture' in reference to the archaic and current meaning of the word 'despite', and with regard to a wealthy businessman named Osei Kwame Despite, who built his business empire despite not having a formal education and is generally considered to be living a Ghanaian dream (Manful, 2019). This architectural style is characterised by trappings and displays of opulence and the use of trendy modern materials in construction markets from factories in China (ibid.). Buildings in this style are often made without the services of trained and registered architects, although not for reasons of affordability. A wealthy businessman who owned several houses that he designed himself, told me he did not like working with architects because of the way they held themselves and seemed to look down on people like him who did not have a formal Western-style education.[12]

There are many such architectures-without-architects or architectures-without-planning-approvals all over the continent, from the flashy-looking and expensively constructed such as the Menzgold building to those gradually built over multiple years and not at all opulent, like Duku's house. Muyenga in Kampala, Uganda, for instance, 'long favoured by elites, became known as the "rich man's slum" due to grand houses built with virtually no planning, often over previously existing roads' (Goodfellow, 2013: 11). Indeed, I would argue that they form the vast majority of homes, places of business, entertainment and worship in urban Africa. Yet, they remain largely absent from critical studies that focus on architecture on the continent, and when they feature, as previously stated, it is through the official lenses of informality and

---

[12]   Interview with businessman, Spintex, Accra, April 2018.

illegality. This is a continuing diminishing and dismissal of whole building sectors, knowledge and related socio-politics.

There are no ready answers, just questions. Could a study of how government workers build their houses in Lagos, Dakar or Abidjan challenge our ideas of the state in those countries? What could studying the material finishes, furniture and decor of buildings in a 'Despite Architecture' style tell us about Ghanaian domestic politics and international relations? What could an analysis of the forms and ornamentations of architecture-without-architects in Bulawayo tell us about identity, being and belonging in Zimbabwe? And what could the tectonics of buildings in Makoko tell us about Nigeria's political transformations and histories? What might the future of our disciplines and fields be if we widen the frame and reject the boundaries of formalisation and *unformalisation* of architecture?

BIBLIOGRAPHY

Abdallah, A. A. (2008). 'State building, independence and post-conflict reconstruction in Djibouti', in Ulf Johansson Dahre (ed.), *Post-Conflict Peace-
Building in the Horn of Africa: A Report of the 6th Annual Conference on the
Horn of Africa, Lund,August 24–26, 2007* (Media-Tryck Sociologen, Lunds
universitet), 269–79.

Abela P. (2002). *Kant's empirical realism* (Oxford: Oxford University Press).

Abiodun, R. (2001). 'African aesthetics', *The Journal of Aesthetic Education*,
35(4): 15–23.

Abubakar, I. R. and P. L. Doan. (2017). 'Building new capital cities in Africa:
Lessons for new satellite towns in developing countries', *African Studies*, 76(4):
546–65.

Accra Archive (2019). About: Building early Accra. *Accra Architecture Archive*.
Available at: www.accraarchive.com/the-project [Accessed 25 November 2021].

Adama, O. (2020). 'Abuja is not for the poor: Street vending and the politics of
public space', *Geoforum*, 109: 14–23.

Addis Tribune (1962). 'Bole international airport, its development projects', *Addis
Tribune*, 18 July.

—— (1997). 'Ethiopia: Ato Hailu Gebre Mariam – The man who looks after
airport project', *Addis Tribune*, 26 December.

Addo, I. A. (2016). 'Traditional earth houses in Vittin, Tamale: Identity and
perception of the tradition-modernity conflict', *Contemporary Journal of
African Studies*, 4(1): 97–128.

Adebajo, A. (2020). 'Daniel Arap Moi: A ruthless dictator', *The Guardian*, 10
February 2020. Available at:https://guardian.ng/opinion/daniel-arap-moi-a-
ruthless-dictator [Accessed 25 November 2020].

Adjaye, D. (2012). *Africa architecture: A photographic survey of metropolitan
architecture* (London: Thames & Hudson).

Adjetey, E. (2019). 'Ghana's plan to build national shrine stirs controversy', *Africa
Feeds*. Available at: https://africafeeds.com/2019/11/21/ghanas-plan-to-build-
national-shrine-stirs-controversy [Accessed 5 November 2021].

Adogla-Bessa, D. (2018). 'Ghana Institute of Architects questions David Adjaye's
selection for national cathedral project', *Citinewsroom*. Available at: https://
citinewsroom.com/2018/11/ghana-institute-of-architects-question-david-
adjayes-selection-for-national-cathedral-project [Accessed 17 November 2019].

AFP (2018), 'Kenyan women lead bold revival of libraries' faded glory', *MailOnline*,
2 August. Available at: www.dailymail.co.uk/wires/afp/article-6017883/Kenyan-
women-lead-bold-revival-libraries-faded-glory.html [Accessed 15 August 2019].

Agyapong, T. F. (1990). *Government policy and pattern of urban housing development in Ghana*, unpublished PhD thesis, University of London.

Agyemang, H. (2021). 'National Cathedral: GHS100 donation drive not a government initiative – Secretariat', *Citinewsroom*. Available at: https://citinewsroom.com/2021/07/national-cathedral-ghs100-donation-drive-not-a-government-initiative-secretariat [Accessed 1 November 2021].

Ahmed, S. (2010). *The promise of happiness* (Durham: Duke University Press).

Akua, M. (1954). 'Homes or mere houses?' *Daily Graphic*, 11 July: 3.

Akyeampong, E. (1999). 'Christianity, modernity and weight of tradition in the life of *Asantehene* Agyeman Prempeh I, c. 1888–1931', *Africa: Journal of the International African Institute*, 69(2): 279–311.

—— (2001). *Between the sea and the lagoon: An ecological history of the Anlo of Southeastern Ghana c. 1850 to recent times* (Athens: Ohio University Press).

Al Jazeera (2012). 'Nigeria forces thousands from floating slum', *Al Jazeera*, 29 July. Available at: www.aljazeera.com/news/2012/7/29/nigeria-forces-thousands-from-floating-slum [Accessed 25 November 2021].

Alexander, J. and C. Anderson (2008). 'Politics, penality and (post-)colonialism', *Cultural and Social History*, 5(4): 391–94.

Allison, H. (2004). *Kant's transcendental idealism: An interpretation and defense* (New Haven: Yale University Press).

Alwang, J, B. F. Mills and N. Taruvinga (2013). *Why has poverty increased in Zimbabwe?* (Washington, DC: World Bank Publications)

Amole, B., D. Korboe and A. G. Tipple. (1993). 'The family house in West Africa: A forgotten resource for policy makers?' *Third World Planning Review*, 15(4): 355–72.

Amnesty International (2020). Nigeria: Time to end impunity. Available at: www.amnesty.org/download/Documents/AFR4495052020ENGLISH.PDF[Accessed 10 November 2020].

Amutabi, M. (2012). 'Buildings as symbols and metaphors of colonial hegemony: Interrogating colonial buildings and architecture in Kenya's urban spaces', in F. Demissie (ed.), *Colonial architecture and urbanism in Africa: Intertwined and contested histories* (Farnham: Ashgate), 325–43.

Anderson, B. (1991). *Imagined communities: Reflections on the origin and spread of nationalism* (London: Verso).

Anderson, C., C. M. Crockett, C. G. De Vito, T. Miyamoto, et al. (2015). 'Locating penal transportation: Punishment, space and place c. 1750–1900', in K. M. Morin and D. Moran (eds), *Historical geographies of prisons: Unlocking the usable carceral past* (London: Routledge), 147–167.

Angelo, A. (2017). 'Jomo Kenyatta and the repression of the "last" Mau Mau leaders, 1961–1965', *Journal of Eastern African Studies*, 11(3): 442–459.

Ankomah, B. (2019). 'Ghana: Asantehene Otumfuo Osei Tutu II – 20 years on the Royal Stool', *New African Magazine*, June, Available at: https://newafricanmagazine.com/18952 [Accessed 15 October 2019].

Ansah, M. (2018). 'Catholic Bishops disappointed they weren't consulted on national cathedral', *Citinewsroom*. Available at: https://citinewsroom.com/2018/09/catholic-bishops-disappointed-they-werent-consulted-on-national-cathedral [Accessed 17 November 2020].

Appadurai, A. (1996). *Modernity at large: Cultural dimensions of globalisation* (Minneapolis: University of Minnesota Press).

Archambault, J. S. (2018). 'One beer, one block: Concrete aspiration and the stuff of transformation in a Mozambican suburb', *Journal of the Royal Anthropological Institute* 24(4): 692–708.

Arhin, K. (ed.) (1991). *The life and work of Kwame Nkrumah* (Accra: Sedco Publishing Limited).

Arhinful, E. and Ziwu, A.-S. (2021). 'Chief Imam donates GHS50K towards the construction of National Cathedral', *Citinewsroom*, 26 August. Available at: https://citinewsroom.com/2021/08/chief-imam-donates-ghs50k-towards-the-construction-of-national-cathedral [Accessed: 10 November 2021].

Arku, G. (2009). 'Housing policy changes in Ghana in the 1990s: Policy review', *Housing Studies*, 24(2): 261–72.

Asante, E. (2017). 'The Participation of the Church in Politics', *E-Journal of Religious and Theological Studies*, 1(1): 72–86.

Asante, N. A. A. (2018). 'A cathedral of lies, waste, and destruction'. Available at: https://justnanaama.com/2018/09/a-cathedral-of-lies-waste-and-destruction [Accessed 1 March 2020].

Asante, S. K. B. (2003). 'NEPAD: A partnership of un equal partners', *New African*, 419: 14–16.

—— (2007). 'Stop the begging bowl syndrome'. *Daily Graphic*, 22 March.

Askouri, A. (2007). 'China's investment in Sudan, displacing villages and destroying communities', in F. Manji and S. Marks (eds), *African perspectives on China in Africa*. (Cape Town: Pambazuka Fahamu).

Assimeng, J. M. (1989). *Religion and social change in West Africa: An introduction to the sociology of religion* (Accra: Ghana Universities Press).

Augé, M. (1995). *Non-places: An introduction to the anthropology of supermodernity* (London: Verso).

Baden, J. S. and C. R. Moss (2016). 'Can Hobby Lobby buy the Bible?', *The Atlantic*. Available at: www.theatlantic.com/magazine/archive/2016/01/can-hobby-lobby-buy-the-bible/419088 [Accessed 20 December 2019].

Bamba, A. B. (2016). *African miracle, African mirage: Transnational politics and the paradox of modernisation in Ivory Coast* (Athens: Ohio University Press).

Barnard, R. (2005). *Apartheid and beyond: South African writers and the politics of place* (New York: Oxford University Press).

Barrett, D., G. Kurian and T. Johnson. (2001). *World Christian Encyclopedia*, Vol. 2, *The world by segments – religions, peoples, languages, cities, topics*, 2nd edn (Oxford: Oxford University Press).

Barsh, R. L. (1993). 'The challenge of indigenous self-determination', *University of Michigan Journal of Law Reform*, 26, 277–312.

Barthes, R. (1972). *Mythologies*, trans. A. Lavers (New York: Noonday Press).

Batsani-Ncube, I. (forthcoming). 'Whose building? Tracing the politics of the Chinese funded parliament building in Lesotho'. *Journal of Southern African Studies*.

Bayart, J-F. (2000). 'Africa in the world: A history of extraversion', *African Affairs*, 99(395), 217–67.

—— (2009) *The state in Africa: The politics of the belly*, 2nd edn (Cambridge: Polity).

BBC (2008). 'Malawi severs links with Taiwan', *BBC Online*, 14 January. Available at: http://news.bbc.co.uk/1/hi/world/asia-pacific/7186918.stm [Accessed 7 October 2021].

—— (2012). 'African Union opens Chinese-funded HQ in Ethiopia', Available at: www.bbc.co.uk/news/world-africa-16770932 [Accessed 30 February 2020].

Beck, U. (1998). 'The open city: Architecture and reflexive modernity', in U. Beck, *Democracy without Enemies* (Cambridge: Polity).

Begum N. and R. Saini (2019). 'Decolonising the curriculum', *Political Studies Review*, 17(2): 196–201.

Bell, C. (1992). *Ritual theory, ritual practice* (Oxford: Oxford University Press).

—— (1997). *Ritual perspectives and dimensions* (Oxford: Oxford University Press).

Bellin, E. (2008). 'Faith in politics: New trends in the study of religion and politics', *World Politics*, 60: 315–47.

Bennett, J. (2010). *Vibrant matter: A political ecology of things* (Durham: Duke University Press).

Berger, P. (1999). *The desecularization of the world* (Washington, DC: Ethics and Public Policy Center).

Bernault, F. (2003). 'The politics of enclosure in colonial and post-colonial Africa', in F. Bernault (ed.) *A history of prison and confinement in Africa* (Portsmouth: Heinemann), 487–92.

—— (2007). 'The shadow of rule: Colonial power and modern punishment in Africa', in F. Dikötter and I. Brown (eds), *Cultures of confinement: A history of the prison in Africa, Asia, and Latin America* (London: Hurst & Co.).

Bevan, R. (2007). *The destruction of memory: Architecture at war* (London: Reaktion Books).

Biney, A. (2011). *The political and social thought of Kwame Nkrumah* (New York: Palgrave Macmillan).

Bjorkdahl, A. (2018). 'Republika Srpska: Imaginary, performance and spatialization', *Political Geography*, 66: 34–43.

Blyden, E. W. (1908). *African life and customs* (London: C.M. Phillips).

Boahen, A. (2000). *Ghana: Evolution and change in nineteenth and twentieth centuries* (Accra: Sankofa Publishing Press).

—— (2004). 'Agyeman Prempeh in the Seychelles, 1900–1924', in A. Boahen, E. Akyeampong, N. Lawler, T. McCaskie and I. Wilks (eds), *'The history of Ashanti kings and the whole country itself' and other writings: by Otumfuo, Nana Agyeman Prempeh I* (Oxford: Oxford University Press).

Boakye, O. (2017). 'Prophets of development: An investigation into Kaiser Industries' economic relationship with Ghana, 1957–1965', *Journal of African Political Economy and Development*, 2(1): 96–124.

Book Bunk (2018). 'Annual Report 2018'. Available at: www.bookbunk.org/impact/annual-reports [Accessed 25 November 2020].

—— (2019). 'Book Bunk explores public libraries'. Available at: www.globalgiving.org/pfil/35790/projdoc.pdf [Accessed 10 November 2019].

Bourdieu, P. (1979). *Algeria 1960: The disenchantment of the world, the sense of honour, the Kabyle House or the World Reversed* (Cambridge: Cambridge University Press).

—— (1993). *The field of cultural production* (Oxford: Polity Press).

Bowdich, T. (1966 [1819]). *Mission from Cape Coast Castle to Ashantee* (London: Frank Cass).

Bowlby, J. (1973). *Attachment and loss* (Volume Two): *Separation, anxiety and anger* (New York: Basic Books).

Bozdogan, S. (2001). *Modernism and nation building: Turkish architectural culture in the early republic* (Seattle and London: University of Washington Press).

Bratton, M. and N. van de Walle (1997). *Democratic experiments in Africa: Regime transitions in a comparative perspective* (Cambridge: Cambridge University Press).

Braun, V. and V. Clarke (2006). 'Using thematic analysis in psychology', *Qualitative Research in Psychology*, 3(2): 77–101.

Brierley, S. and G. Ofosu (2016). '9 things you should know about Ghana's election', *Washington Post*. Available at: www.washingtonpost.com/news/monkey-cage/wp/2016/12/07/nine-things-you-should-know-about-ghanas-election [Accessed 16 January 2021].

Bromley, R. (2003). 'Towards global human settlements: Constantinos Doxiadis as entrepreneur, coalition-builder and visionary', in J. Nasr and M. Volait (eds), *Urbanism imported or exported? Native aspirations and foreign plans* (Chichester: John Wiley & Sons), 316–40.

Brouwer, S., P. Gifford and S. D. Rose (1996). *Exporting the American gospel: Global Christian fundamentalism* (New York: Routledge).

Brown, A. (2001). 'Cities for the urban poor in Zimbabwe: Urban space as a resource for sustainable development', *Development in Practice*, 11 (2/3): 319–31.

Browne, E. A. (1920). *Cocoa* (London: A. & C. Black).

Buchli, V. (2014). *An anthropology of architecture* (London: Bloomsbury).

Buntman, F. (2002). '*Inside apartheid's prison: Notes and letters of struggle*, Raymond Suttner – book review'. *South African Historical Journal*, 47(1): 252–54.

Cajee, I. (2005). *Timol: A quest for justice* (Johannesburg: STE Publishers). Available at www.sahistory.org.za/people/ahmed-timol [Accessed: May 2019].

Chabal, P. and J.-P. Daloz (1999). *Africa works: Disorder as political instrument* (Oxford: James Currey).

Chan, S. and R. Primorac (2013). *Zimbabwe since the Unity Government* (London: Routledge).

Chandler, D. (2010). *International statebuilding: The rise of post-liberal governance* (Abingdon: Routledge).

Charles, E. (2019). 'Decolonizing the curriculum', *Insights*, 32(1): 24.

Chaudhuri, A. (2016). 'The real meaning of Rhodes Must Fall', *The Guardian*, 16 March. Available at: www.theguardian.com/uk-news/2016/mar/16/the-real-meaning-of-rhodes-must-fall [Accessed 25 November 2020].

Cheng, Z. and I. Taylor (2017). *China's aid to Africa: Does friendship really matter?* (London: Routledge).

Ching, F. (2014). *Architecture: Form, space, and order* (Hoboken: John Wiley & Sons).

Chirisa, I. (2014). 'Building and urban planning in Zimbabwe with special reference to Harare: Putting needs, costs and sustainability in focus', *Consilience: The Journal of Sustainable Development*, 11 (1): 1–26.

Choto, R. (2016). 'Zimbabwe's Innscor Africa directors ensnared in Panama Papers'. *VOA News*, 9 May. Available at: www.voanews.com/africa/zimbabwes-innscor-africa-directors-ensnared-panama-papers [Accessed 30 July 2020].

Ciarkowski, B. (2015). 'The post-colonial turn and the modernist architecture in Africa' *Art Inquiry: Recherches sur les arts* XVII: 239–49.

Clapham, C. (1996). *Africa and the international system: The politics of state survival* (Cambridge: Cambridge University Press).

Cohen, A. (1985). *The symbolic construction of community* (London/New York: Routledge).

Coleman, P. (2006). *Shopping Environments: Evolution, Planning and Design* (Amsterdam: Elsevier).

Collier, P. and A. J. Venables (2014). *Housing and urbanization in Africa: Unleashing a formal market process*. Available at: https://openknowledge. worldbank.org/bitstream/handle/10986/18745/WPS6871.pdf?sequence=1 [Accessed 18 June 2020].

Colombijn, F. (2011). 'Public housing in post-colonial Indonesia: The revolution of rising expectations', *Bijdragen tot de taal-, land-en volkenkunde: Journal of the Humanities and Social Sciences of Southeast Asia*, 167(4): 437–58.

Conduah, A. K. (1966a). 'Should Ghana use bricks?' *Evening News*, 23 November: 6.

—— (1966b). 'Ideal roofing materials for Ghana', *Evening News*, 24 November: 6.

Cooper, F. (2001). 'What is the concept of globalization good for? An African historian's perspective', *African Affairs*, 100(399): 189–213.

—— (2002). *Africa Since 1940: The past of the present* (Cambridge: Cambridge University Press).

Coote, J. (1992). '"Marvels of everyday vision": The anthropology of aesthetics and the cattle-keeping Nilotes', in J. Coote and A. Shelton (eds), *Anthropology, art and aesthetics* (Oxford: Clarendon Press), 245–74.

CPG (2014). *Redevelopment of Addis Ababa Bole international airport* (Singapore: CPG Airports).

Crang, M. (1994). 'Spacing times, telling times and narrating the past', *Time and Society*, 3(1): 29–45.

Croucher, S. (2004). *Globalisation and belonging: The politics of identity in a changing world* (Lanham: Rowman & Littlefield).

Curl, J. S. (2006). *A Dictionary of Architecture and Landscape Architecture*, 2nd edn (Oxford: Oxford University Press).

Dadoo, S. (2020). 'How a pro-Israel "spiritual diplomacy" event became a COVID-19 super spreader in South Africa', *Middle East Monitor*. Available at: www.middleeastmonitor.com/20200409-how-a-pro-israel-spiritual-diplomacy-event-became-a-covid-19-super-spreader-in-south-africa [Accessed 2 May 2020].

Daily Graphic (1952). 'Prefab. factories to be built in Kumasi', 11 July: 1.

—— (1954a). 'Housing experts to visit G. C.', 16 August: 1, 12.

—— (1954b). 'Houses for the people', 29 September: 5.

d'Auria, V. (2010). 'From tropical transitions to ekistic experimentation: Doxiadis Associates in Tema, Ghana', *Positions: On modern architecture and urbanism/ histories and theories*, 1: 40–63.

—— (2014). 'In the laboratory and in the field: Hybrid housing design for the African city in late-colonial and decolonising Ghana (1945–57)', *The Journal of Architecture*, 19(3): 329–56.

Dapatem, D. A. (2020). 'Ghana ingests Israeli stone as National Cathedral construction begins', *Graphic Online*. Available at: www.graphic.com.gh/news/ general-news/ghana-ingests-israeli-stone-as-national-cathedral-construction-begins.html [Accessed 1 October 2020].

Daswani, G. (2019). 'Ordinary ethics and its temporalities: The Christian God and the 2016 Ghanaian Elections', *Anthropological Theory*, 19(3): 323–40.

Deacon, H. (2004). 'Intangible heritage in conservation management planning: The case of Robben Island', *International Journal of Heritage Studies*, 10(3): 309–19.

Demissie, F. (2004). 'Editorial note: Social identities on architecture and race', *Social Identities*, 10(4): 435–37.

Dewey, J. (2005). *Art as experience* (New York: Penguin).

Doortmont, M. R. (ed.) (2004 [c.1929]). *The pen-pictures of modern Africans and African celebrities by Charles Francis Hutchison: A collective biography of elite society in the Gold Coast colony*. African Sources for African History series, Vol. 7 (Leiden and Boston: Brill).

Doucet, I and K. Cupers (2009). 'Agency in architecture: Rethinking criticality in theory and practice', *Footprint: Delft School of Design Journal*, 4: 1–6.

Dovey, K. (1999). *Framing places: Mediating power in built form* (London: Routledge).

Dudu, J. E. and B. H. Odalonu (2016). 'Effectiveness of Nigeria's amnesty programme in peace restoration in the Niger Delta', *IOSR Journal of Humanities and Social Science*, 21 (6): 20–33.

Easterling, K. (2014). *Extrastatecraft: The power of infrastructure space* (London: Verso).

Edelman, M. (1995). *From art to politics: How artistic creations shape political conceptions* (Chicago: University of Chicago Press).

Eisenman, J. (2008). 'China's political outreach to Africa', in R. I. Rotberg (ed.), *China into Africa* (Washington, DC: Brookings Institution Press), 230–49.

Elleh, N. (1997). *African architecture: Evolution and transformation* (New York: McGraw-Hill).

—— (2002). *Architecture and power in Africa* (Westport: Praeger).

—— (2014). *Reading the architecture of the underprivileged classes* (Farnham: Ashgate).

Embassy of the FDRE, London, UK (2019). 'Ethiopian Airlines opens new terminal and new Addis Ababa hotel'. Available at: www.ethioembassy.org.uk/ ethiopian-airlines-opens-new-terminal-and-new-addis-ababa-hotel [Accessed 12 June 2020].

Erben, D. (2016). 'Conspicuous architecture: The shopping arcade, the department store, and consumer culture', in A. Lepik and V. S. Bader (eds), *World of malls: Architectures of consumption* (Berlin: Hantje Cantz), 25–34.

Essop, S. (2005). Affidavit. In the High Court of South Africa, Gauteng Local Division, Johannesburg. *In the matter of: Reopened Inquest: Late Ahmed Timol*. Case number 2361/71.

Ethiopian Airlines (2019). 'Ethiopian Airlines Factsheet, November 2019'. Available at: https://corporate.ethiopianairlines.com/docs/default-source/ethiopian-factsheet/ethiopian-factsheet-november-2019-new.pdf?sfvrsn=75c21d45_2 [Accessed 12 June 2020].

Ethiopian Herald (1962). 'Emperor ushers in jets, 720 Bs taxi at Bole', 4 December 1962.

European Committee for the Prevention of Torture and Inhuman or Degrading Treatment or Punishment (2015). Living space per prisoner in prison establishments: CPT standards (Strasbourg: Council of Europe).

Evaristo, B. (2019). 'These are unprecedented times for black female writers', *The Guardian*, 19 October. Available at: www.theguardian.com/books/2019/oct/19/bernadine-evaristo-what-a-time-to-be-a-black-british-womxn-writer [Accessed 25 November 2020].

Evening News (1966a). 'Several foreign students study in Yugoslavia', 23 August: 6.

—— (1966b). 'Germans to build houses in Accra', 23 July: 1.

Falola, T. and M. M. Heaton (2008). *A history of Nigeria* (Cambridge: Cambridge University Press).

Feierman, S. (1990). *Peasant intellectuals: Anthropology and history in Tanzania* (Madison: University of Wisconsin Press).

Forster, G. (2018). 'Bibliothek in Nairobi: Junge Kenianer und ihre Geschichte', *Südwest Presse*, 6 August. Available at: www.swp.de/unterhaltung/kultur/bibliothek-in-nairobi_-junge-kenianer-und-ihre-geschichte-27286016.html [Accessed 20 October 2019].

Foss, S. K. (2005). 'Theory of visual rhetoric', in K. Smith, S. Moriarty, G. Barbatsis and K. Kenney (eds) *Handbook of visual communication: Theory, methods, and media* (New York: Routledge), 141–52.

Foucault, M. (1975). *Discipline and punish* (New York: Vintage Books).

Fox, J. (2008). *A world survey of religion and the state* (Cambridge: Cambridge University Press).

—— (2015). *Political secularism, religion, and the state: A time series analysis of worldwide data* (New York: Cambridge University).

—— (2018). *An introduction to religion and politics: Theory and practice.* 2nd edn (New York: Routledge).

Francis, D. J. (2006). *Uniting Africa: Building regional peace and security systems* (Aldershot: Ashgate).

Freedom Park (n.d. a). Freedom Park information brochure.

Freedom Park (n.d. b). Freedom Park Lagos: Formerly Her Majesty's Prison Lagos, information leaflet.

—— (n.d. c). His Majesty's Prison Broad Street Lagos, information leaflet.

Fry, M. and J. Drew (1956). *Tropical architecture in the humid zone* (London: Batsford).

Fuller, M. (1988). 'Building power: Italy's colonial architecture and urbanism, 1923–1940', *Cultural Anthropology*, 3(4): 455–87.

Galbraith, J. K. (1964). *Economic development* (Cambridge: Harvard University Press).

Gallagher, J. (2017). *Zimbabwe's international relations: Fantasy, reality and the making of the state* (Cambridge: Cambridge University Press).

—— (2018). 'Misrecognition in the making of a state: Ghana's international relations under Kwame Nkrumah', *Review of International Studies*, 44(5): 882–901.

—— (2022). 'Making sense of the state: Encounters between South African citizens and state architecture'. *Political Geography.*

Gallagher, J., D. L. Mpere and Y. A. N'djoré (2021). 'State aesthetics and state meanings: Political architecture in Ghana and Côte d'Ivoire', *African Affairs*, 120(480): 333–64.

Gandhi, L. (2019). *Postcolonial theory: A critical introduction*, 2nd edn (New York: Columbia University Press.

Gatabaki-Kamau, R., and S. Karirah-Gitau (2004). 'Actors and interests: The development of an informal settlement in Nairobi, Kenya', in K. T. Hansen and M. Vaa (eds), *Reconsidering informality: Perspectives from urban Africa* (Uppsala: Nordic Africa Institute), 158–75.

Ghana Information Services Department (1960). 'Ghana: Ten Great Years: 1951–1960', Accra.

Ghana Legal Information Institute (GHALII) (2019). *James Kwabena Bomfeh versus Attorney-General*, Available at: https://ghalii.org/gh/judgment/supreme-court/2019/2-0 [Accessed 1 April 2020].

Ghana Statistical Service (GSS) (2014). '2010 population and housing census: Urbanisation'. Available at: www.statsghana.gov.gh/gssmain/fileUpload/press-release/Urbanisation%20in%20Ghana.pdf [Accessed 13 July 2020].

Ghana Today (1957a). 'Ghana's foreign policy will not be dictated by the need for aid', 20 March, 1(2): 2.

—— (1957b). 'Dr. Nkrumah's arrival in Britain', *Ghana Today*, 26 June, 1(9): 1.

—— (1957c). 'Solving the housing problem in Ghana' *Ghana Today*, 3 April, 1(3): 4–5.

—— (1957d). '"Cheap" sample house on view in Accra' *Ghana Today*, 13 November, 1(19): 7.

—— (1958a). 'The second development plan: Twenty million pounds to be spent annually on various projects', *Ghana Today*, 19 March, 2(2): 2.

—— (1958b). 'New committee to investigate housing problem', *Ghana Today*, 2 April, 2(3): 7.

—— (1958c). 'Houses for the people … Corporation is at work in five towns', *Ghana Today*, 28 May, 2(7): 4–5.

Giddens, A. (1984). *The constitution of society: Outline of the theory of structuration* (Berkeley: University of California Press).

Gidron, Y. (2020). 'Why is Israel in Africa?' *Africa is a country*. Available at: https://africasacountry.com/2020/03/who-is-israel-in-africa [Accessed 2 May 2020].

Gifford, P. (1994). 'Ghana's charismatic churches', *Journal of Religion in Africa*, 24(3): 241–65.

Gilroy, P. (1993). *The black Atlantic: Modernity and double consciousness* (London: Verso).

Goodfellow, T. (2013). 'Planning and development regulation amid rapid urban growth: Explaining divergent trajectories in Africa', *Geoforum*, 48: 83–93.

Goodsell, C. T. (1988). 'The architecture of parliaments: Legislative houses and political culture', *British Journal of Political Science*, 18(3): 287–302.

Government Printing Department (1951). *The development plan, 1951* (Accra: Government of Ghana).

Graphiconline (2019). 'Peace and thankfulness: Ghana's prayer from Jerusalem'. Available at: www.graphic.com.gh/features/features/peace-and-thankfulness-ghana-s-prayer-from-jerusalem.html [Accessed 1 June 2020].

Gready, P. (2003). *Writing as resistance: Life stories of imprisonment, exile, and homecoming from apartheid South Africa* (Lanham: Lexington Books).

Guyer, P. (1983). 'Kant's intentions in the refutation of idealism', *The Philosophical Review*, 92: 329–83.

Gyampo, R. E. V. and B. Asare (2015). 'The church and Ghana's drive toward democratic consolidation', *Journal of Church and State*, 59(1): 1–22.

Gyampo, R. E. V., E. Graham and E. Yobo (2017). 'Ghana's 2016 general election: Accounting for the monumental defeat of the National Democratic Congress (NDC)', *Journal of African Elections*, 16(1): 24–45.

Haarhoff, E. J. (2011). 'Appropriating modernism: Apartheid and the South African township', *A/Z ITU Journal of the Faculty of Architecture*, 8(1): 184–95.

Hanke, S. H. and A. K. Kwok (2009). 'On the measurement of Zimbabwe's hyperinflation', *Cato Journal*, 29(3).

Harris, C. (2007). 'Libraries with lattes: The new third place', *Australasian Public Libraries and Information Services*, 20(4): 145–52.

Harrison, V. (2017). *Little leaders: Bold women in black history* (New York: Little, Brown).

Hartmut, E. (1981). 'Differences in the perception of national socialist and classicist architecture', *Journal of Environmental Psychology*, 1(1): 33–42.

Heidegger, M. (1971). *Martin Heidegger's poetry, language and thought* (New York: Harper & Row).

Held, D., A. McGrew, D. Goldblatt and J. Perraton (2003). 'Rethinking globalization',in D. Held and A. McGrew (eds), *The global transformations reader: An introduction to the globalization debate*, 2nd edn (Cambridge: Polity Press), 67–74.

Hernæs, P. (2005). 'A symbol of power: Christiansborg Castle in Ghanaian history', *Transactions of the Historical Society of Ghana*, 9: 141–56.

Hertz, M., with I. Schröder, H. Focketyn and J. Jamrozik (2015). *African modernism: Architecture of independence* (Zurich: Park Books).

Hess, J. B. (2000). 'Imagining architecture: The structure of nationalism in Accra, Ghana', *Africa Today*, 47(2): 35–58.

—— (2006). *Art and architecture in postcolonial Africa* (Jefferson: McFarland & Company).

Hicks, T. A. (2006). *The Capitol*, Symbols of America series (New York: Marshall Cavendish Benchmark).

Hobsbawm, E. and T. Ranger (eds) (1983). *The invention of tradition* (Cambridge: Cambridge University Press).

Hodder, I. (2003). 'The social in archaeological theory: A historical and contemporary perspective', in L. Meskell and R. Pruecel (eds), *A companion to social archaeology* (Malden: Blackwell), 23–42.

Holmes, C. (2018). 'Ghana–the lynchpin in Israel's attempt to woo Africans', *Africa is a country*. Available at: https://africasacountry.com/2018/05/ghanas-evolving-relationship-with-israel [Accessed 2 May 2020].

Hoskins, J. (2006). 'Agency, biography and objects', in C. Tilley, W. Keane, S. Küchler, M. Rowlands and P. Spyer (eds), *Handbook of Material Culture* (London: Sage Publications), 74–84.

Hsiu-chuan, S. (2007). 'Relations between Taiwan and Malawi unchanged: Maloya', *Taipei Times*, 25 December. Available at: www.taipeitimes.com/News/taiwan/archives/2007/12/25/2003394036 [Accessed 7 October 2021].

Hughes, D. (1997). *Afrocentric architecture: A design primer* (Columbus: Greyden Press).

Hughes, H. F. and J. P. Lomax (1952). 'Houses for the ministers of Gold Coast Government', *Royal Academy Summer Exhibition Catalogue*, Royal Academy, Entry No. 1321. Available at: https://chronicle250.com/1952#catalogue [Accessed 30 May 2020].

Human Rights Watch (2005). '"Clear the filth": Mass evictions and demolitions in Zimbabwe', Human Rights Watch Briefing Paper. Available at: www.hrw.org/legacy/backgrounder/africa/zimbabwe0905/zimbabwe0905.pdf [Accessed 25 November 2021].

Hurd, I. (1999). 'Legitimacy and authority in international politics', *International Organisation*, 53(2): 379–408.

Ibelings, H. (1998). *Supermodernism: Architecture in the age of globalization* (Rotterdam: NAi Publishers).

Ibrahim, J. (2020). 'How to restructure Nigeria (2)', *Premium Times*, 13 November. Available at: https://opinion.premiumtimesng.com/2020/11/13/how-to-restructure-nigeria-2-by-jibrin-ibrahim [Accessed 22 November 2021].

ICAO and UN-Habitat (2018). *Promoting synergy between cities and airports for sustainable development* (Nairobi: UN-Habitat).

Immerwahr, D. (2007). 'The politics of architecture and urbanism in postcolonial Lagos, 1960–1986', *Journal of African Cultural Studies*, 19: 165–86.

Ingold, T. (2007). 'Materials against materiality', *Archaeological Dialogues*, 14: 1–16.

—— (2013). *Making: Anthropology, archaeology, art and architecture* (London: Routledge).

Isichei, E. (2004). *Voices of the poor in Africa: Moral economy and the popular imagination* (Rochester: James Currey).

Iqani, M. (2016). *Consumption, media and the Global South* (London: Palgrave Macmillan).

Jackson, I., O. Uduku, I. Appeaning Addo and R. Assasie Opong (2019). 'The Volta River Project: Planning, housing and resettlement in Ghana, 1950–1965', *The Journal of Architecture*, 24(4): 512–48.

Jackson, W. (2011). 'White man's country: Kenya colony and the making of a myth', *Journal of Eastern African Studies*, 5(2): 344–68.

Jacobs, D. P. (2021). 'National Cathedral will be commissioned on March 6, 2024 – Ofori-Atta', *Citinewsroom*. Available at: https://citinewsroom.com/2021/07/national-cathedral-will-be-commissioned-on-march-6-2024-ofori-atta [Accessed 20 September 2021].

Jacobs, J. U. (1991). 'Confession, interrogation and self-interrogation in the new South African prison writing', *Kunapipi*, 13(1): 115–27.

Jefferson, A. M. and T. M. Martin (2016). 'Prisons in Africa', in Y. Jewkes, B. Crewe and J. Bennett (eds), *Handbook on prisons* (London: Routledge), 423–40.

Jemo, R. M. (2008). 'Public libraries and democracy: The Kenyan experience', paper presented at the Goethe Institute / Kenya National Library service workshop, Ruaraka, July 2008.

Jenkins, P. (2005). 'A provisional survey of nineteenth century photography on the Gold Coast and in Ashanti focused on the Basel Mission Collection, and with special reference to the images linked to the war of 1874', *Journal des Africanistes*, 75(2): 103–06.

Jerusalem Prayer Breakfast (2020). 'Jerusalem Prayer Breakfast 2021'. Available at: www.jpb2021.org [Accessed: 1 November 2020].

Jhetam, D. (2017). Affidavit. In the High Court of South Africa. Gauteng Local Division, Johannesburg. *In the matter of: Reopened Inquest: Late Ahmed Timol*. Case number 2361/71.

Johnson, M. C. and M. Smaker (2014). 'State building in de facto states: Somaliland and Puntland compared', *Africa Today*, 60(4): 3–23.

Kadzanja, F. (2020). 'Chaos in Parliament over HRDC presence', *The Times*, 19 February. Available at https://times.mw/chaos-in-parliament-over-hrdc-presence [Accessed 1 November 2021].

Kaku, D. (2018). 'National Cathedral brouhaha: Apologise to Christian community – Razak Opoku to Chief Imam's PRO', *Modern Ghana*. Available at: www.modernghana.com/news/878798/national-cathedral-brouhaha-apologise-to-christia.html [Accessed 16 November 2021].

Kamete, A. Y. (2013). 'On handling urban informality in southern Africa', *Geografiska Annaler: Series B, Human Geography*, 95(1), 17–31.

Kangondo, F. (2014). 'Sam Levy, the man and his legacy`, *Saturday Herald*, 25 January. Available at: www.herald.co.zw/sam-levy-the-man-and-his-legacy [Accessed 16 November 2021].

Kant, I. (1998 [1781]) *Critique of pure reason*, in P. Guyer and A. Woods (eds), *The Cambridge edition of the works of Immanuel Kant* (Cambridge: Cambridge University Press).

Kapferer, B. and A. Hobart (2005). 'Introduction: The aesthetics of symbolic construction of experience', in B. Kapferer and A. Hobart (eds), *Aesthetics in performance: Formations of symbolic construction and experience* (New York: Berghahn), 109–28.

Khamula, O. (2020). 'Chinese-built Malawi parliament's chamber leaks affect proceedings', *Malawi Nyasa Times*, News from Malawi about Malawi, 14 February. Available at: www.nyasatimes.com/chinese-built-malawi-parliaments-chamber-leaks-affect-proceedings [Accessed 1 November 2021].

Kiereini, D. (2016a). 'McMillan Library is treasure chest of knowledge built from labour of love', *Business Daily*, 10 March. Available at: www.businessdailyafrica.com/McMillan-Library-is-treasure-chest-of-knowledge/539444-3111546-hg2jsp/index.html [Accessed 4 November 2019].

—— (2016b). 'Kaloleni Social Hall: From Kenya's first parliament to just an eyesore', *Business Daily*, 30 September. Available at: www.businessdailyafrica.com/lifestyle/society/-From-Kenya-first-Parliament-to-just-an-eyesore/3405664-3399986-97gp8o/index.html [accessed 5 November 2019].

Killingray, D. (2003). 'Punishment to fit the crime? Penal policy and practice in British colonial Africa', in F. Bernault (ed.), *A history of prison and confinement in Africa* (Portsmouth: Heinemann), 97–118.

King, A. D. (2004). *Spaces of global cultures: Architecture urbanism identity* (London: Routledge).

—— (2015). *Urbanism, colonialism, and the world-economy* (London: Routledge).

Kirk-Greene, A. H. M. (1981). '*Stay by your radios': Documentation for a study of military government in Tropical Africa* (Cambridge, UK: African Studies Centre).

Klinenberg, E. (2018a). 'To restore civil society, start with the library', *The New York Times*, 8 September 2018. Available at: www.nytimes.com/2018/09/08/opinion/sunday/civil-society-library.html [Accessed 5 November 2019].

—— (2018b). *Palaces for the people: How to build a more equal and united society* (London: Bodley Head).

Korboe, D. 1992. 'Family-houses in Ghanaian cities: To be or not to be?' *Urban Studies*, 29(7): 1159–71.

Krupansky, J. (2017). 'Intelligent entities: Principals, agents, and assistants', *Medium*, 15 December. Available at: https://jackkrupansky.medium.com/intelligent-entities-principals-agents-and-assistants-8353639a4092 [Accessed 28 February 2020].

Kultermann, U. (1969). *New directions in African architecture* (London: Studio Vista).

Kusno, A. (2010). *The appearances of memory: Mnemonic practices of architecture and urban form in Indonesia* (Durham: Duke University Press).

Kwawukume, V. (2017). 'Prez cuts sod for National Cathedral', *Graphic Online*, 7 March. Available at: www.graphic.com.gh/news/general-news/prez-cuts-sod-for-national-cathedral.html [Accessed 16 March 2019].

Lammy, D. (2019). 'How Britain dishonoured its African first world war dead', *The Guardian*, 3 November. Available at: www.theguardian.com/world/2019/nov/03/how-britain-dishonoured-first-world-war-african-dead [Accessed 5 November 2019].

Latour, B. (2005). *Reassembling the social: An introduction to actor-network-theory* (Oxford: Oxford University Press).

Lawrence D. L. and S. M. Low (1990). 'The built environment and spatial form', *Annual Review of Anthropology*, 19(1): 453–505.

Lee, J. and T. Ingold (2006). 'Fieldwork on foot: Perceiving, routing, socializing', in S. Coleman and P. Collins (eds), *Locating the field: Space, place and context in anthropology* (Oxford: Berg), 67–86.

Lepik, A. and V. S. Bader (eds) (2016). *World of malls: Architectures of consumption* (Berlin: Hatje Cantz).

Lintao, Y. (2012). 'From aid to cooperation, China seeks to enhance ties with Africa as the West pulls back', *Beijing Review*. Available at: www.bjreview.com/special/2012-02/06/content_453701.htm [Accessed 28 February 2020].

Lloyd, J. (1966). 'Intentions', *Arena: The Architectural Association Journal*, 82(904): 40–41.

Lynch, P. (2018). 'Adjaye Associates unveils design of new Ghana National Cathedral in Accra', *ArchDaily*. Available at: www.archdaily.com/890261/adjaye-associates-unveils-design-of-new-ghana-national-cathedral-in-accra [Accessed 17 March 2020].

Lynch Pinnacle Group (2021). 'About Lynch Pinnacle Group'. Available at: https://lynchpinnacle.com/ [Accessed 20 November 2021].

Macamo, E. (2018). 'Urbane scholarship: Studying Africa, understanding the world', *Africa*, 88(1): 1–10.

Macdonald, S. (2008). *Difficult heritage: Negotiating the Nazi past in Nuremberg and beyond* (London: Routledge).

Mamdani, M. (2013). 'The logic of Nuremberg', *London Review of Books*, 35(21): 33–34

Manful, K. (2015). *Building identity: Ghanaian architects and tropical modernism*. MA dissertation, University of Oxford.

—— (2019). 'Whose style? Taste, class, and power in Accra's architecture', *The Metropole*, 13 November. Available at: https://themetropole.blog/2019/11/13/whose-style-taste-class-and-power-in-accras-architecture [Accessed 25 November 2021].

Mangat, R. (2010). 'Slow death of library that McMillan built', *The East African*, 3 May. Available at: www.theeastafrican.co.ke/magazine/Slow-death-of-library-that-McMillan-built/434746-910652-vufo1l/index.html [Accessed 20 October 2019].

Manning, J. (2007). 'Racism in three dimensions: South African architecture and the ideology of white superiority', *Social Identities on Architecture and Race, Social Identities*, 10(4): 527–36.

Mars, R. (2019). 'Palaces for the people', *99% Invisible Podcast*, 19 March. Available at: https://99percentinvisible.org/episode/palaces-for-the-people [Accessed 1 October 2019].

Marschall, S. (2008). 'The heritage of post-colonial societies', in B. Graham and P. Howard (eds), *The Ashgate research companion to heritage and identity* (Abingdon: Routledge), 347–63.

Martin, A. (2005) 'Agents in inter-action: Bruno Latour and agency', *Journal of Archaeological Method and Theory*, 12(4): 283–311.

Massire, H. (2018). 'Le Palais présidentiel d'Abidjan: la logique de l'opulence', *In Situ: revue des patrimoines* 34. Available at: https://journals.openedition.org/insitu/15837 [Accessed 21 October 2019].

Matambanadzo, P. (2012). 'VP Mujuru consoles Levy family', *The Herald*. Available at: https://allafrica.com/stories/201206081075.html [Accessed 25 June 2020].

Mathews, K. (2005). 'Renaissance of pan-Africanism: The African Union', *India International Centre Quarterly*, 31(4): 143–55.

Mati, J. (2014) 'Neoliberalism and the forms of civil society in Kenya and South Africa', in E. Obadare (ed.), *The handbook of civil society in Africa* (New York, Sage), 215–32.

Mbembe, A. (2001). *On the postcolony* (Berkeley: University of California Press).

—— (2006). 'Variations on the beautiful in Congolese worlds of sound', in S. Nuttall (ed.), *Beautiful ugly: African and diaspora aesthetics* (Durham: Duke University Press), 60–93.

McCaskie, T. (1995). *State and society in pre-colonial Asante* (Cambridge: Cambridge University Press).

McGovern, M. (2011). *Making war in Côte d'Ivoire* (London: Hurst).

Mensah, J. K. (1954). 'Social problems face the people', *Daily Graphic*, 8 September: 1.

—— (1965a). 'Time to uplift the small towns', *Evening News*, 24 August: 3.

—— (1965b). 'The rent office', *Evening News*, 24 August: 3.

Meseret, E. (2019). Anger in Ethiopia as officials demolish hundreds of houses.,*AP NEWS,* 23 February. Available at: https://apnews.com/article/ccc738ec0ea4403f8fc1d617fa52dd72 [Accessed 25 November 2021].

Metcalf, T. R. (1989). *An imperial vision: Indian architecture and Britain's Raj* (Berkeley: University of California Press).

Meyer, B. (2010). 'Aesthetics of persuasion: Global Christianity and Pentecostalism's sensational forms', *South Atlantic Quarterly,* 109(4): 741–63.

—— (2015). 'How pictures matter: Religious objects and the imagination in Ghana', in Ø. Fuglerud and L. Wainwright (eds), *Objects and imagination: Perspectives on materialization and meaning* (New York: Oxford).

Mhazo, T. and V. Thebe (2020). 'Hustling out of unemployment: Livelihood responses of unemployed young graduates in the city of Bulawayo, Zimbabwe', *Journal of Asian and African Studies,* 56 (3), 628–42.

Mhike, I. (2017). 'Political violence in Zimbabwe's National Youth Services, 2001–2007', in L. Oinas, H. Onodera and L. Suurpää (eds), *What politics? Youth and political engagement in Africa* (Leiden and Boston: Brill), 246–64.

Miescher, S. F. (2012). 'Building the city of the future: Visions and experiences of modernity in Ghana's Akosombo Township', *The Journal of African History,* 53(3): 367–90.

Milne, D. (1981). 'Architecture, politics and the public realm', *Canadian Journal of Political and Social Theory,* 5(1–2): 131–46.

Ministry of Information (1967). Patterns of Progress: Ethiopia past and present. National Archive reference: 62.1.26.01 (Addis Ababa: Publications & Foreign Languages Press Dept).

Minkenberg, M. (2014). 'Power and architecture: The construction of capitals, the politics of space, and the space of politics', in M. Minkenburg (ed.), *Power and Architecture: The construction of capitals and the politics of space* (New York: Berghahn), 1–30.

Mitchell, T. (1988). *Colonizing Egypt* (Cambridge: Cambridge University Press).

Mlambo, A. (2008). 'Historical antecedents to Operation Murambatsvina', in M. T. Vambe (ed.), *The Hidden Dimensions of Operation Murambatsvina* (Harare: Weaver Press), 9–24.

Mohan, G. and M. Power (2008). 'New African choices? The politics of Chinese engagement', *Review of African Political Economy,* 35(115): 23–42.

Molefe, P. (1975). Testimony curated by Catherine Kennedy (SAHA), 2007. From the collection of the South African History Archive, William Cullen Library, University of the Witwatersrand.

Momoh, A. and S. Adejumobi (2002). *The national question in Nigeria: Comparative perspectives* (Aldershot: Ashgate).

Moore, H. L. (1986). *Space, text and gender: An anthropological study of the Marakwet of Kenya* (Cambridge: Cambridge University Press).

Morka, F. C. (2012). 'Violent forced evictions of 30,000 people as homes in Nigeria's Makoko community are demolished', *Land Portal,* 21 July. Available at: www.landportal.org/node/8437 [Accessed 25 November 2021].

Moss, C. and J. Baden (2017). *Bible nation: The United States of Hobby Lobby* (Princeton: Princeton University Press).

Mothle, J. (2017). *The re-opening inquest into the death of Ahmed Essop Timol.* High Court of South Africa, Gauteng Division. Case number: IQ01/2017: 118–26.

Mulugeta, D. (2021). 'Pan-Africanism and the affective charges of the African Union building, Addis Ababa', *Journal of African Cultural Studies*, 33(4): 521–37.

Munzwa, K. and W. Jonga (2010). 'Urban development in Zimbabwe: A human settlement perspective', *Theoretical and Empirical Researches in Urban Management*, 5: 120–46.

Murithi, T. 2020. 'The African Union and the institutionalisation of pan-Africanism', in R. Rabaka (ed.), *Routledge handbook of pan-Africanism* (London: Routledge), 373–84.

Murphy, F. A. (2015). 'Christ, trinity and the sacraments', in H. Boersma and M. Levering (eds), *Oxford handbook of sacramental theology* (Oxford University Press), 616–30.

Murray, N. (2010). *Architectural modernism and apartheid modernity in South Africa: A critical inquiry into the work of architect and urban designer Roelof Uytenbogaardt, 1960–2009*. Thesis, University of Cape Town, Faculty of Humanities, School of Architecture, Planning and Geomatics. http://hdl.handle. net/11427/11183.

Musasia, P. (2020): 'Leaders pay tribute to Kenya's ex-president Daniel Moi', *The East African*, 12 February 2020. Available at: www.theeastafrican.co.ke/ tea/news/east-africa/leaders-pay-tribute-to-kenya-s-ex-president-daniel-moi-1436688 [Accessed 25 November 2020].

Mutonga, S. (2020). 'What do a crumbling, embalmed lion head and a photograph of Kenya's first institutional hanging have in common?' *Jalada*, 2 July. Available at: https://jaladaafrica.org/2020/07/02/what-do-a-crumbling-embalmed-lion-head-and-a-photograph-of-kenyas-first-institutional-hanging-have-in-common-by-syokau-mutonga [Accessed 27 November 2020].

Muzulu, P. and Z. Ndlovu (2015). 'Demolitions target the poor', *The Standard*, 23 August. Available at: www.thestandard.co.zw/2015/08/23/demolitions-target-the-poor [Accessed 25 June 2020].

Myburg, J. (2017). 'The Ahmed Timol case'. Available at: www.politicsweb.co.za/ news-and-analysis/the-ahmed-timol-case-I [Accessed 23 November 2021].

MyJoyOnline (2017), 'Curfew in Kumasi as Asantehene makes midnight visit to buried mother', 9 December 2017. Available at: www.myjoyonline.com/curfew-in-kumasi-as-asantehene-makes-midnight-visit-to-buried-mother [Accessed 19 March 2021].

—— (2019). 'Govt explains Akufo-Addo, NAM 1 photo', 11 January. Available at: www.myjoyonline.com/govt-explains-akufo-addo-nam-1-photo [Accessed 25 November 2021].

—— (2021). 'Opoku Onyinah appointed National Cathedral Board of Trustees Chairman', 11 February. Available at: www.myjoyonline.com/opoku-onyinah-appointed-national-cathedral-board-of-trustees-chairman [Accessed 3 November 2021].

Naik, K. (2017). Affidavit. In the High Court of South Africa, Gauteng Local Division, Johannesburg. *In the matter of: Reopened Inquest: Late Ahmed Timol*. Case number 2361/71.

Nartey, T. (1954). 'Plans to produce more houses', *Daily Graphic*, 11 January: 1, 12.

Navaro-Yashin, Y. (2007). 'Make-believe papers, legal forms and the counterfeit: Affective interactions between documents and people in Britain and Cyprus', *Anthropological Theory*, 7(1): 79–98.

—— (2009). 'Affective spaces, melancholic objects: Ruination and the production of anthropological knowledge', *Journal of the Royal Anthropological Institute*, 15(1): 1–18.

—— (2012). *The make-believe space: Affective geography in a postwar polity* (Durham: Duke University Press).

Nelson, L. (2016). *Architecture and empire in Jamaica* (New Haven: Yale University Press).

Newell, Sasha (2013). 'Brands as masks: Public secrecy and the counterfeit in Côte d'Ivoire', *Journal of the Royal Anthropological Institute*, 19: 138–54.

Newell, Stephanie (2013). *The power to name: A history of anonymity in colonial West Africa* (Athens: Ohio University Press).

NewsdzeZimbabwe (2018). 'ED opens Borrowdale Village Walk', 23 May. Available at: www.newsdzezimbabwe.co.uk/2018/05/ed-opens-borrowdale-village-walk.html [Accessed 25 June 2020].

Ngwenya, J. (1981). Testimony curated by Catherine Kennedy (SAHA), 2007. From the collection of the South African History Archive, William Cullen Library, University of the Witwatersrand.

Nielsen, M. (2014). 'A wedge of time: Futures in the present and presents without futures in Maputo, Mozambique', *Journal of the Royal Anthropological Institute*, 20(S1): 166–82.

Njiofor, J. C. (2018). 'The concept of beauty: A study in African aesthetics', *Asian Journal of Social Sciences and Humanities*, 7(3): 30–40.

Norris, P. and R. Inglehart (2011). *Sacred and secular: Religion and politics worldwide* (Cambridge: Cambridge University Press).

Nott, M. (2018). 'Chicken Inn's new Village Walk drive-thru', *Structure and Design Zim*, 5 October. Available at: www.structureanddesignzim.com/2018/10/05/chicken-inns-new-village-walk-drive-thru-text-by-michael-nott [Accessed 30 July 2020].

Nuttall, S. (ed.) (2006). *Beautiful/ugly: African and diaspora aesthetics* (Durham: Duke University Press).

Nwannekanma, B. (2021). 'Lagos residents decry use of abandoned, uncompleted buildings as hideout for miscreants', *The Guardian Nigeria*, 15 November. Available at: https://guardian.ng/news/lagos-residents-decry-use-of-abandoned-uncompleted-buildings-as-hideout-for-miscreants [Accessed 25 November 2021].

Nyabor, J, and E. Washington (2021). 'Ashaiman: Shops at Nii Annang Adjor market demolished by assembly', *Citinewsroom*, 5 July. Available at: https://citinewsroom.com/2021/07/ashaiman-shops-at-nii-annang-adjor-market-demolished-by-assembly [Accessed 25 November 2021].

Nyairo, J. (2015). *Kenya@50: Trends, identities and the politics of belonging*. Nairobi: Contact Zones.

Nyenevi, C. and E. N. Amasah (2015). 'Separation of church and state under Ghana's Fourth Republic', *Journal of Politics and Law*, 8(4): 283–92.

Obeng, H. (2021). 'Ghana National Mosque Complex: Symbol of friendship between Ghana and Turkey', *Ghana News Agency*, 27 July. Available at: www.gna.org.gh/1.21034894 [Accessed 23 March 2022].

Okoye, I. S. (2002). 'Architecture, history, and the debate on identity in Ethiopia, Ghana, Nigeria, and South Africa', *Journal of the Society of Architectural Historians*, 61(3): 381–96.

Olaleye, W. and O. Tungwarara (2005). 'Burning down the house to kill a rat! An analysis of the demolitions in Zimbabwe' (Johannesburg: ActionAid International).

Olaniyan, A. and L. Asuelime (2014). 'Boko Haram insurgency and the widening of cleavages in Nigeria', *African Security*, 7(2): 91–109.

Olufemi, A. (2020). 'Nigeria: Week of jailbreaks – over 2,000 inmates escape from three Nigerian prisons', *Premium Times*, 25 October, Available at: https://allafrica.com/stories/202010260177.html [Accessed 22 November 2021].

Olympio, C. (1966). 'This housing problem must be solved now', *Evening News*, 26 October: 2.

Oquaye, M. (1980). *Politics in Ghana, 1972–1979* (Accra: Tornado Publications).

Osaghae, E. E. and E. Onwudiwe (2001). *The management of the national question in Nigeria* (Ibadan: The Lords Creations).

Owusu, M. A. S. (2009). *Prempeh II and the making of modern Asante* (Accra: Woeli Publishing Services).

Owusu-Addo, J. and J. M. Bond (1966). 'Aspirations', *Arena: Architectural Association Journal*, 82(904).

Oyigbenu, A. (2015). 'A museum of colonial history and national identity: Lokoja and the Nigerian situation regarding preserving the past', *African Studies Bulletin*, 76: 72–84. Available at: https://lucas.leeds.ac.uk/article/a-museum-of-colonial-history-and-national-identity-lokoja-and-the-nigerian-situation-regarding-preserving-the-past-amirikpa-oyigbenu [Accessed 22 November 2021].

Pallasmaa, J. (2012). *The eyes of the skin: Architecture and the senses* (Chichester: Wiley).

Parry, M. (2016). 'Uncovering the brutal truth about the British empire', *The Guardian*, 18 August. Available at: www.theguardian.com/news/2016/aug/18/uncovering-truth-british-empire-caroline-elkins-mau-mau [Accessed 5 November 2019].

Patrick, A. (2020). 'How art, activism and feminist agency shaped a ground-breaking museum', Write-up of 2017 talk at *Museum-iD*. Available at: https://museum-id.com/art-activism-feminist-agency-shaped-ground-breaking-museum [Accessed 27 November 2020].

Patterson, K. D. (1979). 'Health in urban Ghana: The case of Accra 1900–1940 [1]', *Social Science & Medicine. Part B: Medical Anthropology*, 13(4): 251–68.

Pehnelt, G. (2007). 'The political economy of China's aid policy in Africa'. University of Jena Economic Research Papers, no. 2007-051.

Peregrino-Peters, G. (1954). 'New houses for rural people', *Daily Graphic*, 29 July: 5.

Pindula News (2016). 'Zim Twitter criticises disturbing inhumane racism at Sam Levy's Village', 14 October. Available at: https://news.pindula.co.zw/2016/10/14/zim-twitter-criticises-disturbing-inhumane-racism-at-sam-levys-village [Accessed 25 June 2020].

Pobee, J. S. (1987). 'Religion and politics in Ghana, 1972–1978: Some case studies from the rule of General I. K. Akyeampong', *Journal of Religion in Africa*, 17: 44–62.

Poplak, R. (2012). 'Beggar's banquet: The new African Union headquarters', *Daily Maverick*, 30 January. Available at:www.dailymaverick.co.za/article/2012-

01-30-beggars-banquet-the-new-african-union-headquarters [Accessed 28 February 2020].

Potts, D. (1985). Capital relocation in Africa: The case of Lilongwe in Malawi, *Geographical Journal*, 151(2): 182–96.

PRC (2019). 'The Great Hall of the People', in *National People's Encyclopedia* (Beijing: PRC) Available at: www.npc.gov.cn/englishnpc/GreatHall/node_3077. htm [Accessed 2 November 2021].

Rahman, O. A. (2019). 'National Cathedral Obsession: Ken Ofori Atta's embarrassing proselytising in Israel!' *Modern Ghana*, 24 July. Available at: www. modernghana.com/news/946877/national-cathedral-obsession-ken-ofori-attas. html [Accessed 2 March 2021].

Raman, P. (2009). 'Change and continuity in contemporary South African architecture and urbanism', in 'Ora Joubert (ed.), *10 years and 100 buildings: Architecture in a democratic South Africa* (Cape Town: Bell-Roberts), 14–18

Ramseyer, F. and J. Kuhne (1878). *Four years in Ashantee*, 2nd edn (London: James Nisbet & Co.).

Rapoport, A. (1982). *The meaning of the built environment: A nonverbal communication approach* (Beverly Hills: Sage Publications).

Rasmussen, S. E. (1964). *Experiencing architecture* (Cambridge: The MIT Press).

Rent Control Department (2020). Available at: http://rentcontrol.gov.gh/index. php/about-us [Accessed 14 July 2020].

Rich, T. S. (2009). Status for sale: Taiwan and the competition for diplomatic recognition. *Issues & Studies*, 45(4), 159–88.

Rodriguez, J. (1971). Affidavit. In the High Court of South Africa, Gauteng Local Division, Johannesburg. *In the matter of: Reopened Inquest: Late Ahmed Timol*. Case number 2361/71.

Rogers, D., C. L. Lee and D. Yan (2015). 'The politics of foreign investment in Australian housing: Chinese investors, translocal sales agents and local resistance', *Housing Studies*, 30(5): 730–48.

Ross, W. (2014). 'How Nigeria turned Her Majesty's prison into a place of pleasure', *BBC News*, 15 August. Available at: www.bbc.co.uk/news/world-africa-28418685 [Accessed 4 November 2019].

Rotberg, R. I. (ed.) (2008). *China into Africa: Trade, aid, and influence* (Washington, DC: Brookings Institution Press).

Rothberg, M. (2013). 'Remembering back: Cultural memory, colonial legacies, and postcolonial studies', in G. Huggan (ed.), *The Oxford handbook of postcolonial studies* (Oxford: Oxford University Press), 359–79.

Rowlands, M. and F. de Jong (2008). 'Reconsidering heritage and memory', in F. de Jong and M. Rowlands (eds), *Reclaiming heritage: Alternative imaginaries of memory in West Africa* (Walnut Creek: Left Coast Press), 13–29.

Ruddle, D. (1870). *The new Palace of Westminster* (London: Warrington & Company).

Ruskin, J. (1989). *The seven lamps of architecture* (New York: Dover Publications).

Russo, C. (2007). 'The concept of agency in objects', A response to Discussion Week 2: 'Materiality: Ethnographies of material culture', 7 February, in Brown University course 'Material worlds: Art and agency in the Near East and Africa: The concept of agency in objects' (Providence: Brown University).

Rydin, Y. (2007). 'Re-examining the role of knowledge within planning theory', *Planning theory*, 6(1): 52–68.

Sachinkonye, L. (2006). *The impact of Operation Murambatsvina/clean up on the working people in Zimbabwe* (Harare: Ledriz).

Sackeyfio-Lenoch, N. (2017). 'The Ghana Trades Union Congress and the politics of international labor alliances, 1957–1971', *International Review of Social History*, 62(2): 191–213.

Saleh-Hanna, V. (2008).*Colonial systems of control: Criminal justice in Nigeria* (Ottowa: University of Ottowa Press).

Samuels, A. J. (2011). 'The space of control: Fascism and architecture in Libya', *Culture Trip*, 14 September. Available at: https://theculturetrip.com/africa/libya/articles/the-space-of-control-fascism-and-architecture-in-libya [Accessed 25 November 2021].

Sarkin, J. (2008). *Human rights in African prisons* (Cape Town: HSRC Press; Athens: Ohio University Press).

Sarpong, P. K. (1990). 'What church, what priesthood for Africa?' in J. S. Pobee and J. N. Kudadjie (eds), *Theological education in Africa: Quo vadimus?* (World Council of Churches), 6–17.

Schalkwyk, D. (2001). *Apartheid narratives* (Amsterdam: Rodopi).

Schatzberg, M. G. (2001). *Political legitimacy in middle Africa: Father, family, food* (Bloomington: Indiana University Press).

Scott, D. (2003). '"Creative destruction": Early modernist planning in the South Durban industrial zone, South Africa', *Journal of Southern African Studies*, 29(1): 235–59.

Scott, J. C. (1998). *Seeing like a state: How certain schemes to improve the human condition have failed* (New Haven: Yale).

Seers, D. and C. R. Ross (1952). *Report on financial and physical problems of development in the Gold Coast* (Accra: Office of the Government Statistician).

Segal, H. (1986). 'A psychoanalytic approach to aesthetics', in H. Segal, *Delusion and artistic creativity and other psychoanalytic essays* (London: Free Association Books), 185–206.

Segre, C. G. (1972). 'Italo Balbo and the colonization of Libya', *Journal of Contemporary History*, 7(3/4): 141–55.

Shinn, D. (2009). 'Comparing engagement with Africa by China and the United States', China in Africa Symposium, African Studies Program, East Asian Studies Center and the Center for International Business Education and Research (Bloomington: Indiana University).

Shinn, D. H. and J. Eisenman (2012).*China and Africa: A century of engagement* (Philadelphia: University of Pennsylvania Press).

Sizer, S. (2004). *Christian Zionism: Road map to Armageddon?* (Downer's Grove and Leicester: Inter-Varsity Press).

Skelly, L. (2015). 'African libraries that adapt can take the continent's knowledge to the world', *The Conversation*, 24 August. Available at: http://theconversation.com/african-libraries-that-adapt-can-take-the-continents-knowledge-to-the-world-46044 [Accessed 25 October 2019].

Sklair, L. (2005). 'The transnational capitalist class and contemporary architecture in globalizing cities', *International Journal of Urban and Regional Research*, 29(3), 485–500.

—— (2012). 'Iconic architecture in globalizing cities', *International Critical Thought*, 2(3): 349–61.

—— (2017). *The icon project: Architecture, cities and capitalist globalization* (New York: Oxford University Press).

Smith, T. (2020). 'Neil Aggett inquest: How the 10th floor worked', New Frame, 28, January. Available at www.newframe.com/neil-aggett-inquest-how-the-10th-floor-worked [Accessed 8 April 2022].

Sneath, D., M. Holbraad and M. A. Pederson (2009). 'Technologies of the imagination: An introduction', *Ethnos*, 74(1): 5–30.

Songsore, J. (2020). 'The urban transition in Ghana: Urbanization, national development and poverty reduction, *Ghana Social Science Journal*, 17(2): 120–75.

Specter, M. (2014). 'Partial recall: Can neuroscience help us rewrite our most traumatic memories?' *The New Yorker*, 19 May. Available at: www.newyorker.com/magazine/2014/05/19/partial-recall [Accessed 15 March 2020].

Stan, L. and L. Turcescu (2006). 'Politics, national symbols and the Romanian Orthodox Cathedral', *Europe-Asia Studies*, 58(7): 1119–39.

Stanek, Ł. (2015). 'Architects from Socialist Countries in Ghana (1957–67), *Modern Architecture and Mondialisation: Journal of the Society of Architectural Historians*, 74(4): 416–42.

Stoler, A. L. (2008). 'Imperial debris: Reflections on ruins and ruination', *Cultural Anthropology*, 23: 191–219.

—— (2013). 'Introduction "the rot remains": From ruins to ruination', in A. L. Stoler (ed.), *Imperial debris: On ruins and ruination* (Durham: Duke University Press).

—— (2016). *Duress: Imperial durabilities in our times* (Durham: Duke University Press).

Strange, C. and M. Kempa (2003). 'Shades of dark tourism: Alcatraz and Robben Island', *Annals of Tourism Research*: 386–405.

Sudjic, D. (2011). *The edifice complex: The architecture of power* (London: Penguin Books).

Suttner, R. (2002). *Inside apartheid's prison: Notes and letters of struggle* (Melbourne: Ocean Press).

Suttner, R. (2016). *Inside apartheid's prisons: Notes and letters of struggle* (Pietermaritzburg: University of Natal Press; Melbourne and New York: Ocean Press).

Tanizaki, J. (2001). *In praise of shadows*, trans. T. J. Harper and E. G. Seidensticker (London: Vintage Books).

Tekere, M. (2001). *Trade liberalisation under Structural Economic Adjustment: Impact on social welfare in Zimbabwe*, paper for the Poverty Reduction Forum (PRF): Structural Adjustment Program Review Initiative (SAPRI).

Tendi, M. B. (2014). 'The origins and functions of demonisation discourses in Britain–Zimbabwe relations (2000–)', *Journal of Southern African Studies*, 40(6): 1251–69.

Terefe, D. (2020). 'Addis Ababa riverside project gives priority to development over residents', *Climate Home News*, 12 March. Available at: www.climatechangenews.com/2020/03/12/addis-ababa-riverside-project-gives-priority-development-residents [Accessed 25 November 2021].

Terrefe, B. (2020). 'Urban layers of political rupture: The "new" politics of Addis Ababa's megaprojects', *Journal of Eastern African Studies*, 14(3): 375–95.

Tetteh, M. N. (1999). *The Ghana Young Pioneer Movement: A youth organisation in the Kwame Nkrumah era* (Accra: Ghana Publicity Limited).

The Economist (2021). 'Why are there so many unfinished buildings in Africa?' 29 April. Available at: www.economist.com/middle-east-and-africa/2021/04/29/why-are-there-so-many-unfinished-buildings-in-africa [Accessed 25 November 2021].

The New York Times (1976). 'Rhodesia revising laws on blacks', 15 June. Available at: www.nytimes.com/1976/06/15/archives/rhodesia-revising-laws-on-blacks-smith-urges-some-changes-but.html [Accessed 30 July 2020].

Thies, C. G. (2004). 'State building, interstate and intrastate rivalry: A study of post-colonial developing country extractive efforts, 1975–2000', *International Studies Quarterly*, 48(1): 53–72.

Tilley, C. (2001). 'Ethnography and material culture', in P. A. Atkinson, A. Coffey, S. Delamont, J. Lofland and L. Lofland (eds), *Handbook of ethnography* (London: Sage), 258–72.

Turner, J. and K. Peters. (2015). 'Doing time-travel: Performing past and present at the prison museum', in K. M. Morin and D. Moran (eds), *Historical geographies of prisons: Unlocking the usable carceral past* (London: Routledge).

Uduku, O. (2006). 'Modernist architecture and "the tropical" in West Africa: The tropical architecture movement in West Africa, 1948–1970', *Habitat International*, 30(3): 396–411.

Ugwueze, M. I. (2019). 'Trauma and memory – explaining the longevity of the Biafra secessionist movement in Nigeria', *Africa Insight*, 49(2): 56–69.

Vambe, M. T. (2008). *The hidden dimensions of Operation Murambatsvina* (Harare: Weaver Press).

Vale, L. J. (1992). *Architecture, power, and national identity* (New Haven: Yale University Press).

Vale, L. J. (2008). *Architecture, power, and national identity*, 2nd edn (New York: Routledge).

Van der Kolk, B. A. and C. P. Ducey (1989). 'The psychological processing of traumatic experience: Rorshach patterns in PTSD', *Journal of Traumatic Stress*, 2: 259–74.

Venturi, R. (1966). *Complexity and contradiction in architecture* (New York: Museum of Modern Art).

Venturi, R., D. S. Brown and S. Izenour (1977). *Learning from Las Vegas: the forgotten symbolism of architectural form* (Cambridge, MIT Press).

Vogel, S. (1997). 'African art/Western eyes', *African Arts*, 30(4): 64–77.

Walby, K. and J. Piché (2015). 'Carceral retasking and the work of historical societies at decommissioned lock-ups, jails and prisons in Ontario', in K. M. Morin and D. Moran (eds), *Historical geographies of prisons: Unlocking the usable carceral past* (London: Routledge).

Wang, S. and C. Wang (2015). *China and Africa, win-win cooperation* (Beijing: Beijing Times Chinese Press).

Waters, J. (2006). 'Adrian Stanley', Obituaries, *The Guardian*, 9 November.

Watson, V. (2009). "'The planned city sweeps the poor away": Urban planning and 21st century urbanisation', *Progress in Planning*, 72(3): 151–93.

Weizman, E. (2007). *Hollow land: Israel's architecture of occupation* (London: Verso).

—— (2014). 'Anselm Franke, and forensic architecture', Haus der Kulturen der Welt (ed.), *FORENSIS: The Architecture of public truth* (Berlin: Sternberg Press).

—— (2015). 'Forensic architecture: Notes from fields and forums', *Continent*, 4: 81–87.

—— (2017). *Forensic architecture: Violence at the threshold of detectability* (New York: Zone Books).

Weizman, E. and T. Keenan. (2012). *Mengele's skull: The advent of a forensic aesthetics.* (Berlin: Sternberg Press).

Werbner, R. (1998). 'Beyond oblivion: Confronting memory crisis', in R. Werbner (ed.), *Memory and the postcolony: African anthropology and the critique of power* (London: Zed Books), 1–17.

Werlin, H. H. (1972). 'The roots of corruption: The Ghanaian enquiry', *The Journal of Modern African Studies*, 10(2): 247–66.

Will, R. (2012). 'China's stadium diplomacy', *World Policy Journal*, 29(2): 36–43.

Wines, M. (2008). 'Malawi cuts diplomatic ties with Taiwan', *The New York Times*, 15 January. Available at: www.nytimes.com/2008/01/15/world/africa/15malawi. html [Accessed 2 November 2021].

Woodward, S. (2019). *Material methods: Researching and thinking with things* (London: Sage).

World Prison Brief (2020). *World prison brief data: Nigeria.* Available at: www. prisonstudies.org/country/nigeria [Accessed 10 November 2020].

Xinhua (2010). 'China hands over new parliament building to Malawi', *People's Daily Online*, 22 May. Available at: http://en.people.cn/90001/90776/90883/6994852. html [Accessed 2 November 2021].

Yaneva, A. (2016). *Mapping controversies in architecture* (London: Routledge).

Yeboah, I. (2016). 'EC declares Nana Akufo-Addo President-Elect of Ghana', *Graphic Online*. Available at: www.graphic.com.gh/news/politics/ec-declares-nana-akufo-addo-president-elect-of-ghana.html [Accessed 16 November 2019].

—— (2018). 'How can National Cathedral be a "priority among priorities"? – TUC rejects President's position', *Graphic Online*, 15 October. Available at: www. graphic.com.gh/news/general-news/how-can-national-cathedral-be-a-priority-among-priorities-tuc-rejects-president-s-position.html [Accessed: 5 May 2020].

Zewde, B. (2001). *A history of modern Ethiopia, 1855–1991*, 2nd edn (Oxford: James Currey; Athens: Ohio University Press; Addis Ababa: Addis Ababa University Press).

Zhaoxing, L. (2010). 'Remarks at the inauguration ceremony of the new parliament building of Malawi', Embassy of the People's Republic of China in the Republic of Malawi. Available at: http://mw.china-embassy.org/eng/sghdhzxxx/t707837. htm [Accessed 2 November 2021].

Zonszein, M. (2020). 'Christian Zionist philo-Semitism is driving Trump's Israel policy'. *The Washington Post*, 28 January. Available at: www.washington

post.com/outlook/2020/01/28/trump-thinks-supporting-israel-means-letting-it-do-whatever-it-wants [Accessed 1 February 2021].

Zurek, K. (2018). 'How Akufo-Addo intends to fund the National Cathedral', *Graphic Online*, 15 November. Available at: www.graphic.com.gh/news/general-news/budget-2019-how-akufo-addo-intends-to-fund-national-cathedral.html [Accessed 20 November 2019].

—— (2019). 'How NAM 1 met Akufo-Addo – minister reveals', *Graphic Online*, 10 January. Available at: www.graphic.com.gh/news/general-news/how-nam-1-met-akufo-addo-minister-reveals.html [Accessed 25 November 2021].

INDEX

Printed and bound by CPI Group (UK) Ltd, Croydon, CR0 4YY

09/06/2025

14685708-0002